Open Network
of
Four-way
Partial
Dotted Scotch
Page 54

Open
Network
of Four-way
Diagonal
Hungarian
Variation 2
Page 47

Open Network
of Four-way
Hot Wheels
with
Four-way
Tent Clusters
Variation 1
Page 58

Open Network
of Four-way
Enlarged
Hot Wheels
Page 59

Open Network
of
Four-way
Partial
Dotted Scotch
Variation 1
Page 54

Open Network
of Four-way
Enlarged
Hot Wheels
Composite
Pattern
Page 60

Open Network
of Four-way
Hot Wheels
with
Double Cross
Variations 1 and 2
Pages 71-72

Open Network
of
Four-way
Partial
Dotted Scotch
Variation 2
Page 55

Open Network
of Four-way
Diagonal Hungarian
Border 1
Page 124

Open Network
of Four-way
Diagonal Hungarian
Variation 1
Page 46

Open Network of
Four-way Diagonal
Hungarian with
Smyrna Crosses
Variation 1
Page 73

Open Network of
Four-way Diagonal
Hungarian with
Smyrna Crosses
Variation 3
Page 75

Open Network of
Four-way Extended
Diagonal Hungarian
Page 61

Open Network of
Four-way Tied
Oblong Cross
Clusters
Variation 7
Page 117

Open Network of
Four-way Diagonal
Hungarian with
Smyrna Crosses
Page 72

Open Network of
Four-way Diagonal
Hungarian with
Smyrna Crosses
Variation 2
Page 74

Open Network of
Four-way Extended
Diagonal Hungarian
Variation 2
Page 62

Open Network of
Four-way Tied
Oblong Cross
Clusters
Page 116

POTPOURRI OF PATTERN

ANN STRITE-KURZ

*A COLLECTION OF
ORIGINAL OPEN PATTERNS
FOR CANVAS AND
LINEN USE*

First Printing June 1995

This self-published book was prepared with an IBM personal computer, using WordPerfect 5.0 page composition software with graphic elements generated by PC Paintbrush IV Plus software.

Ann Strite-Kurz
3802 Wrenwood Court
Midland, Michigan 48640-2372
Tel. (517)631-2126

ABOUT THE AUTHOR

Ann Strite-Kurz has been an active teacher of canvas embroidery for the past thirteen years. She is certified in canvas by the National Academy of Needle Arts (formerly The Valentine Museum), and she received a Master Craftsman award in canvas from the Connecticut River Valley Chapter of the Embroiderers' Guild of America.

Ann graduated from The Madeira School and has a B.A. degree in American Studies from Sweet Briar College. Her involvement in embroidery was originally the result of her volunteer activities with the Keeler Tavern Preservation Society in Ridgefield, Connecticut. She organized some classes in crewel and canvas as part of her duties as the Chairman of the Docent Training Program in 1974, and this led to her role as one of the founders and eventually a President of the Fairfield County Chapter of EGA.

Ann has had extensive training in many specialized areas of embroidery. These include crewel, counted thread, silk and metal and Japanese embroidery as well as canvas embroidery. Her designs exhibit a unique mixed media approach, and her innovative original style of patterning has become the hallmark of her work.

Ann teaches several correspondence courses on specialized patterning, and she also teaches notebook classes on pattern development. Her first book, *The Heart of Blackwork*, was published in 1992 and focuses on unconventional styles of this unique type of patterning.

Ann currently resides in Michigan with her husband Bill. Their hobbies include travel, photography, and a number of outdoor and underwater sporting activities. They also share three children.

TABLE OF CONTENTS

ACKNOWLEDGMENTS

This book is dedicated to my students whose enthusiasm and support have encouraged me to keep stitching new designs and to keep sharing my expertise. In my twenty years of affiliation with various needlework organizations both on a local and national level, I have seen a steady growth in the interest in embroidery. The availability of widespread learning opportunities through classes sponsored by needlework guilds and shops throughout the country has stimulated this renaissance, and it has been a privilege to have such eager students in the classroom.

I have also seen the development of a new level of technical excellence and originality that has accompanied this growth. Exhibits today demonstrate high calibre work in a wide range of diverse categories. This technical proficiency is also reflected in the many beautiful civic projects that have been produced by needlework groups that are active in community affairs.

One of the greatest gifts that I have received from my participation in these groups has been friendship and comradery. It is a privilege to know so many other creative individuals, and a number of fellow teachers and students have become close personal friends. Some students have graciously offered their expertise and time in piloting some of my new classes and in proofreading my instruction booklets as well.

I particularly want to thank my two editors for *Potpourri of Pattern,* Connie Ashman and Mary Ellen Sand. Their meticulous scrutiny and excellent suggestions were invaluable in making this book more polished and concise, and I am honored to have such generous and conscientious friends.

In closing, I want to acknowledge my husband Bill whose many talents have also contributed to the publication of this book. Not only did he proofread the copy several times, but his photography skills produced all of the transparencies for the color plates. His computer expertise was also a valuable resource, and the book has been the product of a true partnership. I am indeed fortunate to have such a supportive spouse whose ongoing encouragement has made the plans for this project become a reality.

FOREWORD

The main purpose of this book is to provide readers with some innovative ideas for stitch treatments. Today there is a great diversity of materials with which to work. The availability of exciting new threads and fabrics has sparked a new enthusiasm for experimenting with our needles.

Historically embroidery was a functional as well as a decorative art or craft – a way to mark linens or to provide necessary household goods. Every region or civilization had a distinct style or taste that is reflected in its art, and textiles were often embellished with hand embroidery. Much of the finest work was created by professionals for the church or the aristocracies during periods of prosperity.

Today we are fortunate to have access to information on all of these traditional needlework techniques through books and museums. However, it is no longer mandatory to execute contemporary styles in the same manner as our forefathers unless one is fulfilling an academic assignment.

Now we tend to stitch for personal enjoyment and relaxation rather than out of any sense of duty or obligation. Those of us who have made it a profession never lose sight of the fact that it is fun and even addictive to stitch, and the pleasure of sharing this love of needlework offsets the many hours spent preparing lesson plans, etc.

Those who do not know the joy of stitching seldom understand us. One common question we are often asked is: "How do you have the patience to do such intricate work?" My favorite answer is one that I overheard Marion Scoular say once, and that is: "You only have to have patience for things you don't like to do."

There seem to be two distinct predispositions that make a stitcher prefer one type of embroidery over another. Some individuals prefer the freedom of painting with a needle, and these embroiderers favor crewel or surface embroidery on fabric. The other personality prefers more structure and likes the confines of a grid.

I happen to like both, but what attracted me to needlework originally was a love of math and the realization that canvas offered a way to merge this aptitude with an artistic bent that had never found the ideal creative outlet. I often refer to this as my "midlife crisis," and this "late bloomer" has been fortunate to be able to pursue this emerging interest the past twenty years.

My love of history has also made this field a multi-faceted one for me. In the beginning when I still felt clumsy with a needle, I found the origins of this art form fascinating, and my museum work got me involved in conservation and preservation studies.

The ultimate satisfaction, however, has come from merely playing with all sorts of different patterning on a grid. As I often tell my students, I do most of my stitching with a pencil on graph paper, and only a small portion of it finally gets to my canvas. The main goal of this book is to introduce you to some innovative styles of patterning which I hope will lead to new dimensions in your needlework.

Welcome to my world of pattern!

IMPORTANT NOTE TO READERS

Although most of my current work is on canvas, I have studied all of the linen techniques and still do occasional blackwork, hardanger and pulled thread designs. Linen samplers use many of the same stitches that are used on canvas so most of the patterning presented in this book is equally appropriate on this beautiful fabric. Both linen and canvas are available today in a wide range of colors, and the interaction between these colored grounds and open patterning can be dramatic.

Linen is my preferred choice when I want to finish an article as a sewn item such as a tote bag. It is also my preferred choice when I want a ground that is finer than 24-mesh. The main advantage of canvas over linen is its sizing, which allows it to support multilayers of stitching better. Therefore some of the couching patterns may be limited to canvas applications, but all of the other patterning can be used on both grounds if appropriate adjustments in thread weights are made.

The band samplers on the front and back covers are stitched on Zweigart 18-mesh Sage canvas. The samplers on the inside covers of the book are both stitched on Zweigart 18-mesh Evergreen canvas. The reproductions of all four of these pieces are the same size as the actual stitched pieces. All of the color plates are stitched on either 24-mesh Congress cloth or 18-mesh white or colored mono canvas.

LIST OF COLOR PLATES
(Found Following Page 62)

CHAPTER 1 – INTRODUCTION

One of the most respected and coveted books in the libraries of contemporary embroiderers is A *Pageant of Pattern for Needlepoint Canvas*, published in 1973 by Sherlee Lantz and Maggie Lane. Earlier books focused either on stitches and technique or on the history of various types of embroidery. The main thrust of this book, however, is on the history of pattern in general and the adaptation of many rich sources of geometric pattern to a canvas grid. The many examples in this book have been an inspiration to me over the years and became a springboard for investigating the endless possibilities for developing unusual patterning in my own work. I hope my enthusiasm for this subject will turn my readers on to a similar fascination with pattern.

Potpourri of Pattern is the culmination of a decade of research and experimentation. Rather than use strictly traditional stitches and published patterns in my designs, I have discovered that the ultimate satisfaction has been in creating "something different" that meets my needs exactly. Because I have studied a variety of techniques, it seemed natural to try to combine elements from various traditional styles to produce a new "mixed media" approach. Couching techniques from silk and metal embroidery and laidwork fillings from crewel embroidery both transplant well to a canvas grid. Traditional counted thread techniques like blackwork, darning and pulled thread are also effective on canvas, and each style creates its own unique visual effect.

The *Blue Oriental Lantern* (Color Plate I) represents my first attempt to combine several different techniques in a mixed media canvas embroidery. Only a few of the patterns used are ones that I developed for this particular design, but I adapted the design from a Chinese papercut so I enjoyed selecting appropriate treatments that would transform the silhouette into a sophisticated multicolor interpretation.

Each stitch treatment shows a distinct style of patterning and each technique is usually repeated at least once to better integrate the design. There are two different blackwork patterns and three different pulled thread patterns. These mix well with the laidwork and other scattered elements.

Since this design is a symmetrical one with a bilateral axis, a certain amount of repetition is automatic within the left and right sides of the lantern. I have found, however, that too much symmetry can make a design monotonous so random elements like the birds and flowers were added as bits of asymmetry to keep the design from being static. The birds are balanced on both sides and the flowers are balanced on the top and bottom of the lantern, but the arrangements are not identical "mirrored" images like the geometric elements in the design.

This visual trick of adding some asymmetrical elements to relieve the monotony of total symmetry is one that I learned from the fascinating work of wildlife artist Charles Harper. *Br-r-r-rdbath* (Color Plate II) is my interpretation of one of his delightful serigraphs. The geometric proportions of Charley's abstract views of animals and birds are a joy to adapt to canvas, but notice how much the scattered leaves and snowflakes enhance the other carefully balanced elements in the design.

Today I not only combine different techniques in a single design, but I also combine different techniques in a single pattern to produce a unique effect. By arranging canvas stitches in an open network it is possible to add other treatments to the exposed areas. Further variations can be produced by changing these accent fillings. The following series of simple open Scotch stitch networks illustrates the infinite potential of open patterns to form interesting composite patterns when two different styles of patterning are combined.

Example 1

Example 2

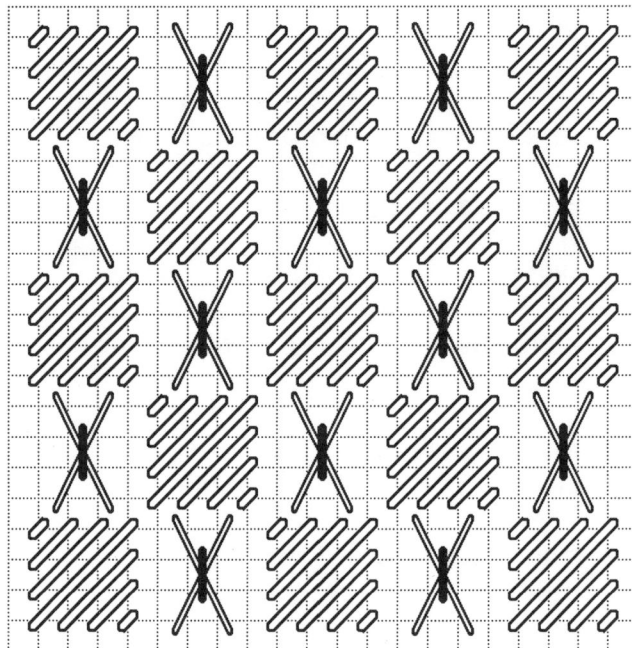

Example 3

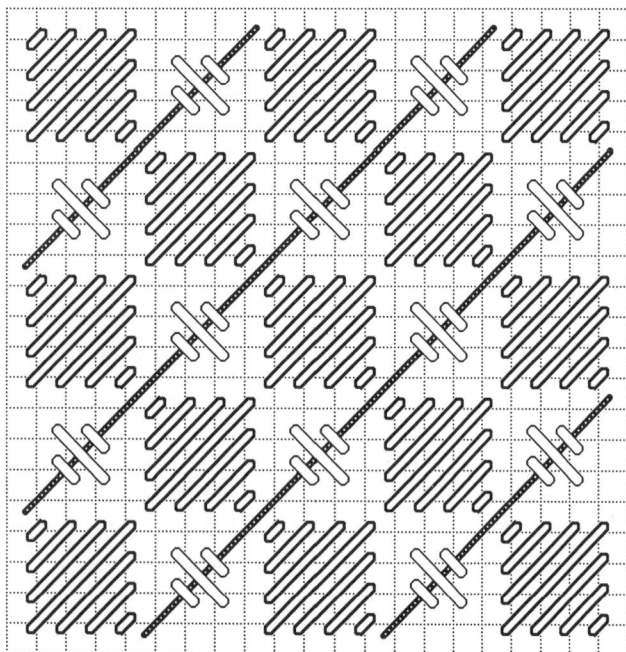

Example 4

Example 5   **Example 6**

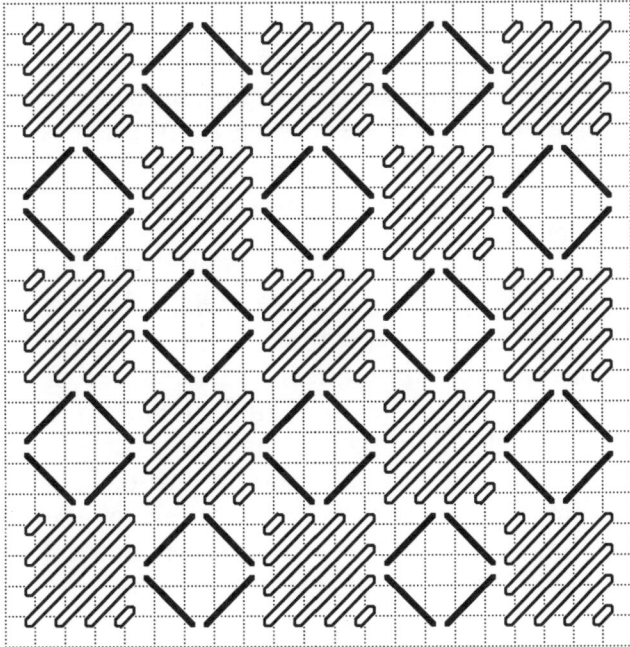 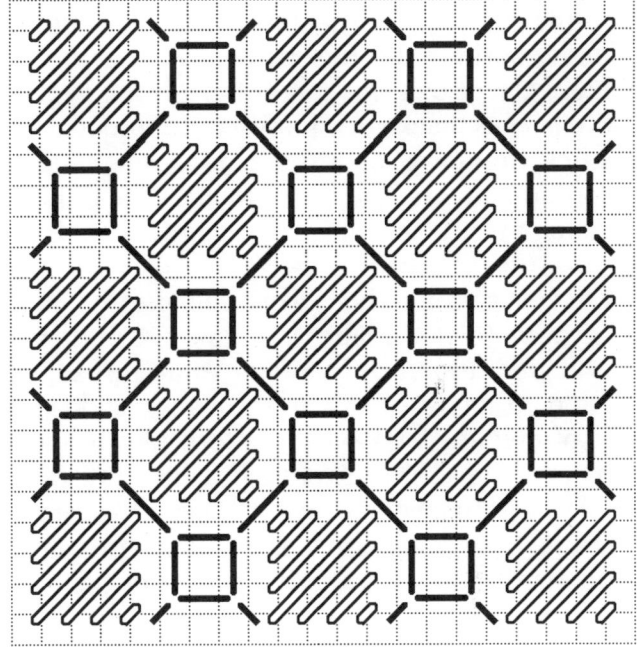

Example 1 shows Scotch units combined with Mosaic units, and Example 2 shows Scotch units combined with Upright Oblong Crosses. The addition of smaller canvas stitches to the open pattern makes an attractive checkerboard arrangement of alternating texture stitches.

Examples 3 and 4 show additions of laidwork patterns in the open areas. Example 3 has a one-way tramé arrangement which tends to produce a stripe unless the tiedown stitches are done in a contrasting color that interrupts the directional flow of the laid thread. Example 4 shows a two-way tramé pattern with the open Scotch network. Couching patterns produce a completely different look to a composite pattern since the layers, especially those done in two colors, add depth and dimension. If the laid thread is a metallic, the effect is even more elegant.

Laidwork rows also provide a barrier or solid path that will conceal the traveling threads of other fillings. This is a particularly important feature when patterns are done on canvas. A 24-mesh canvas has a comparable grid to a 24-mesh linen or cotton fabric, but the canvas threads are usually thinner and the holes are bigger than those of the same count unsized fabric. Therefore any visible traveling threads are more conspicuous on canvas, so I prefer to create a sequence that will either conceal the traveling threads or minimize their visibility if they cannot be eliminated completely. A more casual approach is feasible on fabric, but the structured sequences provided in this book can be used on any ground.

Examples 5 and 6 show two open Scotch networks combined with blackwork elements. Example 5 shows isolated diamonds inside the open squares whereas Example 6 shows a four-way continuous network that fits nicely in the exposed areas. When the pattern is continuous, I usually use a reversible double running sequence to add the blackwork. When isolated units are added, I find the reversible technique less efficient so modified approaches are used.

Blackwork is distinctive in that it is an outline technique whereas other treatments use masses of stitches to create a pattern or special effect. The thin lines and the dark color usually used for this type of embroidery make it stand out when combined with other types of patterning. Notice how effective it is in *Hungarian Hootenanny* (Color Plate XII) in defining the patterning in the four corner squares and in the center and side diamonds. Watercolours was used for the main outlines of this geometric design, so any strong patterning created by the Flip-Flop Hungarian rows was somewhat diluted by the overdyed thread. To restore the shapes in the open areas, the blackwork motifs were added. The strong lines in the star patterning are the Cross stitch tie-downs of a dense four-way couching pattern. Most couching patterns have a more spread out arrangement, so the linear flow of the tramé rows is usually interrupted by the couching stitches and is not continuous like the lines in this pattern.

I have also found blackwork very useful in background treatments on canvas. In the *Blue Oriental Lantern* (Color Plate I) it makes a perfect mat around the design. In other instances I have executed a pattern in a light value thread, so it is not obvious that the pattern is blackwork. A good example of this is the background pattern around the butterflies in *Flurry of Butterflies* (Color Plate VII). The pattern of alternating large and small diamonds is done in reversible blackwork, so no traveling threads show in the open areas. The use of the pale blue threads in this pattern and the other canvas pattern around the Imari plate intensifies the effect of the strong patterning elsewhere. A background should compliment but not overwhelm the main focal points of a design, and the choice of the light value keeps the patterning soft and unobtrusive.

GOALS OF THIS BOOK

In setting the specific goals of this book, I have tried to evaluate what is already available on patterning for counted work today. There are a number of books that can be purchased on pattern in general, and I have included a bibliography of these for your convenience. There are also a number of recently published books on stitches and patterns for specialized uses on even weave fabrics and/or canvas; I have included these in a separate bibliography.

Few books, however, have dealt specifically with open patterning, so I will focus on this topic. My first book, *The Heart of Blackwork*, explored one particular type of open patterning and unconventional uses of it on canvas. This book will deal with open patterning that begins with an open arrangement of one stitch or a combination of stitches. I think I have developed some innovative approaches to developing such patterns along with some unusual ways to execute them so that the traveling threads can be concealed.

Unlike other forms of surface embroidery, traditional needlepoint usually requires complete coverage of the canvas, and the quality of this coverage has always been a major judging point in evaluating its technical excellence. Stitches are usually laid side by side in sequential order, and thread weights are adjusted to attain good coverage. With the advent of today's wide selection of colored fabrics and canvas, it is no longer imperative to cover the canvas, and allowing the background to interact with the patterning can be both attractive and different. In the past the actual stitch was the focus of the pattern, and the visual impact was limited to both the shape and the texture of the individual stitches. In open patterning the negative space around the actual stitches adds a new dimension to the overall visual effect.

In counted thread techniques, the background has always been an integral part of the patterning. In blackwork, the actual outlines are formed by the dark stitches, but the shapes or motifs inside are the repeated elements that form the patterns. In pulled thread, the actual stitches are distorted by the exertion required, and the pattern is formed by the negative space inside the pulled paths along with the holes or perforations created by the tightly pulled stitches. In hardanger, the kloster blocks are quite functional since they support the fabric and allow threads to be removed so that additional fillings can be added to the inside areas. These kloster blocks are also decorative since they appear embossed against the surrounding fabric and the delicate inner fillings. These three examples illustrate how the background or ground fabric can be an integral part of the patterning either as negative space or as a contrast to the raised areas of stitching.

In surface embroidery, the background can be either quiet and recessive like most tightly woven fabrics or it can be softly patterned like the twill weave of traditional crewel linen. It can also be made more conspicuous with painting or dying techniques, marbling, stenciling or other deliberate alterations to the fabric surface done to enhance the overall design. Similar effects can be applied to evenly woven fabrics as well, so "anything goes," and the ground is no longer merely something to support the stitches. It becomes an important part of the total design.

In deciding how to organize this book, I isolated several goals which have influenced the choices of the patterns presented. Instead of bombarding you with an overwhelming number of miscellaneous open patterns (which to me is more of a "pattern for the sake of pattern" approach), I have selected specific patterns that have been particularly useful to me in more than one design situation. I have also presented patterns that demonstrate new ways to execute stitches. In order to eliminate the visibility of traveling threads, I often manipulate a common stitch in such a way that this can be accomplished.

Developing an original pattern is usually quite easy, but developing appropriate stitch sequences for such patterns is more challenging. In single stitch patterns stitches usually build in sequential order back and forth in rows that are either horizontal, vertical or diagonal, and there are a number of stitch encyclopedias that provide numbered sequences for these traditional stitches. Open patterning is more complex, and priorities change somewhat because of the additional need to control the path of the traveling thread. If only a single thread is visible between stitch units, no special measures need to be taken. However, when open holes are present, it is necessary to structure a sequence more carefully. Cluttered open areas detract from the beauty of the surface embellishment. If such areas are clean, one can use a contrasting backing fabric behind the open areas to further enhance the impact of the patterning. Notice how pronounced the open background pattern is in *Oriental Butterfly* (Color Plate X) with a teal backing fabric behind the design.

I will also stress patterns that maneuver well in difficult shapes. Many patterns are beautiful, but because of the stitches incorporated, their use is limited to geometric shapes that conform to the repeats. I personally enjoy designs with curves in them, but handling them on a grid requires patience and imagination. By sharing some of my solutions and by providing patterns that compensate easily in irregular and curved shapes, I hope to give you some good ideas for future uses in your own work.

I will also share some of my concepts for developing original patterning. One can either copy patterns from non-embroidered sources and translate them on a grid, or one can use a more spontaneous approach of just playing with familiar stitches and changing the way they are arranged. I call this "doodling," and I usually find that I use more of these types of stitches in my pieces than I do the ones that are inspired by external sources. Since all of the fillings in a specific design should relate to each other in a comfortable way, a variation of a pattern that has already been used is generally a suitable choice for another area.

No discussion of pattern is complete without an understanding of the structure of pattern. To create original patterning for a grid, it is essential to be able to identify what is commonly called the "eight basic pattern networks." Every pattern incorporates at least one of these networks. When one is browsing for patterns with potential use on canvas, it helps to be able to isolate these "underlying" geometric structures in order to transfer such patterns to a grid. The information presented on the next few pages is gleaned from Richard Proctor's *Principles of Pattern Design,* which to me is the "bible" on the structure of pattern.

IDENTIFICATION OF EIGHT BASIC PATTERN NETWORKS

The eight basic pattern networks include the following geometric shapes that form the understructure of all repeat patterns: the square, the diamond, the brick, the half-drop, the triangle, the hexagon, the ogee, and the scale. The illustrations that follow show these networks as blackwork outlines since this technique is the easiest way to record such outlines on a grid.

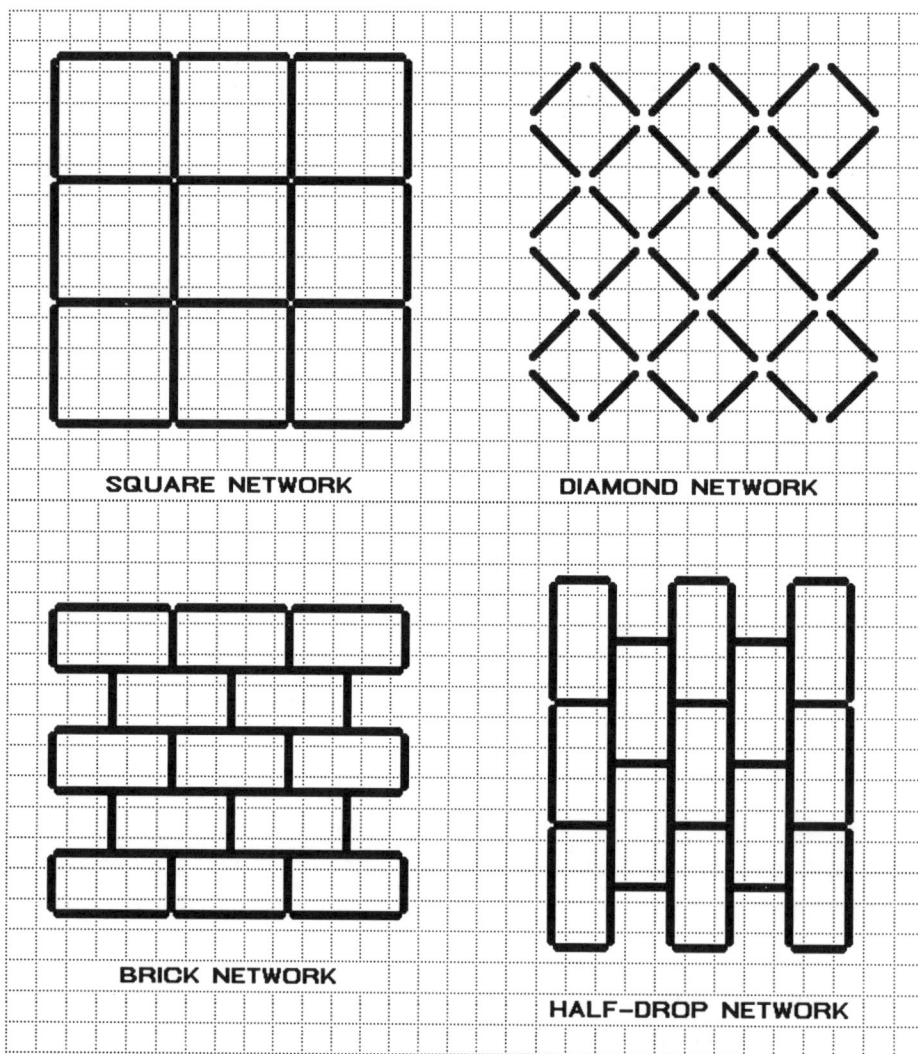

SQUARE NETWORK   DIAMOND NETWORK

BRICK NETWORK   HALF-DROP NETWORK

The chart above shows the first four basic pattern networks, and these are common in many canvas embroidery patterns. There are many box-shaped stitches that form a square network when they are stitched as a solid filling. These include Scotch stitch, Mosaic stitch, Rice stitch and Smyrna Cross. There are also many diamond-shaped stitches that form diamond networks when stitched as solid fillings. These include Diamond Eyelet, Hungarian, Upright Cross and Double Straight Cross.

The brick and the half-drop networks are "cousins" in that if either network is rotated 90°, it will form the other. Both networks are derived from simple variations of square or rectangular units that are arranged so that the alternating rows are staggered in either a horizontal arrangement for brick networks or in vertical arrangements for half-drop patterns. Although half-stepping is the usual proportion for these arrangements, many other combinations are common. In canvas embroidery, the Cashmere stitch, or any rectangular or square unit, can be used to form either of these networks.

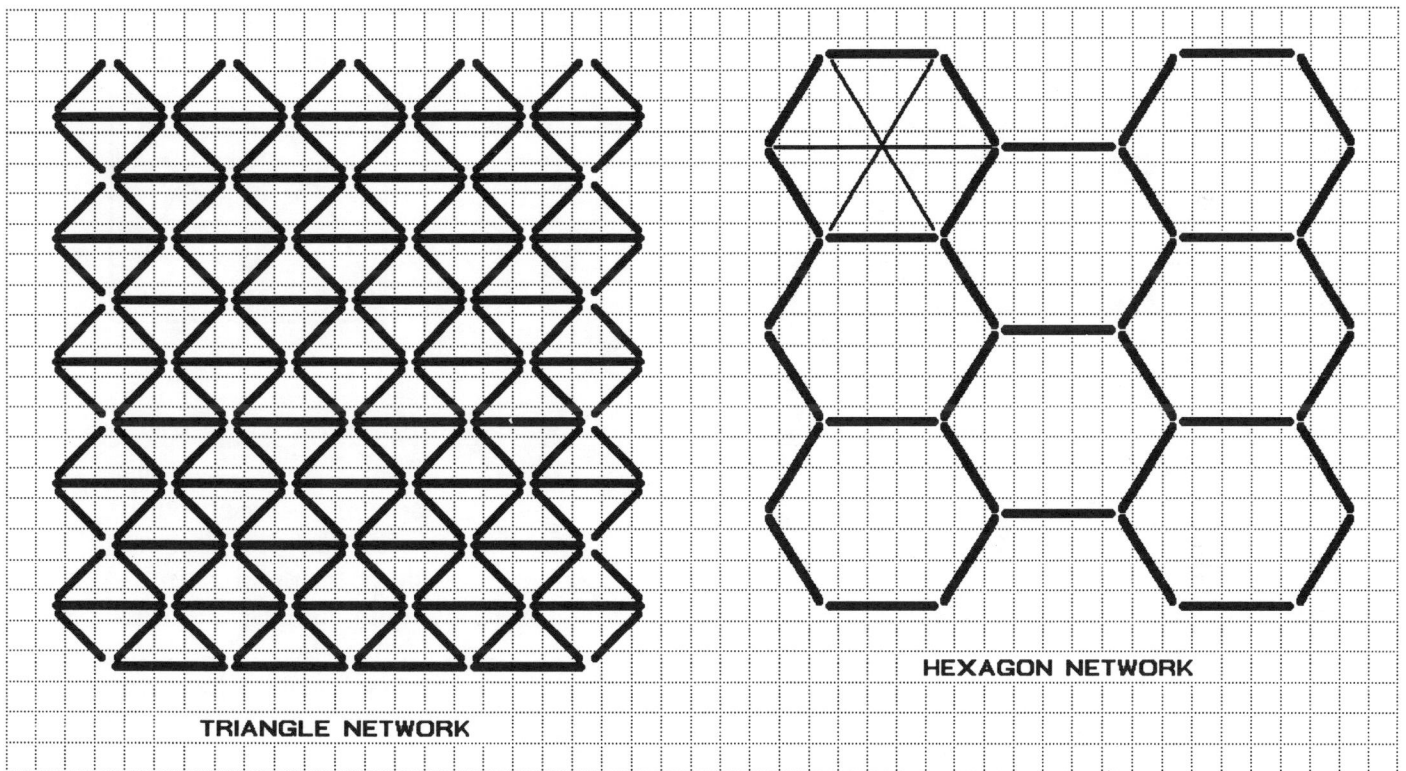

TRIANGLE NETWORK

HEXAGON NETWORK

The triangle is merely a half of a diamond shape, and the Milanese stitch is the "classic" canvas stitch that forms a natural right triangle. Combinations of parallel satin stitches can also be used to form triangles of all sorts (isosceles, equilateral, etc.).

The hexagon is a six-sided shape that can be formed by six triangles – hence the network chart above shows one unit that is divided into six equal size triangles. Any hexagonal pattern can be copied on canvas by using satin block triangles to form the hexagons and by changing colors at strategic points to follow the pattern repeats. As a matter of fact, there is a book called *Trianglepoint* that explores this premise (see the canvas bibliography).

The last two pattern networks are not common to actual canvas stitches, but they are very common in a category of canvas embroidery called Florentine Embroidery. Both the ogee and the scale pattern networks have curves in them that do not maneuver well on a grid.

However, straight stitches used in step formations can create lovely soft curves, so many Florentine or bargello patterns use these shapes.

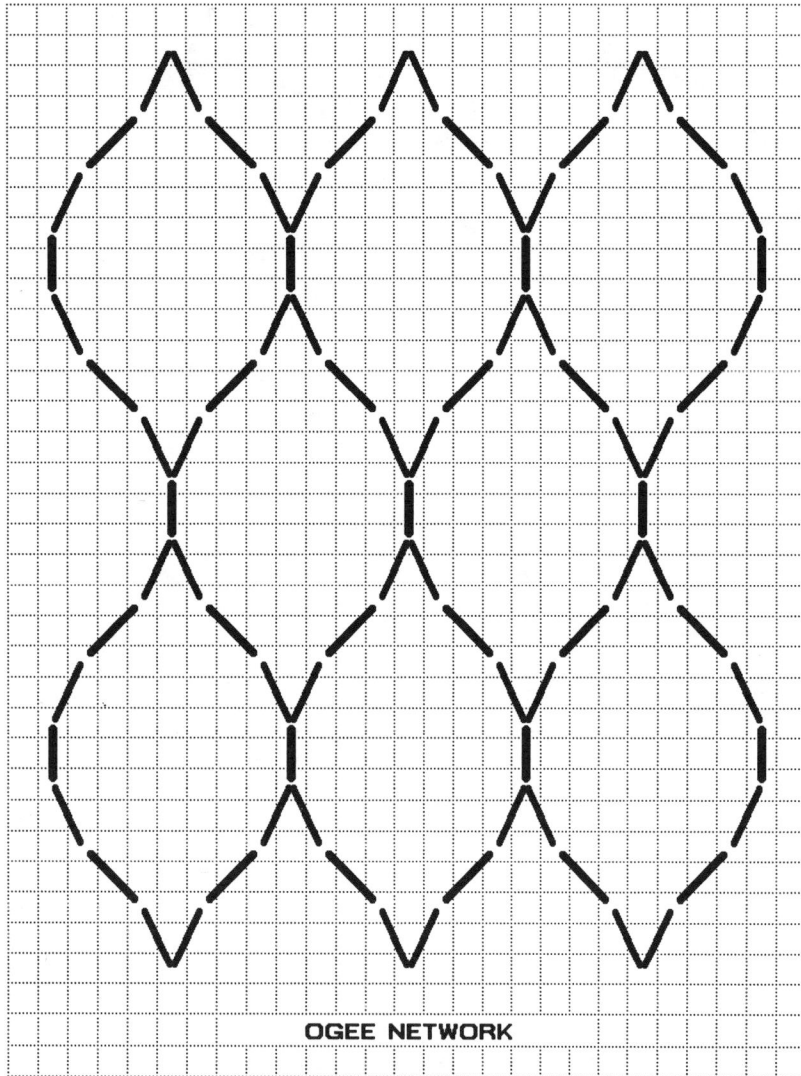

OGEE NETWORK

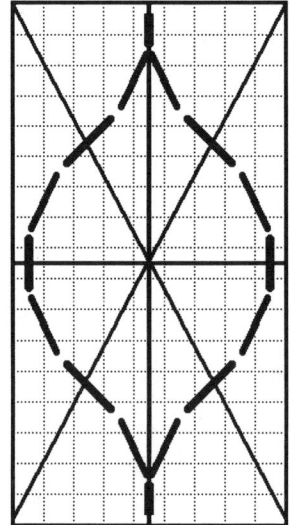

The inset chart above shows how the ogee network is based on the S curve. A diamond shape is divided into 4 equal shapes, and each shape has the same wavy line that has been rotated to form the ogee.

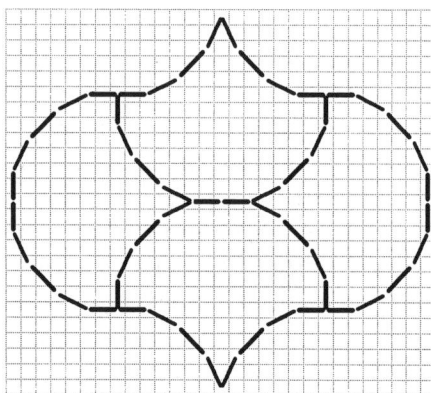

This elongated ogee is commonly associated with Christmas tree ornaments. However, the chart to the left shows a wide ogee that is formed with a four-way arrangement of scale units.

A Tent stitch outline can also be used on canvas to define this shape, but notice how attractive the contours are in blackwork outlines that use a Slanted Gobelin stitch to suggest the curves.

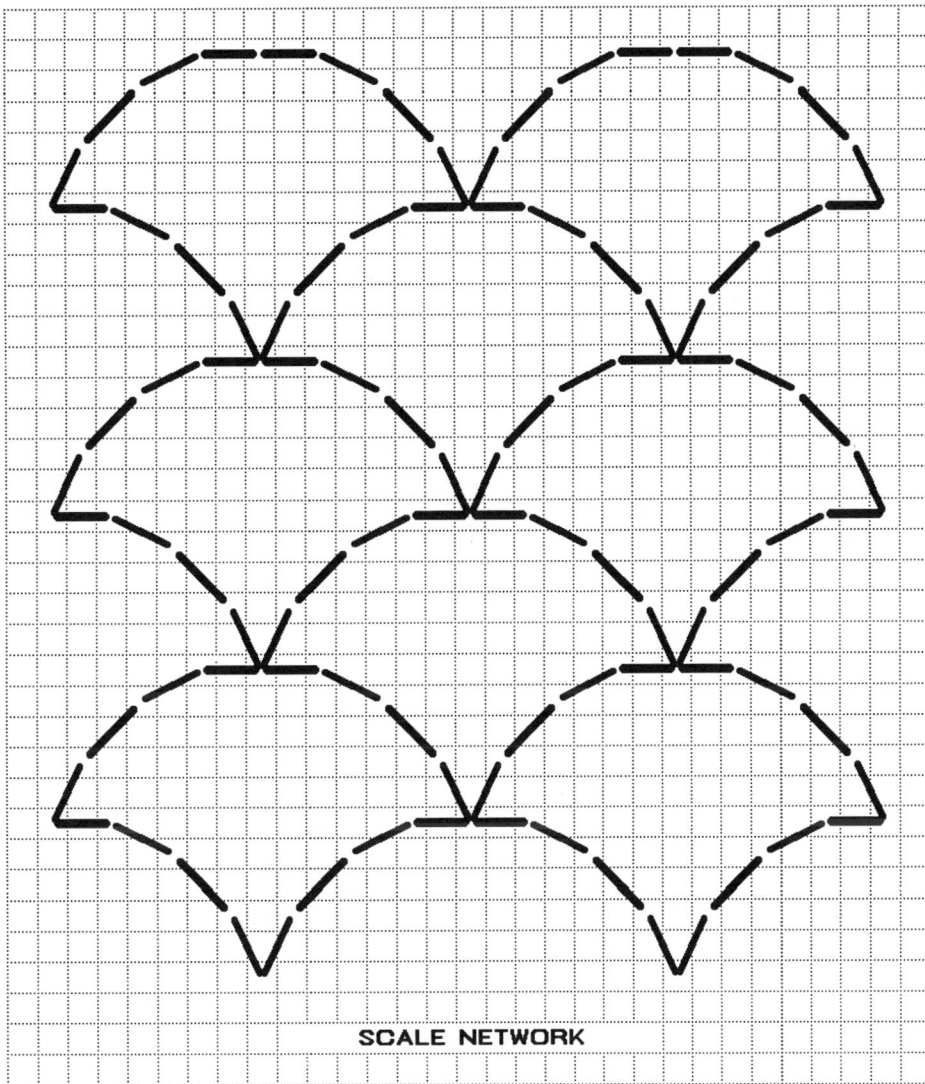

SCALE NETWORK

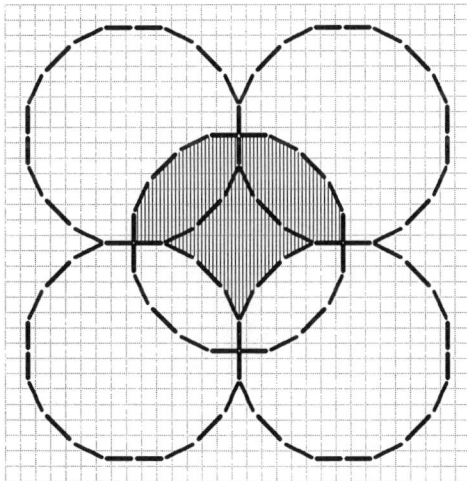

The chart above displays a scale pattern executed in a blackwork outline. The chart to the left illustrates the fact that a scale network is derived from a pattern of overlapping circles. The circle itself is not a basic pattern network because any arrangement of circles that are tangent to each other produces a pattern with negative or leftover spaces between the units (notice the small diamond that is part of the shaded scale). Therefore a circle cannot create a true "interlocking" network when it is repeated. A basic network must connect endlessly in any direction, but other types of networks can be constructed of non-interlocking shapes. For further study, please see the bibliography for pattern at the end of the book.

9

OPEN PATTERN NETWORKS

Adapting pattern to canvas and linen stitches largely depends on what we see when we view pattern. The following comparisons exhibit how the same pattern network can be stitched several different ways. The blackwork example is usually the best way to transplant a pattern to a grid since this technique will capture the main outlines of a pattern best. The other examples emphasize different elements in the pattern so the dominance changes.

BLACKWORK PATTERN
EXAMPLE 1

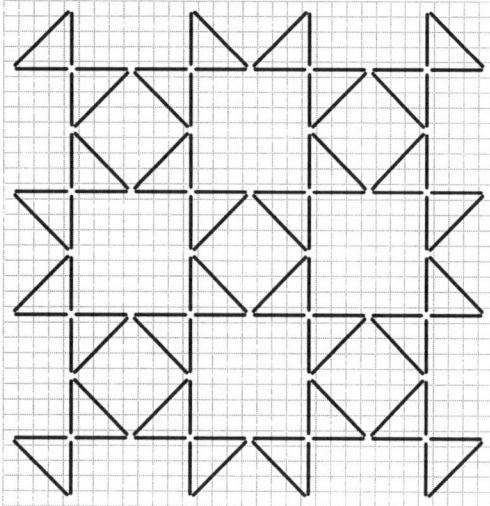

This pattern features a square network of alternating elements. Empty squares alternate with squares with a diamond inside. By adding half units along the outer edge, the eye can now see a star motif formed by the triangles around the empty squares. These shapes emerge only if the diamond units repeat more than twice.

Below are two interpretations of the same pattern network in Milanese and Scotch stitches. Since a Milanese stitch is also a partial Scotch unit, the textures of both patterns are similar. However, Example 2 depicts the pattern as an arrangement of hourglass shapes positioned in a four-way relationship to each other. Example 3 interprets the square and diamond shapes, and the hourglass shapes are the negative spaces or open areas around the stitched areas.

TEXTURE STITCH INTERPRETATIONS

EXAMPLE 2

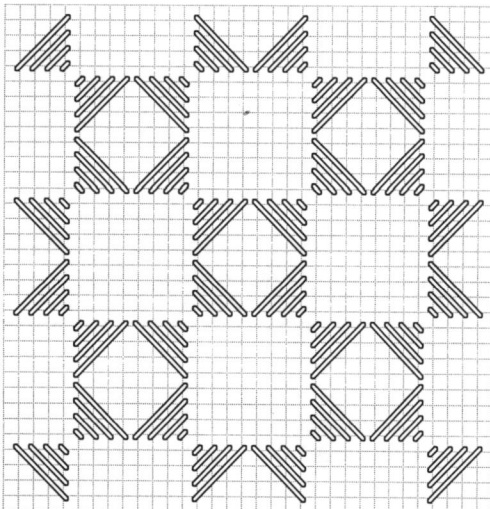

EXAMPLE 3

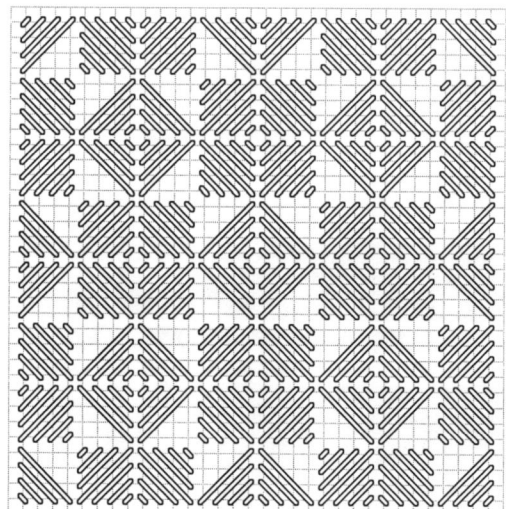

What one actually sees when one views pattern is determined by what dominates or by what the eye finds first. (Optical illusions can be frustrating, but some of us find puzzles fascinating!) To transfer pattern to stitches, it is necessary to both analyze the negative space as well as the obvious linear outlines seen. Linear outlines can also be interpreted in either blackwork or Tent outline, but the masses of negative space can be interpreted in texture stitches.

To the right is another allover blackwork pattern with a checkerboard arrangement of alternating units. The same repeat unit is used, but since it is not symmetrical, it can be rotated to produce a second element. Below is both a Tent stitch interpretation and a texture stitch interpretation of the same square network.

The scale of the blackwork pattern is slightly different from the other two examples (the square is one thread larger). This is inevitable when different stitch treatments are used to form the same pattern. Sometimes certain shapes can be clumsy in one style of treatment but quite successful in another, so try several different approaches until a satisfying version emerges. I always record patterns that I see in blackwork first since the outline technique is the easiest way to capture it. Then I doodle on my graph paper to create other possibilities.

BLACKWORK PATTERN

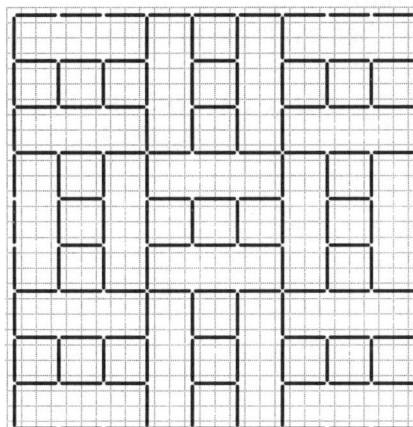

TENT STITCH PATTERN

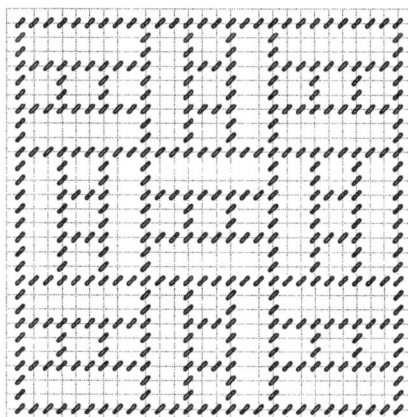

TEXTURE STITCH PATTERN

PRINTED PATTERN

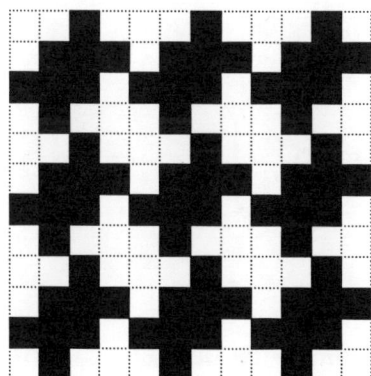

The next comparison shows a remarkable difference in scale between two texture stitch interpretations of the same pattern. Both patterns shown at the top of the next page are adapted from the printed counterchange pattern shown to the left. The motifs are arranged "Escher style" in interlocking units, and alternating rows of the oblong "X" units slant in the opposite direction.

Each shape in the black and white pattern is made up of eight squares so the first example on the next page shows the pattern motif stitched in eight units of Smyrna Cross. The second example shows the pattern motif interpreted in long satin stitches, and the squares have been merged, but the size of each invisible "square" is now three threads rather than two.

EXAMPLE 1

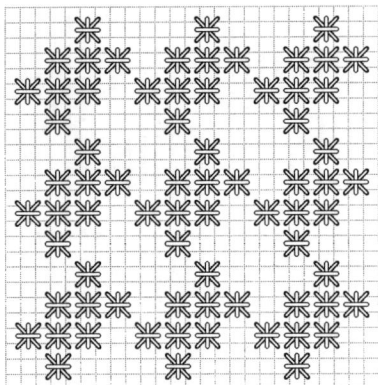

Instead of stitching the alternating rows of flip-flop units in a different color to form a counterchange pattern, the canvas is left exposed to produce the same effect.

EXAMPLE 2

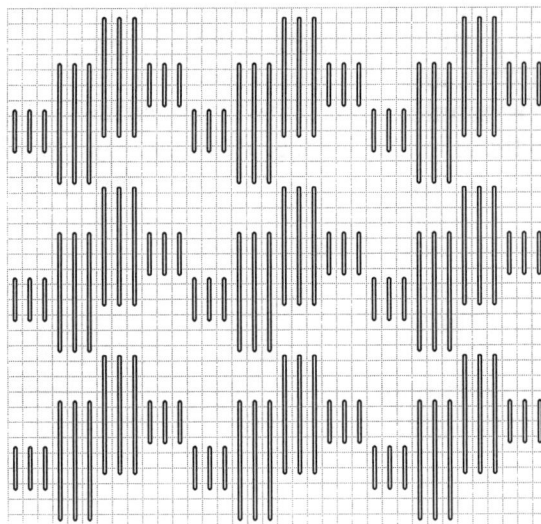

NOTE. The term "unit" will be used throughout the book to identify composite stitches or elements that are made up of more than one stitch. This seems more logical to me since such stitches are also shapes, whereas a single stitch is merely a line.

Being able to adjust the scale of a pattern is important in its effective use in an embroidery. By seeing the shapes in a pattern rather than just the outlines, one can choose an appropriate stitch or combination of stitches that will fulfill one's needs.

Because of its spread out elements, open patterning will be larger in scale than the same arrangement in a solid pattern. Changing the relationship between the repeated units of an open pattern will also alter the scale and the shape of the negative space between these units. Below are several examples of a pattern repeat that combines alternating units of Hungarian stitches with a Pavillion variation. Both stitches form diamonds, so the pattern is an arrangement of large and small diamonds.

EXAMPLE 1

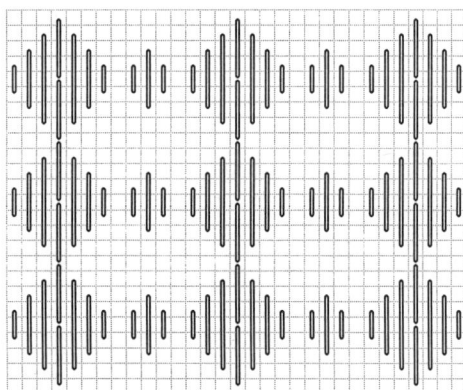

EXAMPLE 2

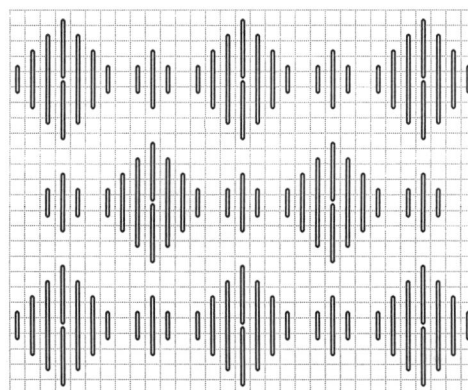

Example 1 arranges horizontal rows of these alternating units directly under each other, whereas the rows in Example 2 are staggered. The negative space changes dramatically, but the scale of both arrangements is still the same.

In the example to the right, however, the two open threads between the horizontal rows have been removed so the units of separate rows are now contiguous. The scale of the pattern has now been reduced in the "compressed" pattern, and the open space is a smaller version of the one in Example 2 since the arrangement is still staggered. All of these patterns are attractive, but they are different in spite of the fact that the components are the same.

Shifting the arrangement of an alternating repeat is another way to create variations, and these patterns can be varied further by adding secondary elements to the open areas. Try adding flip-flop units of Double Tent stitches to the rectangles in Example 3. Beaded Brick stitches would be attractive between the rows of Example 2.

Example 1 has a large negative space; therefore a number of secondary units could be added to make interesting variations. The enlarged chart below shows several possibilities that emerged from my doodle cloth.

EXAMPLE 3

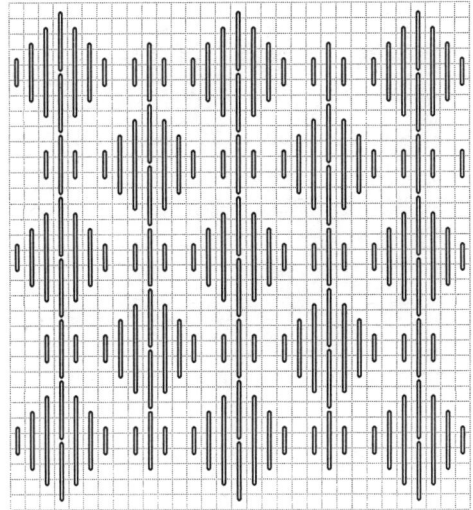

VARIATIONS OF EXAMPLE 1

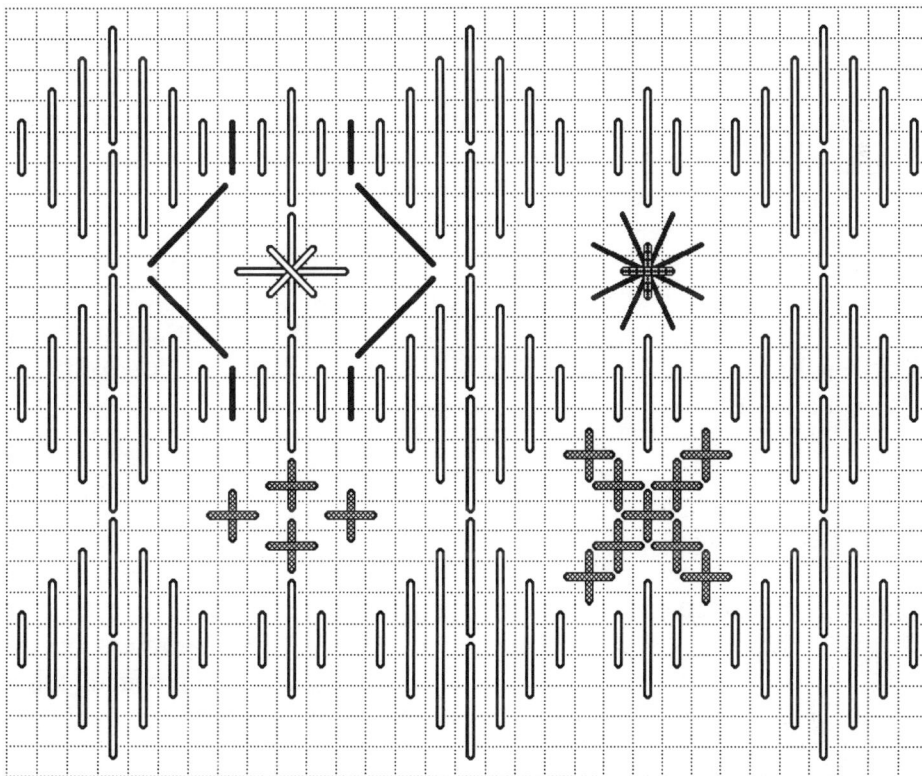

Incidentally, Example 3 of this pattern is used in *Strawberry Delight* (Color Plate VIII) to embellish some of the green triangles in the border. Notice how well the pattern contours to the shape, and this is a policy I consistently follow. In explaining this concept to students, I usually say that **a pattern should always reinforce a shape rather than antagonize it.**

TWO APPROACHES TO PATTERN DEVELOPMENT

The more one studies books on pattern structure, the more one grows in one's awareness of ways to vary pattern and the easier it becomes to develop useful original patterning with stitches. There are also many books available on historical styles of ornament, but these are often expensive "coffee table" editions. I use shapes found in non-embroidery sources such as tiles, wallpapers, batiks, baskets or quilts. I collect lots of potential pattern inspiration from magazines, catalogues, cards, etc. I always carry graph paper with me so I can quickly record various "sightings" of interesting pattern when I spot a unique blouse or tie or an unusual architectural feature in my travels. Pattern is ubiquitous, so it must also be popular. The desire to embellish things seems to be a universal human trait, and as stitchers, we merely use the unique symbols of stitches to express ourselves.

The easiest way to create original treatments, however, is not by copying other patterns. Much of my own experimentation has used a more intuitive approach. I merely play with stitches and use them as building blocks to construct patterning. I have always been an incessant doodler, and exploring pattern in this way is as satisfying as any finished piece I have ever done.

Most of my "needle play" is initially done with a pencil on graph paper. This kind of doodling is fast (no ripping!), and good results have come from just scribbling and trying to arrange the basic stitches in a different way. Over the years I have developed an extensive menu of ways to vary stitches. By applying a step-by-step "what if" approach to classic stitches, I have created some interesting new stitches (new to me anyway and unpublished as far as I know). These and many original arrangements of familiar stitches will be shared in the pattern chapters that follow.

Some stitches seem to have endless potential, whereas others are less versatile, but most stitches can be altered in some way to create a slightly different look from their traditional appearance. In addition, stitches can be combined to produce interesting composite patterns. Once I have scribbled several workable patterns that appear promising, I stitch them several times to see how changes in the thread, color or values used can alter the appearance of a pattern. There are lots of wonderful surprises along the way as the patterns are "tested," and eventually each new offspring will find its way into a finished piece.

Two of my doodle cloths are shown in Color Plate XIV. The top one shows variations of Partial Pavillion units combined with zigzag rows of long diagonal stitches (series covered in pages 81-90). The patterns in the bottom group all have open networks of Extended Diagonal Hungarian units (series covered in pages 61-64). The samplers on the inside of the front and back covers were prepared to illustrate some specific patterns featured in the pattern chapters. The naked open pattern network is usually presented next to several composite stitch patterns that use the open network as Step 1.

The band samplers on the front and back covers are more formal and were developed to showcase some of the treatments included in the book. I also chose this format to encourage lovers of historic samplers to try something different. Traditional samplers are beautiful and nostalgic, but one can make a more personal statement by designing an original sampler, using elements and stitches that reflect your own interests and taste.

HOW TO CREATE AN OPEN NETWORK BY DOODLING

The easiest way to create an open network is to lay rows of a familiar stitch but leave out every other row. The examples of Scotch variations presented on pages 2 and 3 are examples of square networks that use an alternating "checkerboard" arrangement. To connect these open units, a diagonal path must be used since a vertical or horizontal sequence would place traveling threads in the open areas.

To the right is an example of an open diamond network, using Double Straight Cross units. The remaining open areas are the same size and proportion as each individual stitch unit, and smaller stitch treatments like an Upright Cross or a Mosaic stitch can be added to these empty diamonds to create a more intricate open pattern.

My favorite stitches for open networks, however, are those that do not form a smooth diamond or a square. Units that form irregular shapes are more versatile. When arranged in networks that rotate the units, the negative space is full of "surprises" and tends not to resemble the shape of the stitch itself in the way symmetrical stitches do.

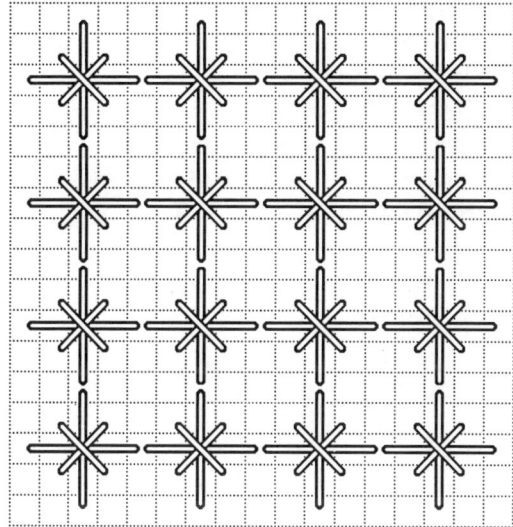

Such unique open areas are exciting by themselves, but they also form great foundations for intricate composite patterns. Some of my favorite irregular diagonal units are shown below, and examples of patterns developed with these stitches are found in the pattern sections. I have drawn a square outline around each stitch to indicate the "indentations" or potential negative space around the shapes if they are used in a square network.

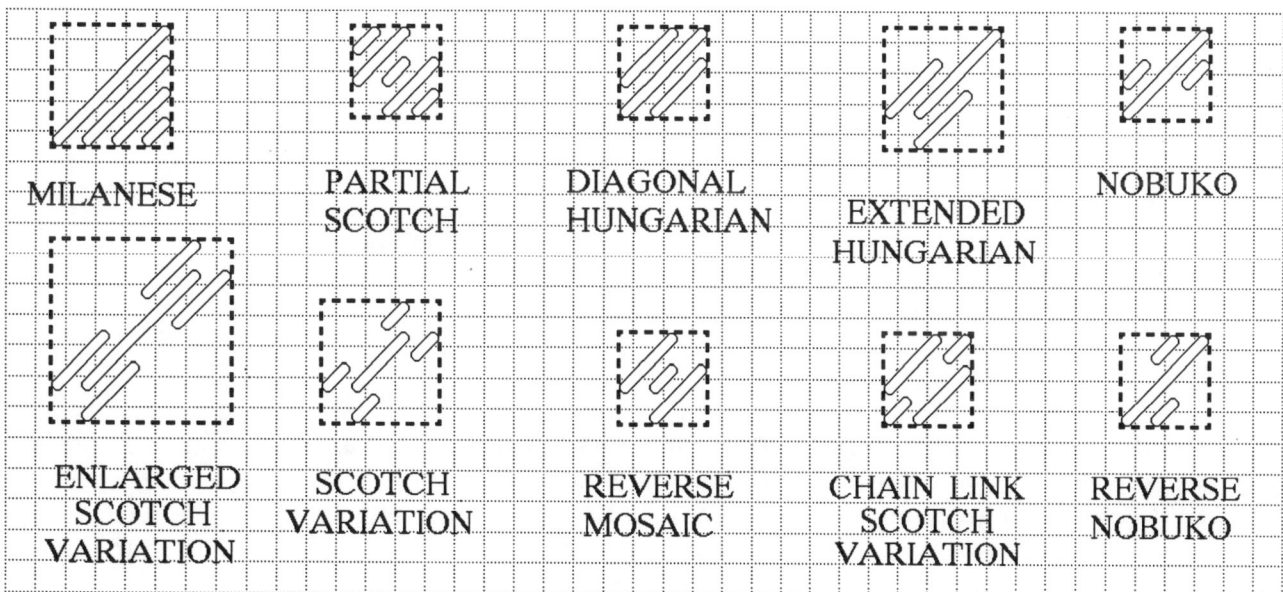

MILANESE PARTIAL SCOTCH DIAGONAL HUNGARIAN EXTENDED HUNGARIAN NOBUKO

ENLARGED SCOTCH VARIATION SCOTCH VARIATION REVERSE MOSAIC CHAIN LINK SCOTCH VARIATION REVERSE NOBUKO

All of these stitches could be labeled derivatives of Scotch stitches since they are constructed with parallel diagonal stitches and they fit inside an imaginary square. Milanese is a half unit of Scotch. Partial Scotch is really a Dotted Scotch unit with the corner Tent stitches removed. Chain Link and Reverse Mosaic are similar variations of Dotted Scotch with sections removed. Diagonal Hungarian is a Scotch unit without the Tent stitches in the upper left and lower right corners, but its proportions more closely resemble a rotated Hungarian – hence the choice of names. Calling all of these stitches Scotch variations is too confusing, so when I could think of a more appropriate name, I used it.

NOTE. Four-way arrangements or clusters of these irregular stitches are particularly attractive. Units combined in this way usually create a natural lattice or framework in which thread tails can be secured. When units connect in this way, it is always easier to create efficient sequences that will conceal traveling threads as well. When stitches with indentations are rotated and combined in clusters of four units, two different shapes usually emerge. This means that two alternating negative spaces will form when these clusters are repeated in an allover pattern. The chart below shows pairs of clusters of some of the stitches featured on the previous page.

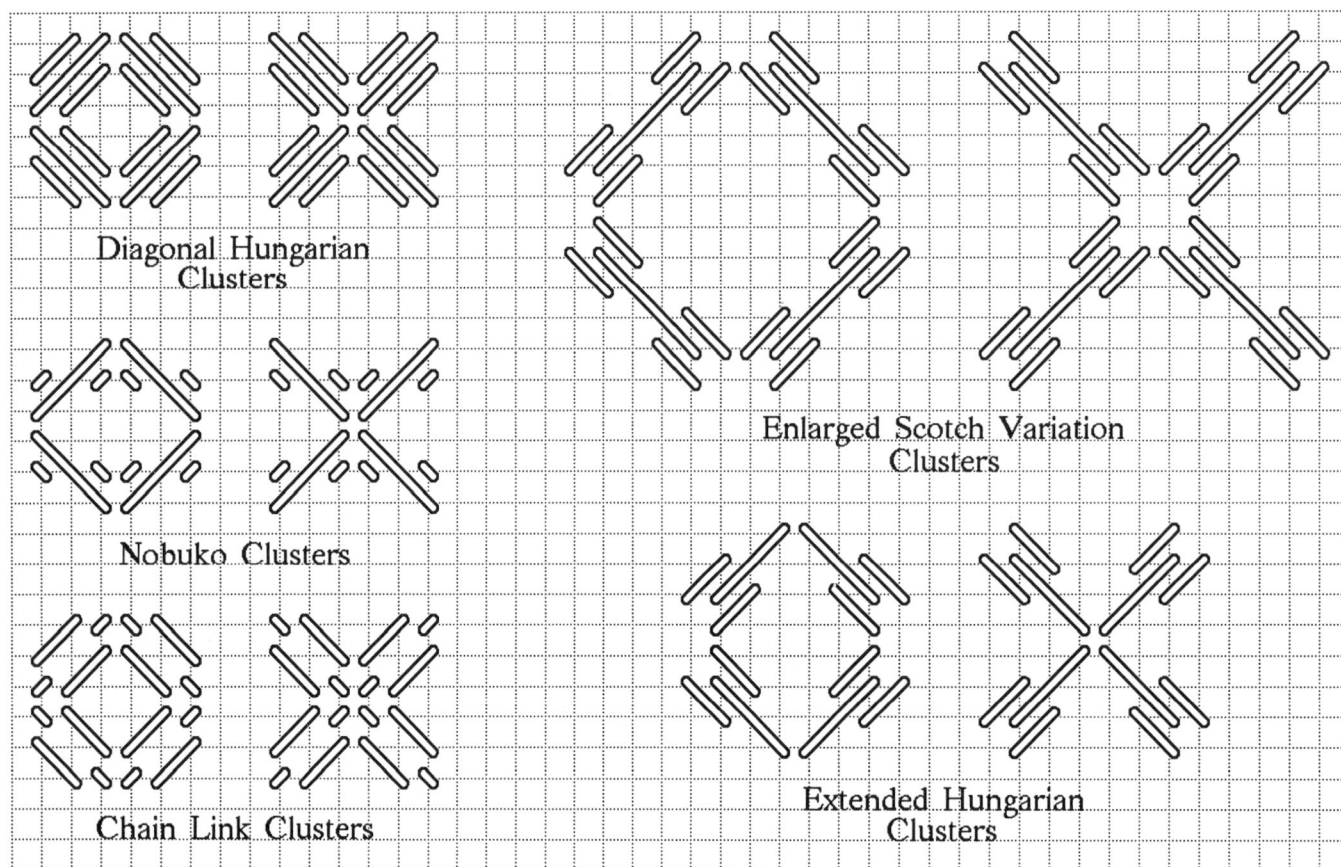

Diagonal Hungarian
Clusters

Enlarged Scotch Variation
Clusters

Nobuko Clusters

Chain Link Clusters

Extended Hungarian
Clusters

A third way to create an open network is to combine two different stitches in an alternating sequence. An example of this kind of arrangement was discussed on pages 12-13, and a number of other patterns are included in the chapter of combination networks. I also use four-way clusters for these arrangements, and one of these patterns is shown on page 72. Scattered stitches that do not touch or form some type of solid row or trellis make it difficult to connect the elements without leaving a visible trail, so the concept of a lattice with built-in converging paths is ideal for open patterning.

Sometimes I combine what I call two separate patterns that have compatible counts. In this case I usually develop one of these networks first. In the process of embellishing the negative space of this network, I end up creating a continuous pattern rather than fillings of isolated units (see the example on page 109). I will then see if I can use these two networks separately as foundations for other variations. One thing always leads to another, and that's why doodling can be addictive and fun.

THREADS FOR DOODLING

I generally choose a very simple thread range when I first stitch my graph paper doodles. I work with perle cotton because it is an inexpensive cotton thread that is quite versatile since it comes in 4 different sizes (#3, #5, #8 and #12). I gather every value of each color I want to work with in every size that will fit my canvas. Since my work is primarily on 18-mesh and 24-mesh, I usually eliminate the #3 skeins for 24-mesh and save them for occasional upright stitches on 18-mesh. I seldom use a #12 perle on 18-mesh either, but it is wonderful for certain effects on 24-mesh.

Because perle cotton is a twisted thread, no special care has to be used in laying it, so it is a fast and efficient thread with which to work. An added advantage of the twisted thread is that one can stitch with either end of a single thread with no obvious difference in the sheen or in the wear of the thread. One priority in planning open patterning is to minimize the number of starting and ending threads, so I often start with a double length thread. I use half of the thread to stitch in one direction. Then I use the second half of the thread to add stitches in the opposing direction.

This technique is particularly useful in borders, and I always use it in fillings for my first row. I start in the middle of the area with the long thread and work half of it in one direction and the other half in the other direction. Starting in the middle also allows me to center the pattern accurately, which is another important priority. After the first row is completed, one end of the thread will continue below the first row and the other end will continue above the first row. In small areas one can often complete a whole sequence with a single thread.

Using this method does require proficiency at turning corners and ease with handling compensation, but the tips on handling such maneuvers in the specific patterns presented should provide a good base for applying the same principles to any pattern. One minor shortcoming of perle cotton is that it seems to knot more than some other threads, but I am willing to put up with this drawback to enjoy the other fringe benefits.

I also gather a range of coordinating metallics in the various sizes that fit the canvas comfortably. Occasionally I use a soft overdye like Watercolours for a special effect. However, I want to caution readers about mixing variegated threads with patterning. These streaky threads tend to "dilute" or interrupt the patterning, and they are more desirable when used for random effects like shading. Sometimes I can't resist using one for my main outline. However, I will choose either a pastel combination or one with another close value range so that contrasts are minimal. A subtle ovedyed thread will not streak or blotch the pattern, so its rhythm is not interrupted.

When I work my initial samples in this limited range of threads, I use the following guidelines for selecting thread weights for open patterns. I am less concerned about coverage in open patterning because that is irrelevant. However, if threads do not fill the holes in open patterning, there is a risk that stitches will not lay straight. This is more conspicuous in upright stitches and in units of parallel satin stitches. If distortions occur, a heavier thread must be used to correct this flaw.

In general, on 18-mesh canvas I use the following thread weights:

1. #5 perle and #16 Balger metallic braid for upright stitches, and #3 perle when stitches lean improperly. A relatively new thread called Pavanne (slightly heavier than #5 perle cotton but with a similar twist) is another thread I like for both upright and diagonal stitches. It is ideal when #5 perle is too light but #3 is too heavy. It also comes in soft muted overdyed colors which blend well with matching perle cottons.

2. #8 perle and #8 Balger braid for small cross stitches and for diagonal stitches used as tiedown stitches over laid threads or as the top layer of layered stitches. Heavier threads tend to muddy the definition of such superimposed units.

3. For diagonal stitches, #5 perle would be the normal choice, and Watercolours fit well. However, I often use #8 perle when I want a light airy effect. It combines well with the heavier weights in composite patterns, and units with overlapping stitches like Ray, Diamond Eyelet, Rhodes, or Oblong Cross are more clearly defined with the lighter weight thread.

4. If large stitches are used, I generally work them in a heavier weight like #5 perle unless there are radiating stitches that share a center hole and less bulk is desirable.

When working on Congress cloth or linen, one would use the next size down in the perle cottons. One always has the option to use plied threads like Medici, cotton floss, or floche and fine weights like flower thread or metallic blending filament. These can be adjusted to exact needs or desired looks, and they are relatively inexpensive threads to doodle with as well.

I usually work a new pattern several times in my limited palette of threads, changing only the color and value distribution, and sometimes the weight of the perle cotton, to get different looks. Next I work additional samples of it, trying other thread choices. By then, I may have a specific use for the pattern in a design, so I may use threads and colors that suit those plans.

One reason that I prefer to work on canvas is that there is a wider choice of suitable threads available for this sized fabric. One may use any of the fine threads that are appropriate for linen and fabric use, but in addition, there is a whole range of natural and synthetic threads that are heavier and therefore limited to canvas use. A canvas embroiderer has a "complete palette," and the unique look that Velour or Rachel can give a pattern cannot be duplicated on evenweave fabrics. Fabrics also cannot support the weight of some of the multinetwork patterns. However, many of these composite patterns are attractive when only a few steps are combined, so do not hesitate to use partial segments of some of the more intricate patterns.

Specific design needs may force one to alter a pattern even further. One must consider the other elements that it will be used with and reassess the role of the pattern. I am constantly amazed at how much the feeling and dominance in a pattern can shift with simple changes, and because of this, a favorite pattern can usually be manipulated to suit any need or mood desired.

To me, there is no such thing as a bad pattern. I merely keep working with it until I find the right combination of colors, threads, and values to make it successful.

The most consistent observation I have made is that the dark and light areas will always draw more attention than medium value areas, and the way to emphasize different elements is to alter the contrasts in a pattern to achieve it. A white canvas tends to keep the colors clearer in a pattern so color interaction is less likely in open patterns with a white ground. Pastel and ecru canvasses are pale so only light colors are usually affected by the ground. Today, however, there are several canvasses that are a middle value and a medium intensity. The Levantine, Aquamarina, and Lavendula shades can be tricky to use because of these two characteristics. Similarly if the canvas is dark, the contrasts with the medium and light threads are intensified, and a light thread will dominate.

Conventional guidelines do not apply to these colored grounds. The relativity of color affects all of our decisions about color and value, and if you do not understand pertinent phenomena like color interaction, I encourage you take a color class. One can waste a lot of time trying to work out patterning with a trial-and-error approach, and an understanding of some basic principles is invaluable.

One of my favorite demonstrations in my notebook classes about pattern is to give students a composite pattern to stitch. I provide sequence instructions but no guidelines about color and value distribution. Invariably twenty totally different interpretations develop, and everyone is amazed that they all came from the same black and white chart. Seeing such variety awakens students to the inherent potential of every pattern and proves the value of doodling. In comparing the samples and analyzing the different visual effects, everyone learns much more about managing color and value and about controlling dominance in a pattern so this is an ideal group exercise. As a designer, it would be a luxury to have a few "elves" at home to stitch variations for me. Time constraints make it impossible to exploit every stitch or pattern to its fullest potential!

SPECIALIZED TECHNIQUES FOR OPEN PATTERNING

Open patterns require a somewhat different set of rules from those that apply to regular canvas. I do not like the word "rules" and prefer to call these "priorities" instead. Because the canvas is no longer completely covered, a number of aspects of the stitching become more conspicuous. Therefore it is necessary to take measures that will make the open stitches look totally consistent.

In the past, a thread was supposed to fit a mesh exactly to achieve full coverage, but this requirement is not mandatory in open patterning so varying weights of threads can be used together to add distinction to a pattern. The main requirement is that a thread must be heavy enough to lay straight and to resist any lean that the tension on the traveling thread may cause. The thread must also be light enough to not distort the holes in the fabric. In traditional canvas embroidery, the threads of the mono canvas will shift somewhat to accommodate varying weights of threads; as long as tension control is uniform and coverage is good, minor discrepancies will not be obvious. However, in open patterning the background is exposed so any enlarged holes are an eyesore.

Stitch Sequences. In conventional canvas patterns, stitches are usually executed in parallel rows back and forth until an area is filled. The one consistent rule that is followed is to always come up in an empty hole when adding stitches and sink into the filled areas. In open patterning, the elements are spread out, so patterns no longer build in this way. Usually a main network is created as Step 1, and it is a spread out lattice or group of rows with open areas between the elements or "outlines." When additional accents are added, it is necessary to both come up in and sink into prefilled holes. Therefore an important priority is to keep these shared holes uncluttered. My way of accomplishing this is to always maintain a back stitch pull on both ends of every stitch. If there is tension on both ends, all stitches will be snugly wrapped, and repeated stitches will look consistent and uniform in size.

Most stitch encyclopedias provide good logical sequences for executing stitches. However, they seldom deal with the need to turn corners with stitches and the need to compensate the stitches around various contours in a design area. Often it is necessary to do what I call a pivot stitch to maintain the correct tension on a stitch, and this usually occurs at the end of one row or at the beginning of a new row. In solid patterning, it is possible to exit a row and weave either in an outline or in a surrounding pattern to get to a new entry point. In open patterning, I often construct an outline to provide an area for traveling and for securing thread tails, but sometimes such a convenience is not available, so the traveling or necessary changes are made within the pattern itself. In the patterns that follow, you will see many instances where pivot stitches are used. Rather than discuss theoretical concepts here, I will let the actual patterns illustrate these points.

In open patterning, it is sometimes necessary to add various parts of a stitch in separate sequences rather than completing a unit in sequential order. Stitches are often constructed in a completely different manner in order to conceal the traveling threads. I also incorporate certain strategies into the planning of my patterns that will allow elements to be added as side trips rather than as a separate sequence later. In my ten years of experimenting with such patterning, I have come up with a number of creative solutions to various recurring problems, and these will be shared in the individual patterns. The main guideline that I follow is to be flexible and use logical practical solutions to the challenges presented.

Starting and Ending Threads. Another priority in planning open patterns is to create solid paths for threads that will accommodate thread tails comfortably as well as provide convenient paths for traveling. Both starting and ending tails are buried after the pattern is completed, so I do not recommend the use of waste knots. Few patterns have wide rows of stitching that will comfortably wrap a thread tail laid in front of its path, so there is always a risk of piercing such a thread. Any waste knot would have to be positioned perfectly to avoid such split threads. I prefer to use what I call "away tails" that do not interfere with the stitching. I park the starting tail at least 3" away from the direction that the stitching will follow. This length will provide a long enough tail to rethread once the stitching is completed.

When starting and ending tails are buried, simple weaving is often not feasible in open patterns. If the backing is sparse, it is more effective to whip or wrap the tails in the backing instead. If weaving can be used, I usually take a locking back stitch midway along the path to add a measure of additional security to keep tails from wiggling loose. Wool threads naturally cling to each other but other threads do not, and the less dense backings of open patterns need extra help.

Another priority in open patterning, that is of particular concern when several sequences are combined, is to spread out the paths of the traveling threads on the reverse side. In multicolor patterns, I usually recommend that thread tails always be secured within the paths of the same color. This automatically keeps threads separated and prevents areas from becoming overpacked. Sometimes excess bulk can be eliminated by merely working sequences in different directions when they are flexible. Paths will only overlap where the rows converge, and no part of the backing will be strained.

DESIGNING WITH PATTERN

This segment could be a book in itself. It is impossible to cover design adequately without dealing with color as one of the elements of design. Therefore I urge anyone with an interest in creating original designs to take courses in both color and design in order to acquire both the skills and the confidence to take this step. Since the main thrust of this book is to share ideas and methods to create original patterning, the discussion of design will be limited to patterning as one of the elements of design.

Once a design has been selected or planned as a line drawing, and once the ground and the threads have been chosen, the next task is to plan the stitch treatments or patterning for the design. As stressed earlier, there is great potential for endless variety but achieving success also requires discipline and control. It is easy to create or select an interesting pattern or a series of patterns, but getting several patterns to work in an overall design can be both a challenge as well as an overwhelming task. This selection process requires a balance of color, a balance of value and a balance of scale. Some patterns maneuver well in almost any shape, whereas other patterns are best used in geometric shapes that fit them since they do not compensate easily within irregular shapes.

One reason why I teach canvas rather than crewel or Japanese embroidery is that I am better able to stitch plan a canvas design. Because I have doodled so much, I am familiar with all of the basic stitches, and I understand the limitations of a grid. My experience allows me to be daring, and my first instinct is usually the right instinct now, but it took many years of "trial and error" as well as study to attain this level of expertise. In the other mediums, I find that I can regain my technical skills reasonably quickly after a long layoff, and I thoroughly enjoy designing since curves can be used freely on fabric. However, the stumbling block is usually the stitch planning since there are so many choices, and I have not spent the same amount of time experimenting with those treatments as I have my canvas doodles.

One cannot expect to achieve what I call a level of comfort and "fluidity" in a field without "paying one's dues" so to speak. As one who loves physical activities, I like to compare the growth of a competent stitcher to the development of a fine athlete. When one first learns a sport, it can be overwhelming to remember and apply all of the necessary movements and strategies. In much the same way, a new stitcher feels clumsy and uncoordinated with a needle at first. As skills develop, suddenly all of those individual steps become second nature to the "intermediate" student, and one can maneuver with ease and confidence. All of the training and practice pays off, and the skills acquired eventually appear refined and sophisticated. What is so remarkable about professional athletes is how easy they make their performances look. We are dazzled and tend to forget about the long hours of training and discipline involved in gaining such maturity!

21

HUNGARIAN HOOPLA

One way to design pattern is to make a complete design that incorporates only one specific stitch. The geometric design shown to the left was created for a contest that restricted entries to just such a requirement. I used nothing but Flip-flop Diagonal Hungarian stitches to outline the shapes.

I worked with a basic nine-patch square to begin with, and five of the original squares are still visible. By adding the triangle shapes to the four corner squares and by creating the "tab" patterning in the middle sections, I was able to create a circular design that fit the band box top that I had planned.

This kind of outlining technique can be very useful in planning a design. In this case, no further embellishment was added, but interior fillings would be appropriate for other situations.

MILANESE MUTATIONS

Another way to design with a single stitch is to play with clusters (units created by rotating and combining stitch units into four-way groups). The design to the left is composed of nothing but Milanese stitches. I doodled a lot of different cluster shapes on graph paper first. Next I worked out the framework or border for the nine-patch outline, using a handsome "star octagon" as the corner motif. Then each of the three interior squares was planned to make sure the border dimensions were compatible with the inside fillings. Once assembled, the design resembles lace.

This piece was also finished as a round band box top, so the triangle patterning along the sides of the border was added to make the design fit a circle. A nice surprise was seeing the dimension that these simple elements added – the nine-patch square then looked superimposed on top of the "diamond doily."

Milanese is a particularly striking stitch to use in clusters, but try using some of the stitches shown on page 16 for a similar experiment. Any stitches with irregular shapes will form interesting four-way clusters and can be combined in this way.

22

EXTENDED CROSS STAR

Another way to design with stitches is to take advantage of the natural contours of a stitch pattern. When I work with a new stitch, I change its placement to see what lines or shapes will form. The three examples on this page are doodles of some shapes made from groupings of Extended Cross stitches. The large star has parallelograms that are formed with an allover arrangement of these units. The diamond points are formed from a pair of mirrored outline rows of the same stitch. The offset alignment used produces a natural slant.

The small star below on the left is formed with the same stitch, but this time an encroaching placement is used. Mirrored pairs of stitches are combined to create a thicker outline too.

The extensions of the pairs lay side-by-side and form a "ladder." The slanted line is different from that used in the first star, but the ladder can be mirrored in each quadrant to form a different star.

EXTENDED CROSS STAR

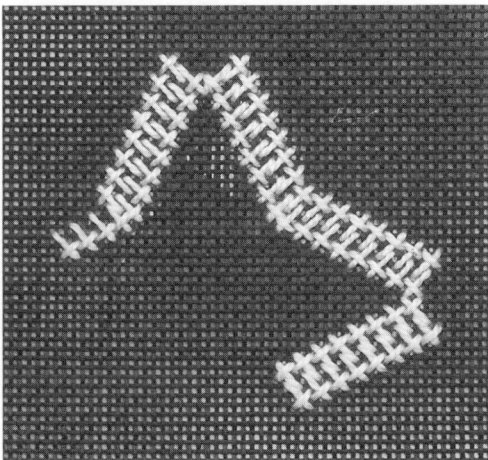

The diamond pattern to the right is also formed from the same Extended Cross units in an encroached position. A second cross is added to the extension this time to increase the density. Simple changes in a stitch can create a slightly different look, and new shapes result from different placements.

EXTENDED CROSS DIAMONDS

These three examples illustrate how the game of "what if" can lead to promising patterns. Each doodle could become the focal point of a whole design, and someday they will.

A few additional patterns that form unusual shapes are shown below. By letting such patterns be used in a design in its natural shape, there is no need to distort the pattern by having to compensate it.

CABLE LINK OUTLINE **STRETCHED STEM OUTLINE** **MIRRORED CHEVRONS**

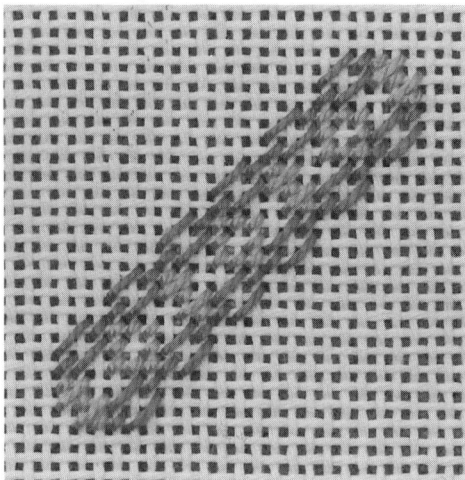

The Cable Link pattern forms a natural diagonal ribbon with an undulating edge. The Stretched Stem pattern forms a natural parallelogram shape, and this is further emphasized by the blackwork outlines that divide the stripe rows into small parallelograms. The Mirrored Chevron pattern forms a natural diamond, but like the Cable Link outline, this edge also has a wavy or undulating quality.

CORNER MOTIF OF FOUR-WAY DIAGONAL HUNGARIAN WITH BLACKWORK ACCENTS

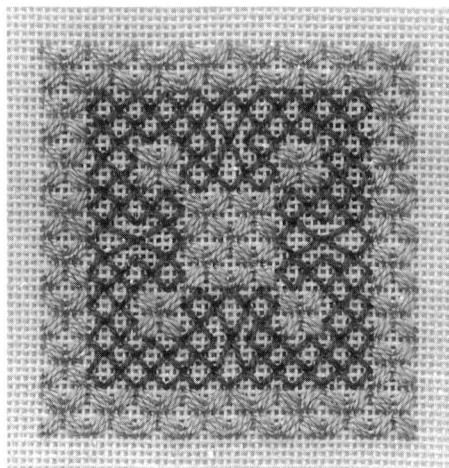

Another way to create interesting shapes is with shading rather than with outlines. In the small square to the left, I used an outline of Four-way Diagonal Hungarian units. Inside I placed a small square of the same four clusters and added a single cluster to each corner. The negative space was not very interesting until the diamond repeats of the blackwork were added. By interrupting this allover pattern and adding the four-way Oblong Crosses in the space where some diamonds were eliminated, the patterning becomes more exciting.

FLIP-FLOP HUNGARIAN CLUSTERS

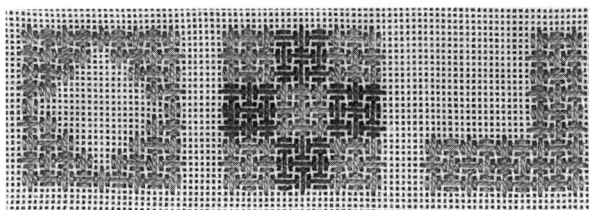

In the series of patterns on the right side above, I used an allover arrangement of Flip-flop Hungarian units to form three different shapes. The left square has an open diamond in the center, and the right square is an L-shape. Both of these shapes were created by eliminating some repeats of the original solid square. The center square, however, is a checkerboard of alternating small squares created by shading within the overall square.

The center square shows how simple changes of value within a pattern can alter its visual impact. The examples that follow also illustrate how a difference in emphasis can result from alterations in the value contrasts. Color and texture are additional factors that can enhance contrasts, but the samples presented will show the patterns either as black and white photographs or black and white charts, so that the values are clear.

BYZANTINE VARIATION

The composite pattern to the left has natural contours that create the unusual diamond shape shown. All of the stitches in the pattern are diagonal stitches of varying lengths, and the color treatments used are identical except for the zigzag rows (which are obvious in the lower half of the shape).

In the top half of the pattern, these rows are executed in two contrasting values (one middle and one light). The pattern here is an allover diaper repeat. In the bottom section, these rows are done in two close light values of the same color, and the pattern is a chevron stripe.

Simple changes in value contrasts not only alter the dominance within a pattern, but such changes can also change its classification. Sometimes the same texture stitch pattern can be manipulated to form three different types of canvas patterning – groundings, stripes or diapers.

A grounding is an allover pattern that is stitched in one color or in two close values of one color, and it is usually used as a background. A stripe is a pattern with a strong linear thrust whether it is a straight line, a zigzag path, or an undulating wave. It usually has strong contrasts but some patterns like Hungarian Grounding can form stripes with texture contrasts as well as value changes. A diaper pattern is a network of allover repeats that form visual diagonals in both directions. A diaper must have clear contrasts, which can be achieved with either two colors or two values of one color.

EXAMPLE 1 - THREE VARIATIONS OF ONE PATTERN
NETWORK WITH ALTERNATING ROWS OF MOSAIC AND REVERSE MOSAIC

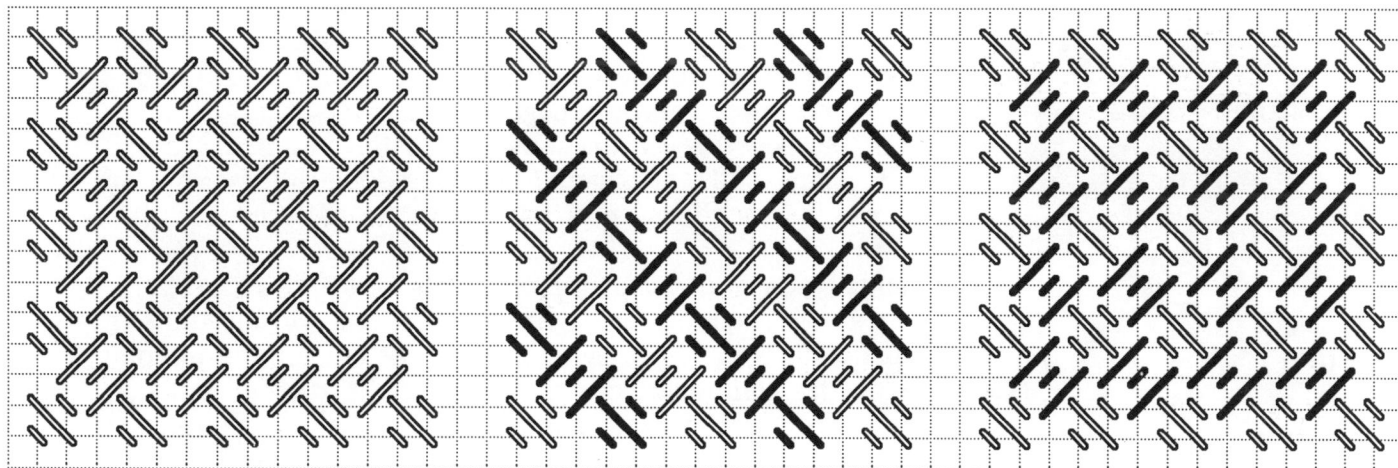

GROUNDING   STRIPE   DIAPER PATTERN

25

This pattern is a solid version of the open network featured in the middle of page 44. A different dominance occurs when the solid one-color or one-value pattern (the grounding) is executed in two colors or values. When the contrasts occur in diagonal rows, the pattern becomes a stripe. When the contrasts occur in vertical and horizontal rows, the pattern becomes a square lattice or diaper arrangement.

EXAMPLE 2 - THREE VARIATIONS OF ONE PATTERN
NETWORK OF DOTTED SCOTCH UNITS

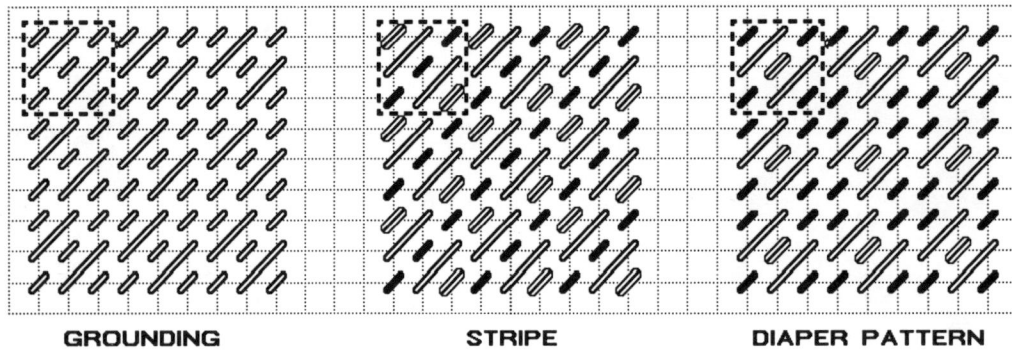

| GROUNDING | STRIPE | DIAPER PATTERN |

Dotted Scotch is a variation of Scotch stitch. The usual long middle stitch has been divided into three Tent stitches. One whole unit is identified with the dotted outline in the upper left corner of each chart to clarify the single repeats. The left pattern is done in one value or color and is a grounding. The middle pattern emphasizes the diagonals formed by the dark value used for the middle stitches of Tent so it is a stripe. The right pattern has no continuous directional flow. Its alternating elements form a diaper.

OPEN NETWORK OF FLIP-FLOP OFFSET MOSAIC

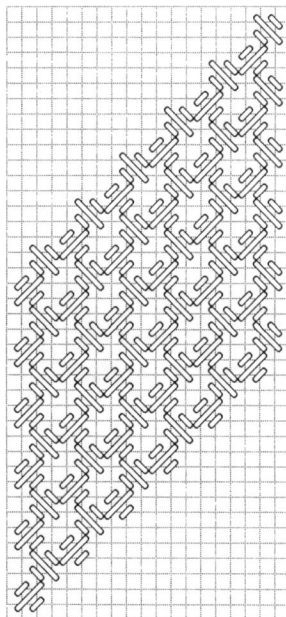

The next comparison features an open pattern that has an alternating repeat. The network combines flip-flop units of Mosaic stitches that are placed in an offset position. If this pattern were executed in a light pink thread on a pale pink canvas, it would appear to be a grounding (with diaper potential, however!). If the pattern were stitched in two colors or values in alternating diagonal rows, it would become a stripe. If the pattern were stitched in a light thread and placed on a dark canvas, one would see a clear diaper repeat in two colors or values.

The negative space could also be embellished further. Additional variations are shown in the charts that follow. Pairs of Oblong Cross units are used to fill the negative space in several different ways, but the coverage is not complete so the patterns are still open. By changing the arrangement of the added fillings, one can also change the classification of this composite pattern.

An enlarged view of the chart to the left appears on the next page. There is also a sequence chart for the Flip-flop Mosaic units in the upper left corner. No sequence is provided for the Oblong Crosses in the additional charts. They can be stitched with no changes in the usual method of executing crosses. Keep the top cross consistent throughout the pattern, and be careful to work the rows so that no traveling paths will show in the open areas.

EXAMPLE 1 - GROUNDING
OPEN NETWORK OF OFFSET
FLIP-FLOP MOSAIC UNITS
WITH A SEQUENCE CHART

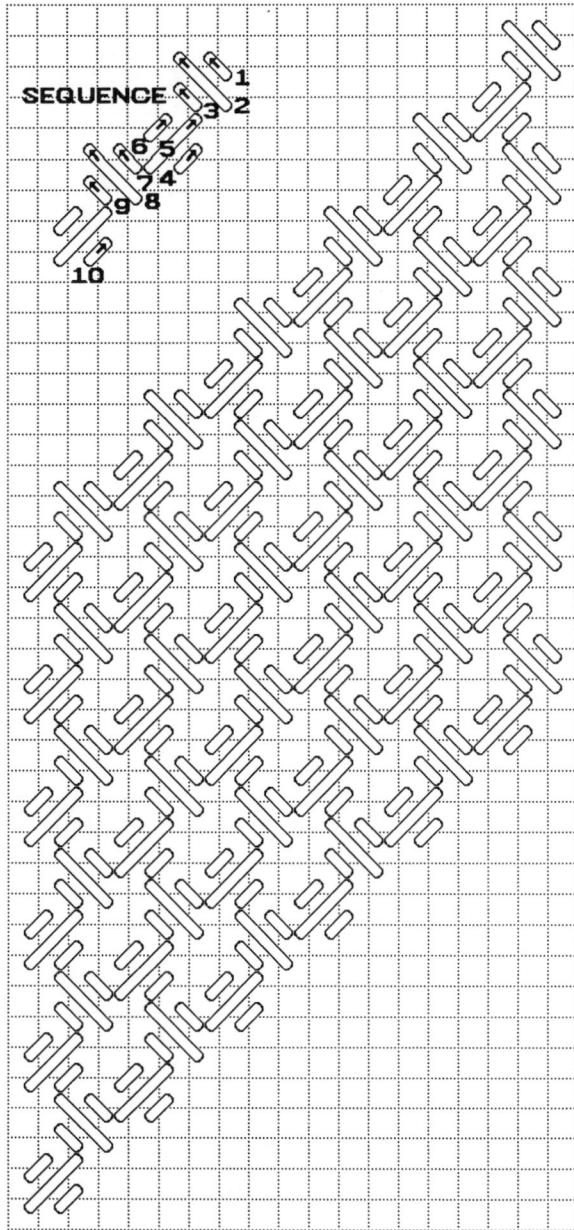

EXAMPLE 2 - STRIPE
COMPOSITE PATTERN WITH
PAIRS OF OBLONG CROSSES ADDED
IN LINEAR BANDS

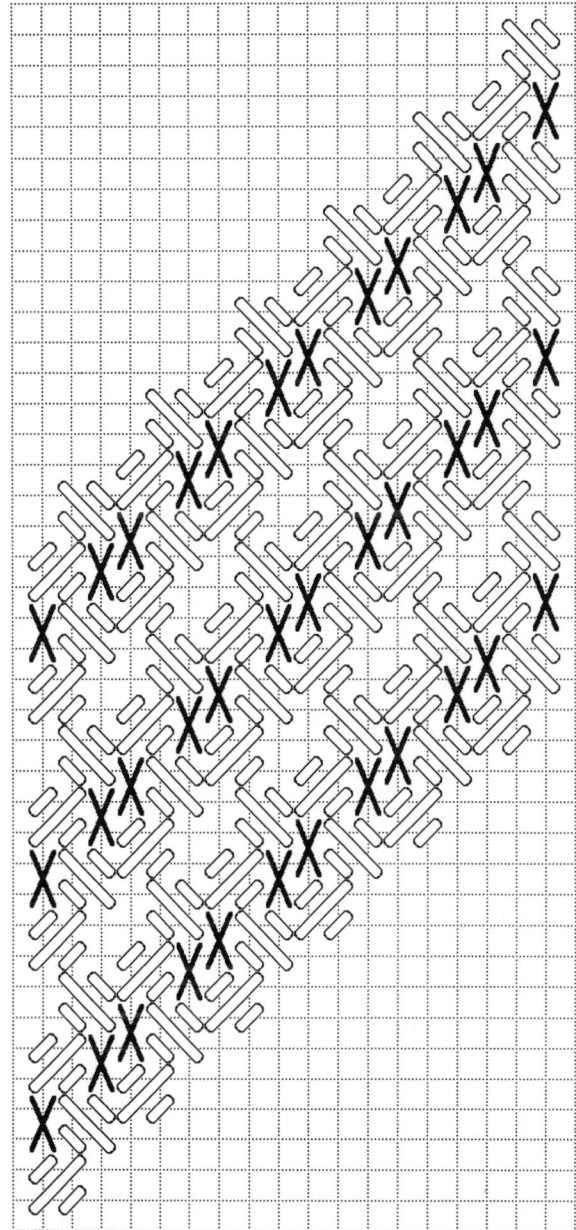

On the next page, there are two different diaper pattern variations. The one on the left is a dense allover arrangement, and every space has a pair of Oblong Crosses. The example on the right is an open diaper with enlarged repeats. Further variations could be created by changing the accent filling so perhaps you would like to doodle or stitch some other combinations.

27

EXAMPLE 3 - DIAPER PATTERN COMPOSITE PATTERN WITH PAIRS OF OBLONG CROSSES ADDED TO EVERY OPEN AREA

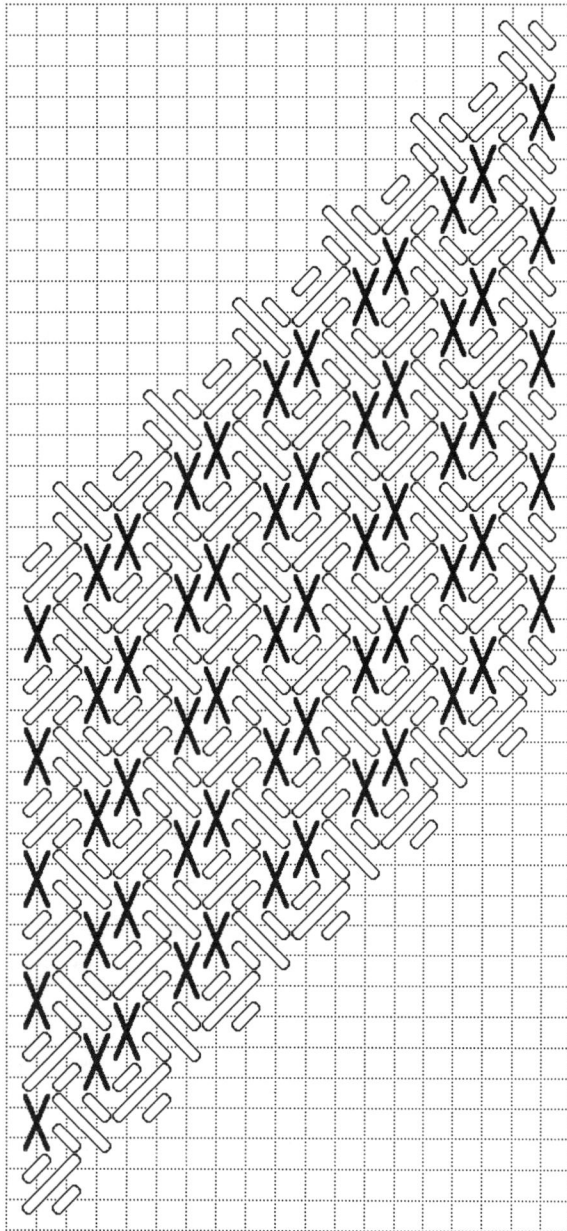

EXAMPLE 4 - DIAPER PATTERN COMPOSITE PATTERN WITH PAIRS OF OBLONG CROSSES IN AN OPEN ARRANGEMENT

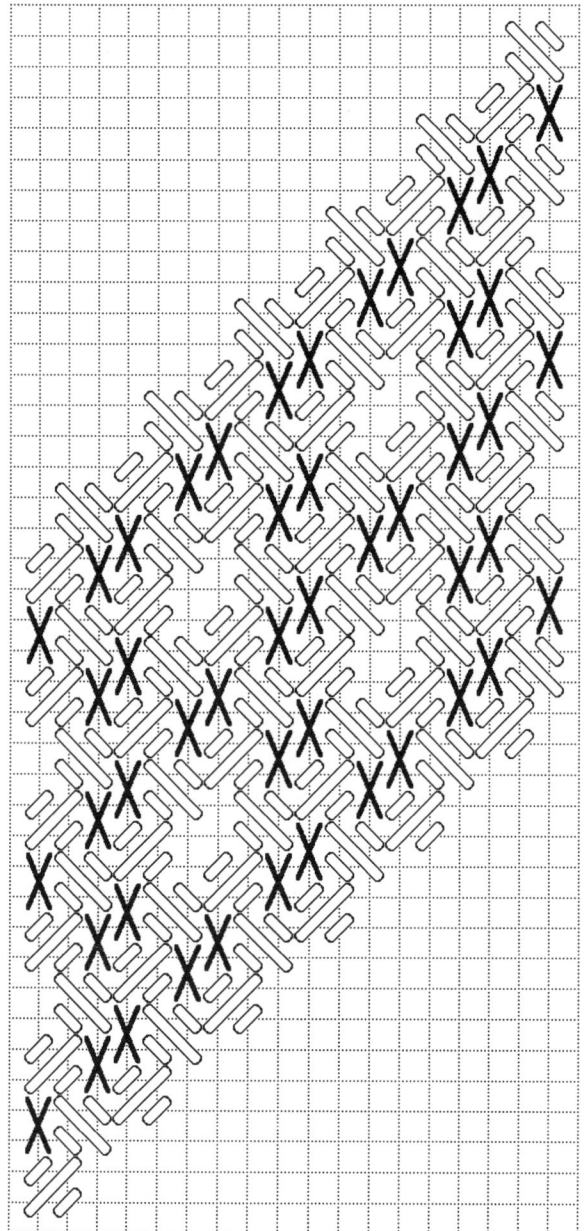

One final comparison will illustrate another point regarding value contrasts and how they can alter the appearance of a pattern. Some open patterns have potential variations that can be created by merely isolating a portion of the network and highlighting it with a contrasting value or color. One example that can be used in this way is Pattern 1 on page 42. On the next page, there is a chart showing an enlarged example of this overall pattern. A secondary diamond path has been darkened to indicate how a contrasting value or color can create a combination network.

When this dual combination is actually stitched, one path will appear superimposed on the other one. Try doing one sample with the dark outline slightly darker than the light outline. Then do a second sample with a reversal in the values. Does this alter the visual effect and which value appears on top in the two examples? Then do a second series of both treatments using stronger contrasts. This sort of optical play makes canvas stitching fun - pattern will continually surprise you, and you often get a different dominance than is anticipated.

EXAMPLE 1 - DIAMOND LATTICE IN TWO VALUES
The dark path is continuous and uninterrupted.

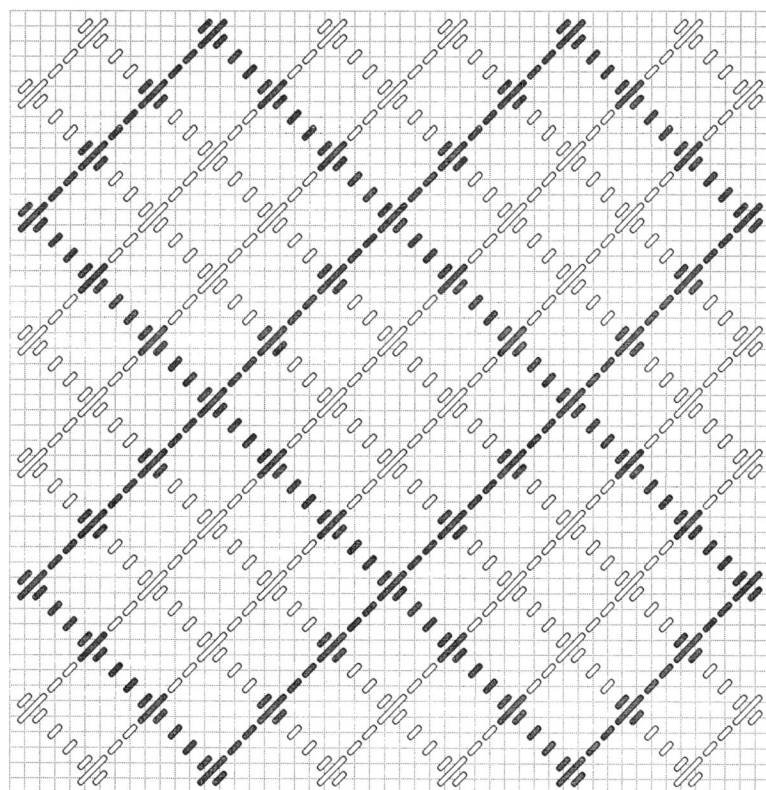

In the bold pattern to the left, the dark value is the "unbroken" path. Below is a two-value example of the smaller scale version of the open pattern to the left (featured on page 43). In this sample, the contrasts are reversed, so the lighter shade is the "unbroken" path.

EXAMPLE 2
DIAMOND LATTICE
(Smaller in Scale)
Light path is continuous.

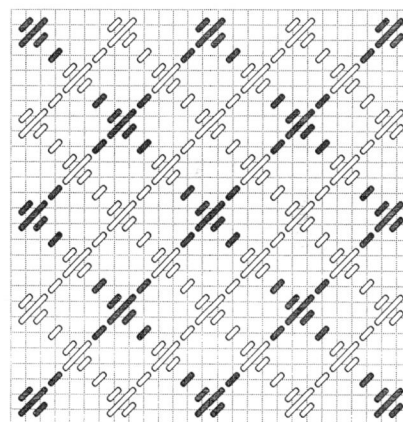

As you can see, it is the unbroken path that dominates in the chart, and this will occur in the thread samples as well, regardless of the values combined. Other optical results are less easy to predict, and the surprises that occur when patterns are stitched in multiple interpretations is part of the fascination of pattern. Expect the unexpected and enjoy!

These comparisons have demonstrated some of the variety that can be achieved in designs by exploiting pattern in simple ways. By showing some actual stitched samples in black and white photographs, I hope I have also reaffirmed the importance of value in determining the final impact of a pattern. In the pages ahead, I will introduce you to a variety of unusual patterns, and I hope you enjoy bringing them to life with color and thread. Let's chart some new territory together (who could resist that pun!); and I hope my examples point the way to new dimensions in your future needle expressions.

29

Most stitch encyclopedias begin with the category of upright stitches, so it seemed logical to start with open networks that use either vertical stitches or horizontal stitches in their composition. Stitches from other categories are added as accents in some of the open areas, but the Step 1 outline that forms the basic pattern contours will be a series of straight stitches in one or both of these directions.

1. Open Old Florentine. This is a simple pattern, but I included it to illustrate how the arrangement of a regular solid pattern can be spread out to form an open variation. In this case, one open thread of canvas is left between the horizontal rows of Old Florentine. Such an arrangement is particularly dramatic in a light thread on a dark fabric since the contrasts are heightened. I often enhance the contrasts further by using perle cotton for such patterns since they make the parallel satin stitches appear embossed against the flat background. Patterns with units of parallel satin stitches are also ideal for silk or cotton floss since the flat stitches allow a maximum play of light on the smooth strands.

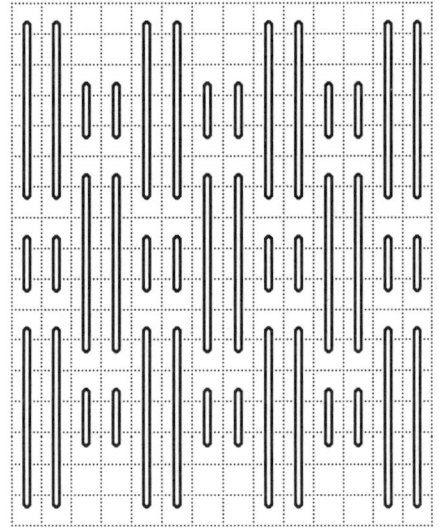

Open patterns with only upright stitches tend to resemble darning patterns, and one could certainly execute this example in vertical rows of running stitches. On canvas, however, I prefer to stitch them in horizontal rows of snugly wrapped stitches. The patterns look "crisper" when the open holes are not cluttered with traveling threads, and it is also easier to end threads in the stronger backing of the wrapped stitches.

Almost any stitch pattern that is laid in horizontal rows can be varied in this way. Some interesting possibilities include Pavillion, Hungarian Ground or Parisian. One could also leave more than one thread between the rows for a more open effect.

2. Straight Gobelin Variation. Gobelin Steps. This pattern repeats clusters of four Gobelin stitches that straddle three threads. Each cluster forms a parallelogram and the units overlap each other in the horizontal rows and appear to "stack" since the high stitch of one group is always above the low unit of the next group. The negative space between the rows is an attractive parallelogram of a different scale.

The overall chart to the right provides sequences for doing this pattern in horizontal rows. The left to right row proceeds in sequential order, but the right to left row needs an adjustment to make the downhill steps connect gracefully when the stacked pairs meet.

On the next page, there is second sequence that executes the pattern in diagonal rows. This option is more efficient, but both sequences keep the open areas clear, and all stitches are snugly wrapped.

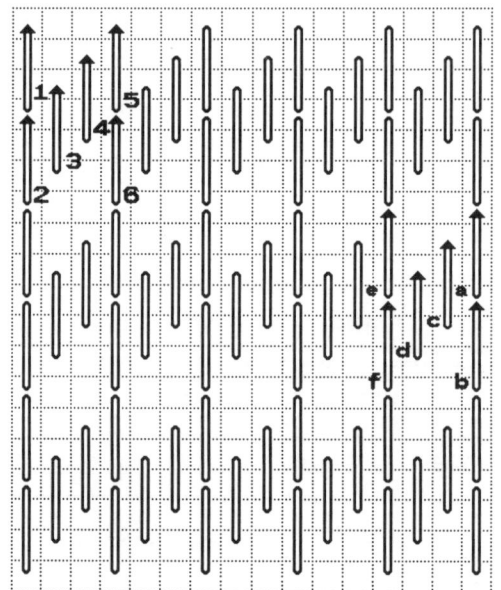

DIAGONAL SEQUENCE

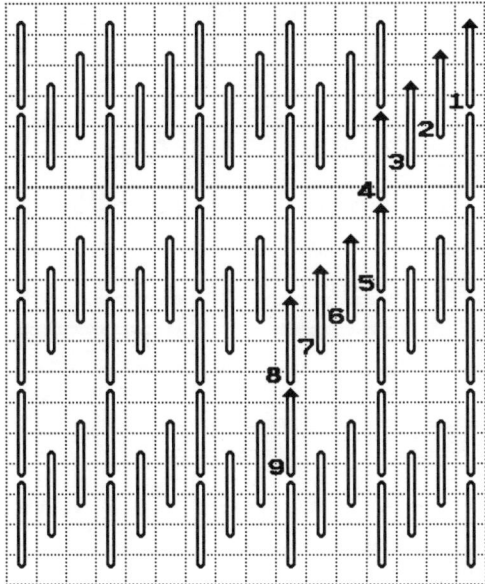

Execute the stitches in Option 2 in sequential order, as numbered for the downhill rows in the chart to the left. To add the uphill rows, rotate the chart 180° and use the same sequence to stitch in the reverse direction. If it is difficult to read the numbers upside down, rotate the canvas 180° instead.

NOTE. When a pattern is flexible, I usually let the shape where it is used influence the sequence chosen. The first option is a better choice when the area is more horizontal than vertical since fewer total rows would be required. Conversely, the vertical path is better for a tall narrow shape. **Traveling from row to row in open patterning is not always easy, so fewer rows is a definite advantage, especially when convenient outline areas around a shape are not available.**

Notice how many of the designs in the color plates have bold outlines. These are functional as well as decorative "devices" that provide areas for securing thread tails as well as for traveling between rows.

3. Brick Variation. Brick Diamonds. This pattern is similar to the one used in the background of *Blue Oriental Lantern* (Color Plate 1). The diamonds are slightly smaller in this version and less elongated.

For background treatments, I usually use a pastel thread on a white ground or a thread of the same color in a slightly darker value when the ground is pastel. These subtle contrasts keep the patterning quiet, adding a pleasing surrounding area that does not overwhelm or compete with the foreground.

Execute each zigzag row of Brick stitches as a separate row, as shown to the right.

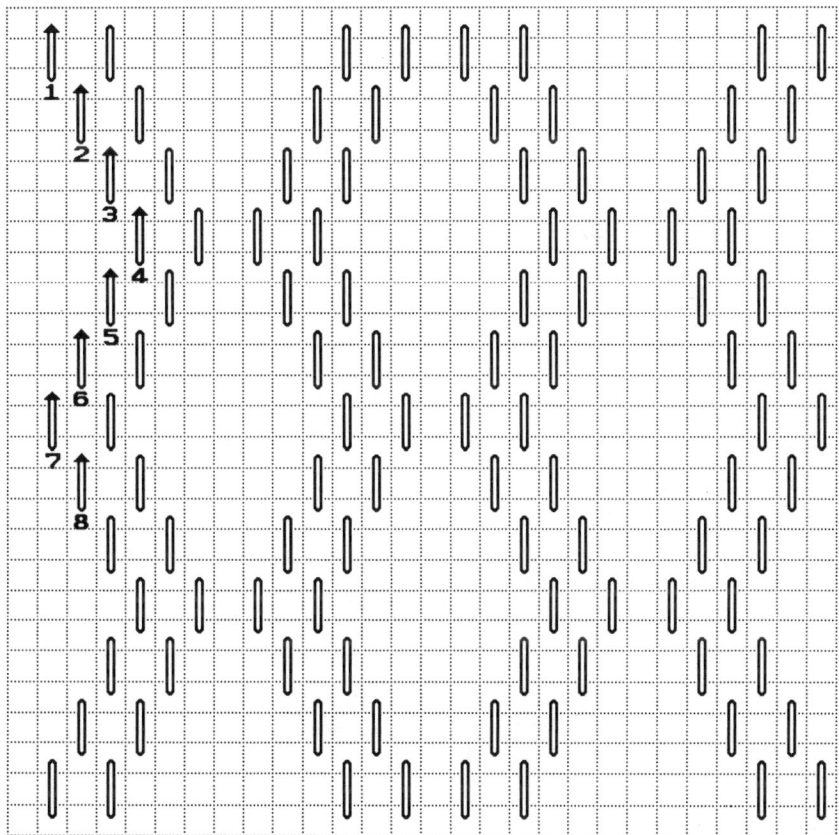

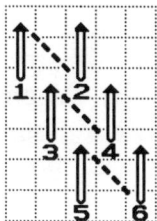

On linen or cotton evenweave fabrics, this pattern could be executed in combined vertical rows, which are more efficient (see the alternative sequence to the left). Notice that the diagonal path of the traveling thread, as indicated by the dotted line, shows between each pair of parallel Brick stitches. Fabric threads are generally thicker, so the holes between the threads are smaller than those of comparable size canvasses. Therefore such traveling paths would not be conspicuous. On canvas, however, any threads that cross open holes will show, so

31

it is important to avoid any clutter that will detract from the surface patterning. **The sequences charted for the patterns in this book will always conceal traveling paths and can be used on any ground.**

4. Flip-flop Straight Gobelin. To my knowledge, you will not find the term "flip-flop" in any other stitch encyclopedia. Because a number of my variations involve rotating a stitch unit and combining the units into an alternating arrangement, this label seems like a logical way to identify such patterns.

In this pattern, pairs of long straight stitches are combined in an alternating arrangement, leaving one open thread between the flip-flop pairs. This pattern could be executed in rows of running stitches in two different directions, but it is more efficient to use a sequence that does not require separate paths to connect the flip-flop units. The numbered sequence shown connects the units in vertical rows. To cover the unavoidable exposed traveling threads, add flip-flop rows of Tent stitches as Step 2. Work these in vertical rows of running stitches.

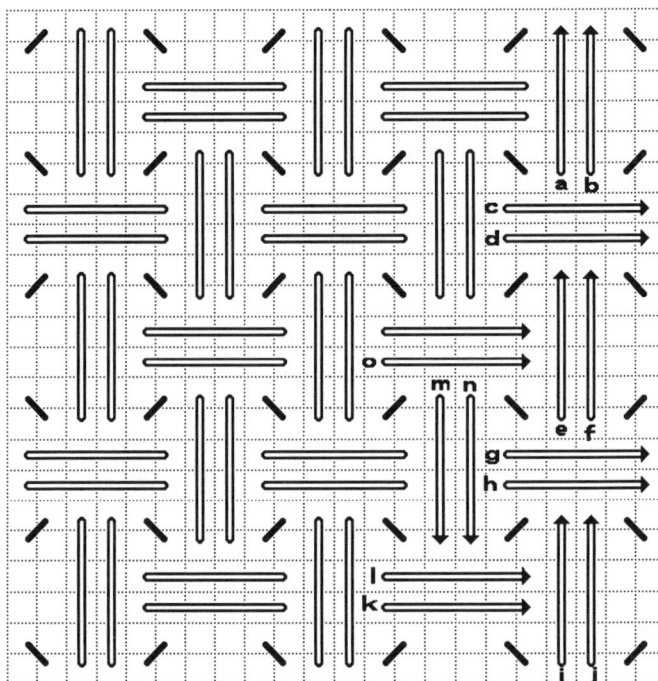

5. Alternating Hungarian and Brick Network. This pattern is formed by combining two different straight stitches in alternating horizontal rows. When brick stitches are in a pattern, it is fun to add beads to these stitches; the right side of the chart shows the pattern with this variation. Use either #8 perle or 2-3 strands of floss for beaded stitches on 24-mesh.

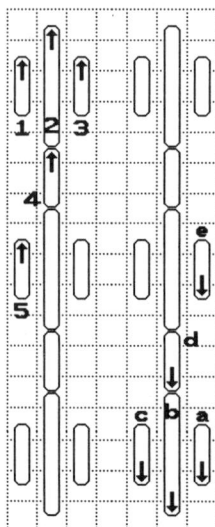

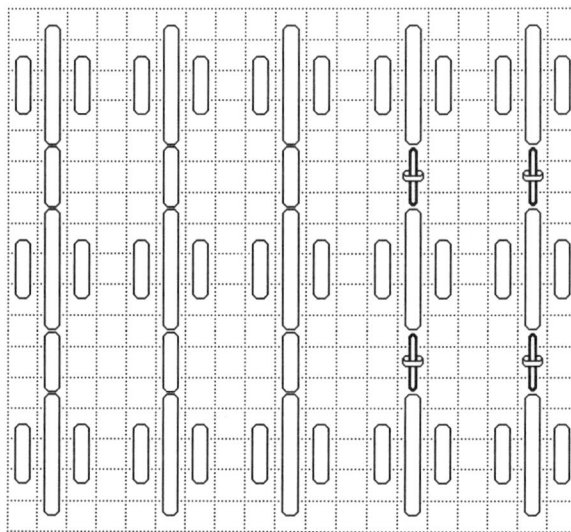

A vertical path is used to connect these rows, and this sequence is shown to the left. If beads are planned, use a #28 tapestry needle and add a bead to each brick stitch as it is laid. Tighten the bead on the next stitch to keep it from drooping.

NOTE. Since one stitches with the frame or hoop in a relatively flat position, it is difficult to judge the appropriate tension for securing beads. Therefore move the frame to a vertical position occasionally to evaluate this. Some authorities recommend wrapping beads twice to anchor them securely. When #8 perle is used, and the bead is seated firmly, I do not find the more tedious method necessary. The bead nests securely in the "hammock" or open hole behind the Brick stitch, and no extra effort is required.

This pattern is used in *Flurry of Butterflies* (Color Plate VII) in the light blue area between the wings of the border butterflies. The area called for an upright pattern in a pastel treatment that would echo the background areas, and this small repeat adapted well to the tapered shape.

6. Alternating Enlarged Pavillion Variation and Hungarian Units.

This pattern has shapes of large and small diamonds that alternate in both a horizontal and a vertical direction rather than just one direction like the previous pattern. This same arrangement is shown on page 13 without beads. The Pavillion unit is also solid there.

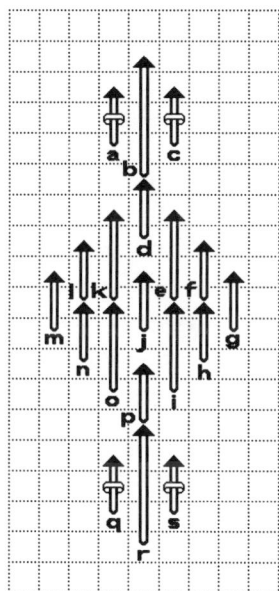

The staggered rows form an unusual and attractive negative space. Either the side stitches of the Hungarian units or the center stitches of the open Pavillion units can be beaded, but only the Hungarian stitches are shown with beads in the overall pattern to the right.

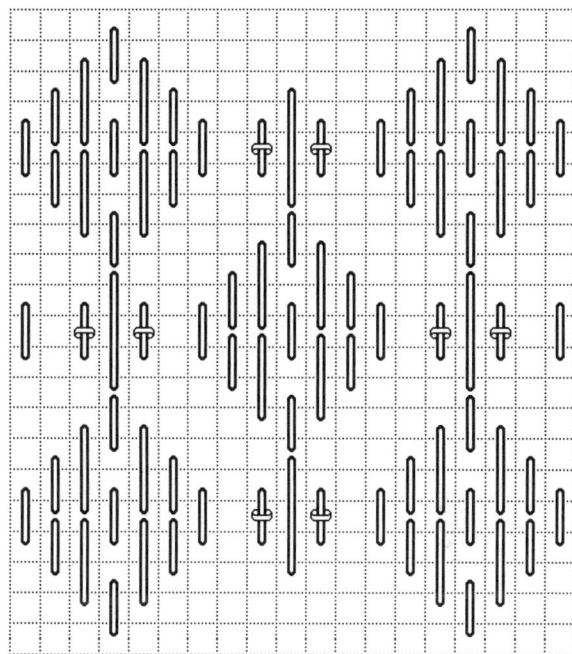

Execute this pattern in vertical paths, as lettered to the left. Use the same sequence to execute the reverse rows by rotating either the canvas or the chart 180°. The large scale of this pattern makes it especially useful as a background. I also used it in the center area of *Twickenham* (Color Plate XIII). Notice how well the pattern fits the unusual shape to reinforce its contours – an ideal goal when possible!

Another variation of this pattern is shown to the right. A second row of "middle" stitches is added to both the Pavillion and Hungarian units. The altered stitched areas are denser, but the negative space between the stitches is unchanged. The most efficient sequence for this variation and its "parent pattern" is a "figure-8" path, as shown. All stitches are snugly wrapped, and open areas are clean. In a finished piece, the negative space can be highlighted further with the addition of a dark backing fabric. Notice the enhanced contrasts in the background of *Oriental Butterfly* (Color Plate X).

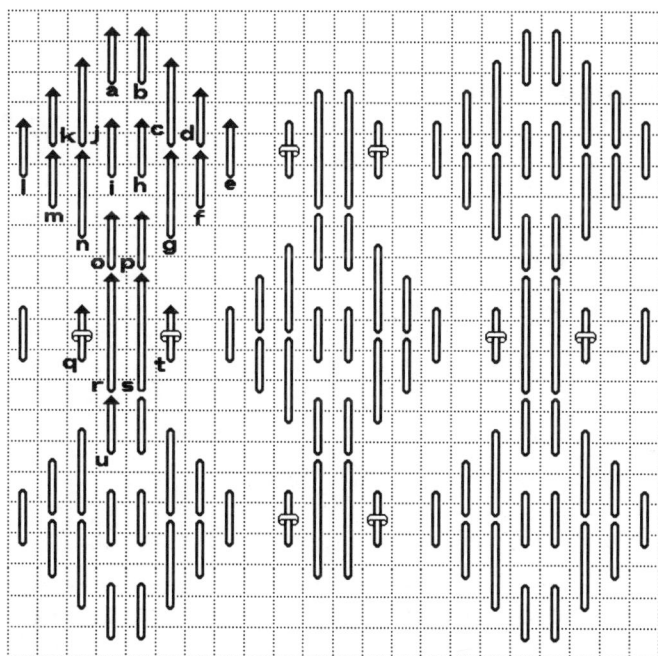

This design was actually the reason this expanded variation evolved. It has bilateral symmetry, and the center of the vertical axis of the canvas is a center thread rather than a hole. In order to make the original pattern fit gracefully as a background pattern, the extra middle stitches were needed to create a center thread. The altered pattern not only looks comfortable, but an added benefit is that the strategic placement of the beads in one Hungarian unit also gives the butterfly a pair of elegant eyes!

7. Open Straight Gobelin Network with Beaded Brick Stitches. This arrangement of upright stitches has alternating rows of two different cluster units. The large clusters of five stitches suggest a spool shape, and these "spools" are placed three threads apart in one row. The in-between rows have pairs of vertical stitches that overlap the spool rows on both sides. A diagonal sequence connects the elements most efficiently, and the traveling threads will automatically be concealed. Add beads to the middle stitch of each spool unit as the units are laid. This pattern is ideal for a background, but the odd number of open threads between the units will limit choices for additional accent fillings in these open areas.

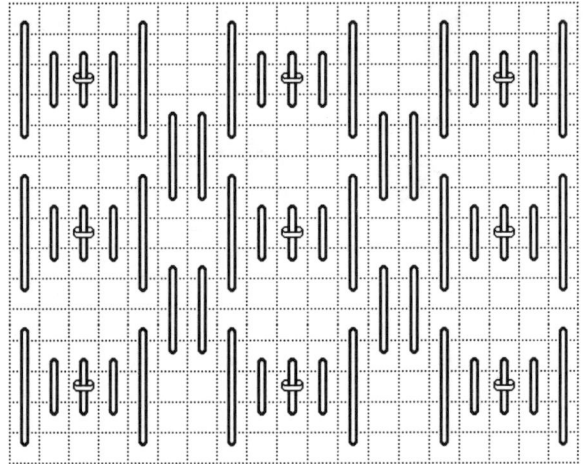

No numbered sequence is provided since the diagonal rows are simple to execute.

8. Open Pavillion Pattern with Two Pavillion Variations. Pavillion is an enlarged Hungarian unit, and both of the units combined in this pattern are partial Pavillion "diamonds" arranged in an alternating repeat. There are open threads between the horizontal rows of staggered units, so a horizontal path connects the units in the most efficient sequence.

As an open pattern with no other embellishments, it is impossible to connect the units without having traveling threads show between the side Brick stitches of adjacent units. However, I was able to eliminate the visibility of any traveling threads inside the open diamond motif by using two paths to connect each row. Use

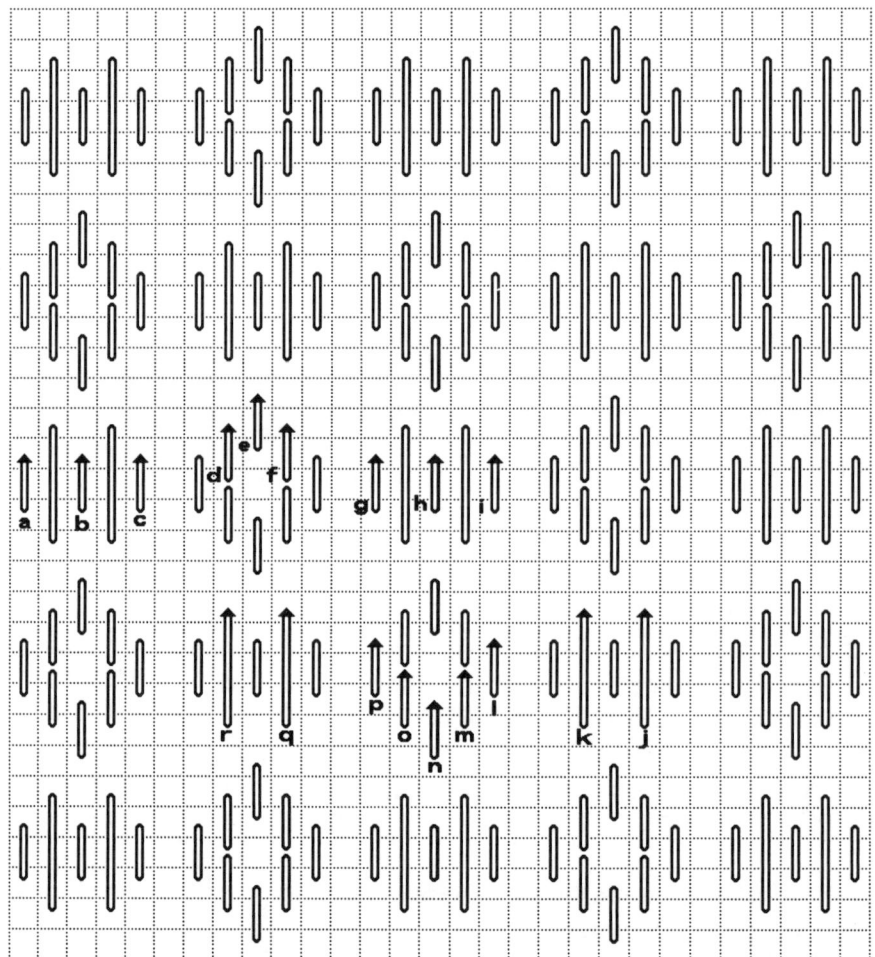

the a-i sequence for the left-to-right rows and the j-r sequence for the right-to-left rows. To conceal the other traveling threads merely add the Tied Oblong Cross units shown below in horizontal rows. Use a lighter weight thread and a slightly darker value to use this for a background pattern.

Variation. Open Composite Pattern. This pattern has lots of potential as an intricate composite pattern since the open areas are bold. To the right is a fancy combination that I doodled. I encourage you to try to see how many interesting color and value combinations you can create. The stitches are all simple familiar ones so no numbered sequences are needed. Below, however, I have provided directions for a suggested order in executing the steps along with some recommendations for the direction of the stitch paths. No color or value suggestions are made because many combinations could be successful. This is a good pattern for learning how to manage such decisions.

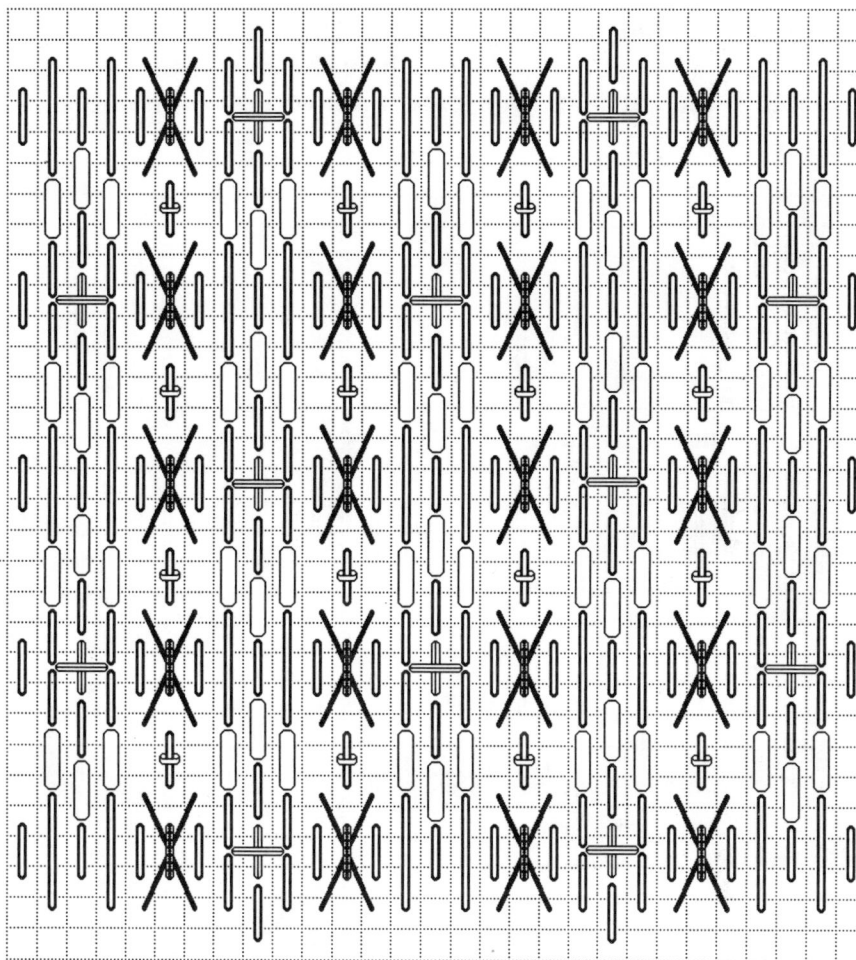

Step 1. Complete the open pattern, as shown in the chart on the previous page.

Step 2. Add the clusters of three Brick stitches between the alternating units of each row. Work each group left to right in vertical paths. The traveling paths will automatically fall behind the partial Pavillion units.

Step 3. Add the Upright Crosses inside the open diamonds. Execute these in vertical rows to conceal the traveling threads.

Step 4. Add <u>only</u> the crosses of the Tied Oblong Cross units. Work these with the usual rhythm in horizontal rows. The traveling threads will all be hidden behind the partial Pavillion units.

Step 5. Add the Brick tiedowns to the Oblong Crosses as back stitches in vertical rows, if these stitches are combined with the Beaded Brick stitches. If a separate journey is needed for the beaded stitches, execute the tiedown stitches in horizontal paths instead.

Step 6. Add the Beaded Brick stitches as back stitches in vertical rows.

As presented, this pattern would be an allover repeat or an open diaper pattern. All of the elements repeat diagonally, vertically, and horizontally with no strong stripe in the arrangement if different hues or values are used for every step. If the Tied Oblong Crosses and the Beaded Brick stitches are both the same hue and value, a strong vertical linear thrust will result. The pattern will become a stripe unless the background fabric is a strong contrasting color that keeps the stitches from merging visually.

9. Straight Gobelin Double Diamonds. The pattern below is adapted from a printed pattern that is a counterchange pattern. Notice how the repeat unit or shape, which I call a "dog bone," is horizontal in the stitched arrangement but vertical in the open areas.

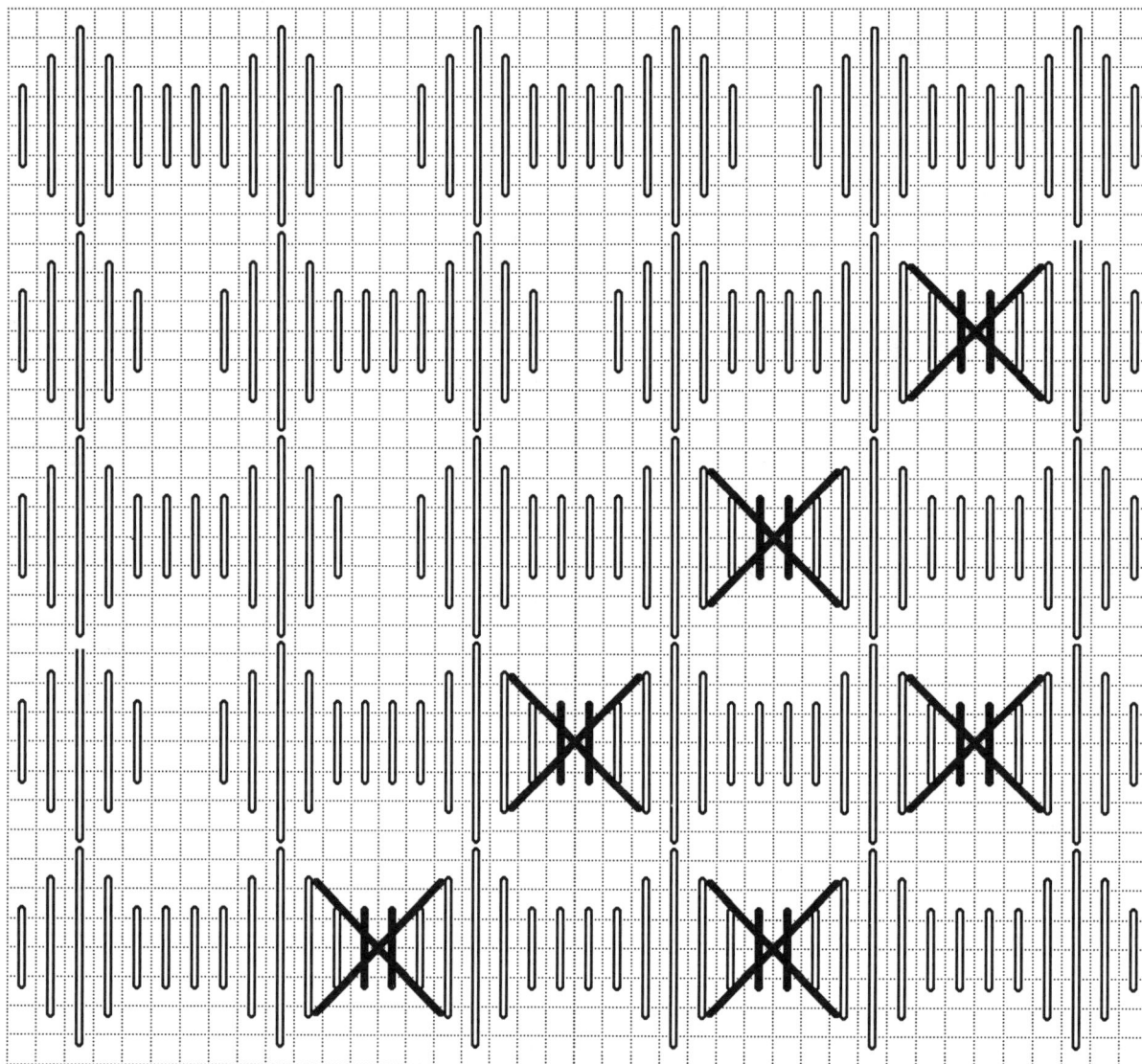

In the lower right hand corner of the overall pattern, a Double Tied Cross has been added between the "dog bone" units. Notice how the negative space changes completely with this addition, and I think the pattern is more attractive with this accent filling in a contrasting color or value. Often a new pattern or stitch is created by a desire to fill an existing open area. This unusual cross is an example of such a byproduct. The crosses straddle five threads in both directions, so two vertical tiedown stitches are needed in the middle to keep the unit symmetrical.

On the next page, there is a sequence chart for the overall pattern and a second chart for adding the contrasting crosses, if desired.

DOG BONE SEQUENCE DIAGONAL ROWS

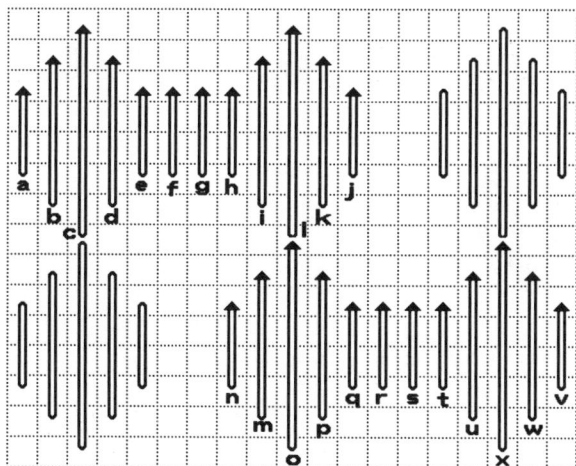

DOUBLE TIED CROSS SEQUENCE DIAGONAL ZIGZAG ROWS

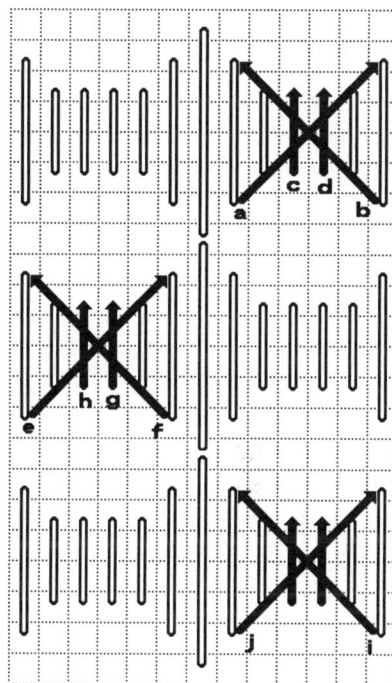

NOTE. The adjustments from j-p are a slight improvement over doing the units in the normal sequential order. Either sequence will conceal the traveling threads, but this alteration is cleaner since it keeps the hole between stitches l and o uncluttered.

In the Double Tied Cross sequence, the last Brick stitch laid is always the one farthest from the next unit since it provides the best angle to conceal the traveling path.

10. Open Pattern of Partial Pavillion. This pattern is not that exciting by itself, but I have used the composite version several times. The core stitch looks like Mirrored Upright Milanese stitches, but I prefer to call it a Partial Pavillion since the triangle shape can also be called a half unit of this diamond stitch. This simple arrangement is worked in sequential order in horizontal rows, so no numbered sequence is needed.

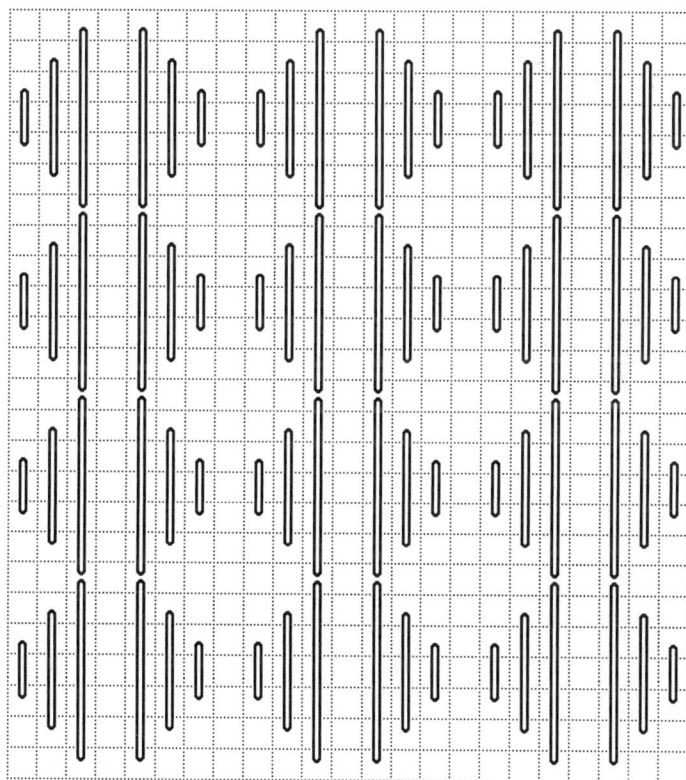

Additional elements are added in the composite pattern shown on the next page. Both the plain and the fancy versions appear in the sampler on the inside of the back cover. I featured them because I wanted to show examples of straight stitches done with pairs of #8 perle in the plain example and with veloura in the composite pattern - two different but attractive looks to consider on 18-mesh canvas. Two strands of #12 perle or Pebbly Perle will duplicate the same "pair" effect on Congress cloth.

The patterns on the sampler are high contrast versions, and the composite stitch version appears to be a stripe since the Tied Oblong Crosses and the beaded Brick stitches are the same color. If the beaded stitches and the tiedowns are the same color, but the Oblong Crosses are in a different color, the pattern will appear as an allover one.

Add the Step 2 Brick stitches in the open vertical rows in a running stitch path if a heavy thread or a metallic is used. (A red 1/16" double face ribbon is used in the sampler.) The stitches will look bigger, and the path will show in the open holes between stitches as "darning." To conceal the traveling thread, these stitches can be added in horizontal rows as well.

In *Br-r-r-r-rdbath* (Color Plate II), this composite pattern is used in the trapezoid shapes of the border sides. Contrasts are minimal with neutral gray and white threads against the gray Congress cloth. A silver metallic is used for the Step 2 Brick stitches, and the running stitch paths allow a glimmer of silver to show in the open holes.

A combined sequence is used to execute Steps 3-4 (the Tied Oblong Crosses and the Beaded Brick stitches). A lettered sequence for the Oblong Crosses is shown below on the left side.

After the Oblong Crosses are laid in two vertical trips of running stitches (stitches a-j), a third trip of back stitches will add all of the tiedowns and Beaded Brick stitches. No traveling threads will show since there are only open threads between units (no open holes). The running stitch paths force the traveling threads of the Oblong Crosses to lay behind the sides of the Step 1 units. The top crosses are not consistent, but this discrepancy is hidden by the tiedowns so does not matter.

In the sequence to the right, Cross stitches are substituted for the beaded Brick stitches of the previous composite pattern. This pattern forms a strong stripe and is shown as a horizontal ribbon in pink on the sampler. A rose metallic tramé thread is also laid behind the sequence to further embellish it.

Since no tiedowns are used in this combination of alternating crosses, the top crosses of both the oblong and regular Cross stitches must slant in the same direction. Therefore a different running stitch sequence is used, and all of the traveling threads fall behind the Cross stitches instead of the surrounding Brick stitches. This sequence requires four paths rather than three, and it is reversible except for the partial units at both ends.

NOTE. In open patterning, a variety of practical solutions are available that manipulate stitches in new ways in order to hide the traveling threads. As long as the sequence is consistent, one can take liberties with the usual method of constructing a stitch to accomplish this "higher priority."

38

11. Open Heart Pattern. Almost every stitcher likes patterns with heart motifs, so I want to share one that I created. This pattern was developed for the background area of *Hungarian Hootenanny* (Color Plate XII). It is a combination of alternating hearts and what was previously referred to as Partial Pavillion stitches, but the units are placed sideways here. The heart outline is composed of horizontal Brick stitches, so all of the straight stitches in the pattern are horizontal rather than vertical.

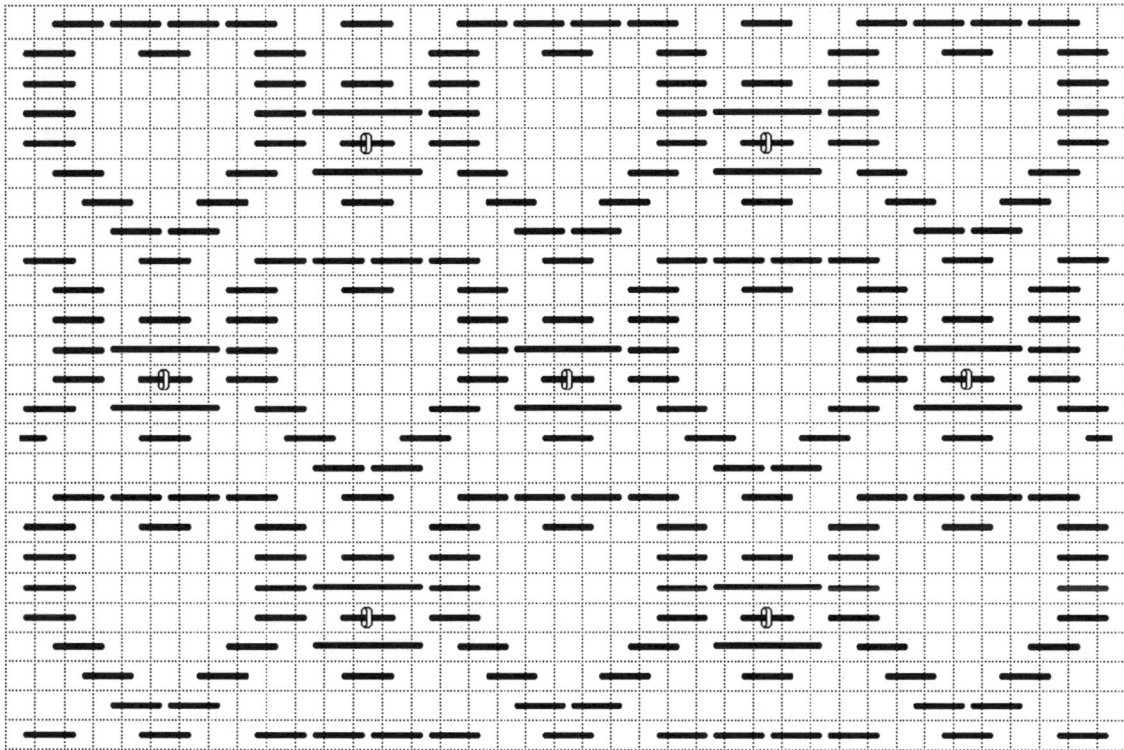

PATTERN SEQUENCE

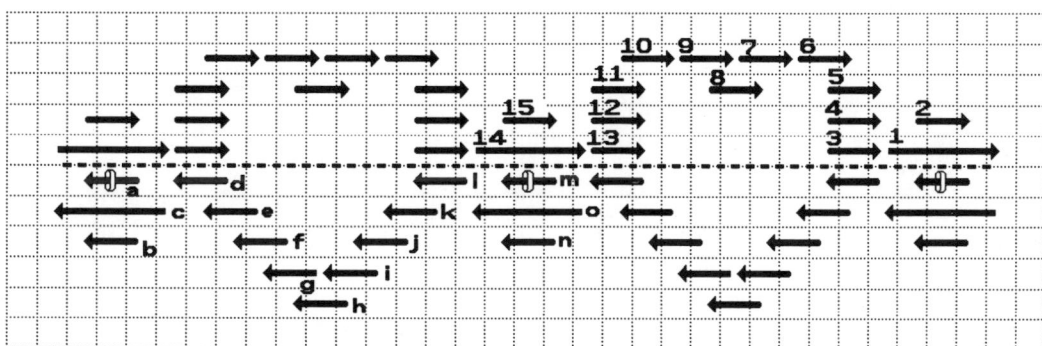

The pattern is worked in horizontal rows. The top part of the heart is worked from right to left, using the numbered sequence, and the bottom part is worked from left to right, using the lettered sequence. Stitch 14 is the repeat point of the numbered row, and stitch m is the repeat point of the lettered row.

The Partial Pavillion stitch serves as a "bridge" to keep the sequence flowing smoothly. Such stitches are often strategic choices that I make to provide smooth transitions from one motif

39

to another. The heart is the dominant motif here, but an alternating pair of motifs generally makes a more interesting pattern. A sideways Hungarian would have served the same purpose to connect the hearts, but the larger unit creates a more balanced negative space.

NOTE. Stitch a and m (or the center brick stitch of every Partial Pavillion stitch) is beaded. Add the bead as the stitch is taken, and seat it firmly on the next stitch.

Compensating this pattern along the sides and changing directions to add the next rows can be tricky even in a symmetrical shape. If the pattern is being used as background and there is no surrounding outline in which to pivot, one can continue the prescribed rhythm by taking pivot stitches in the selvedge area around the design. For example, at the end of the first row in the overall pattern provided, one would travel several threads from the edge and take a horizontal back stitch (right to left) over a single thread in the bald canvas. Then travel to the starting point of the return row, and the needle is in the correct position to take a back stitch on the first stitch. Sometimes two pivot stitches may be necessary if there is a wider gap between edge rows, but it is important to keep a consistent tension on both ends of every stitch.

This pattern demonstrates the need to be creative when planning sequences. Because the heart unit has a large empty center area, it was necessary to use a split sequence to navigate gracefully around the outlines.

12. Square Network of Alternating Pavillion Variations and Hungarian Units. This pattern is similar to the one shown on page 13 but the Pavillion units are omitted in the second and fourth rows so the open areas are now larger.

To partially fill this space, I added an Enlarged Double Straight Cross. It is not part of the square network, but it will be part of the Step 1 sequence. This is a functional filling as well as a decorative one because it enables the main network to be stitched in efficient alternating vertical paths with no side trips.

A sequence chart follows on the next page.

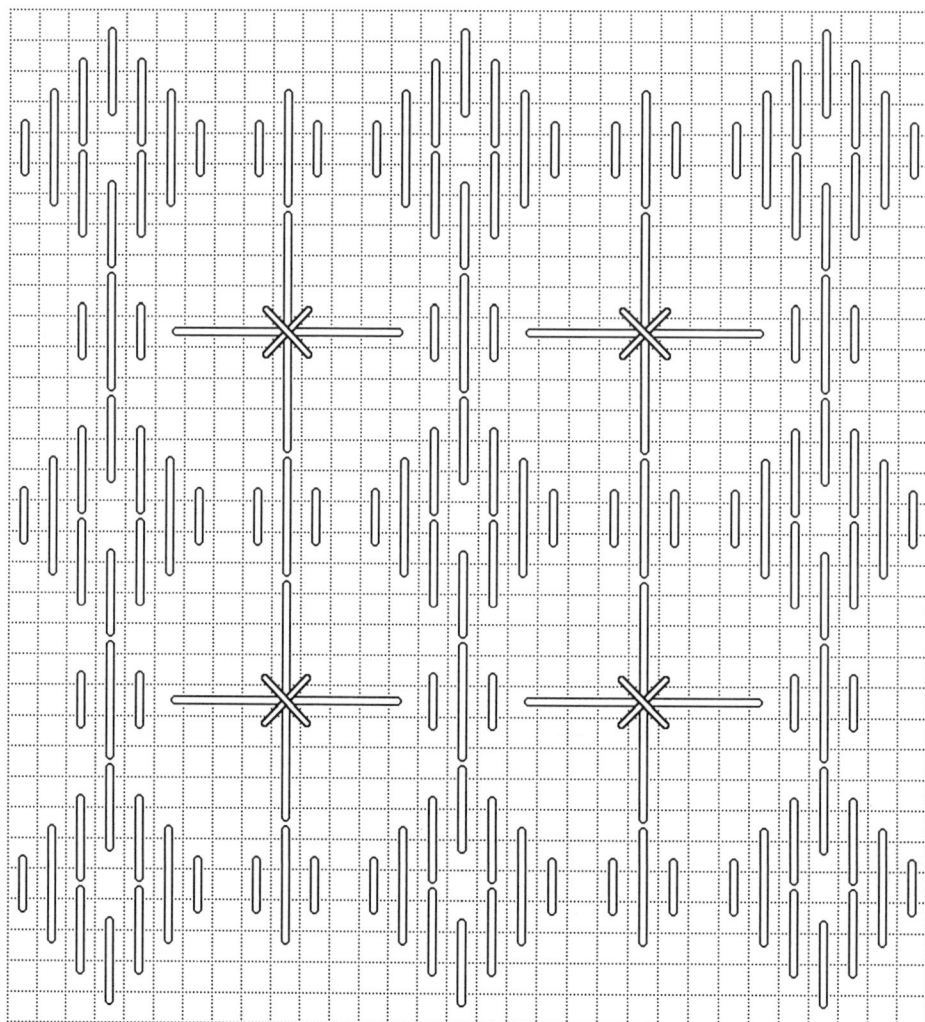

40

Step 1. Two separate vertical sequences are shown in the chart to the right to connect the main elements of this pattern. The lettered sequence connects the large Pavillion "diamonds" and the Hungarian units above and below them. The numbered sequence connects the remaining Hungarian units and the Enlarged Double Straight Crosses, which serve as a "bridge" between these units.

These two sequences are more efficient if they are combined in continuous alternating rows to build a complete pattern. To add the numbered sequence after the first row of the lettered sequence is completed, merely rotate the canvas 180° and work the chart as shown.

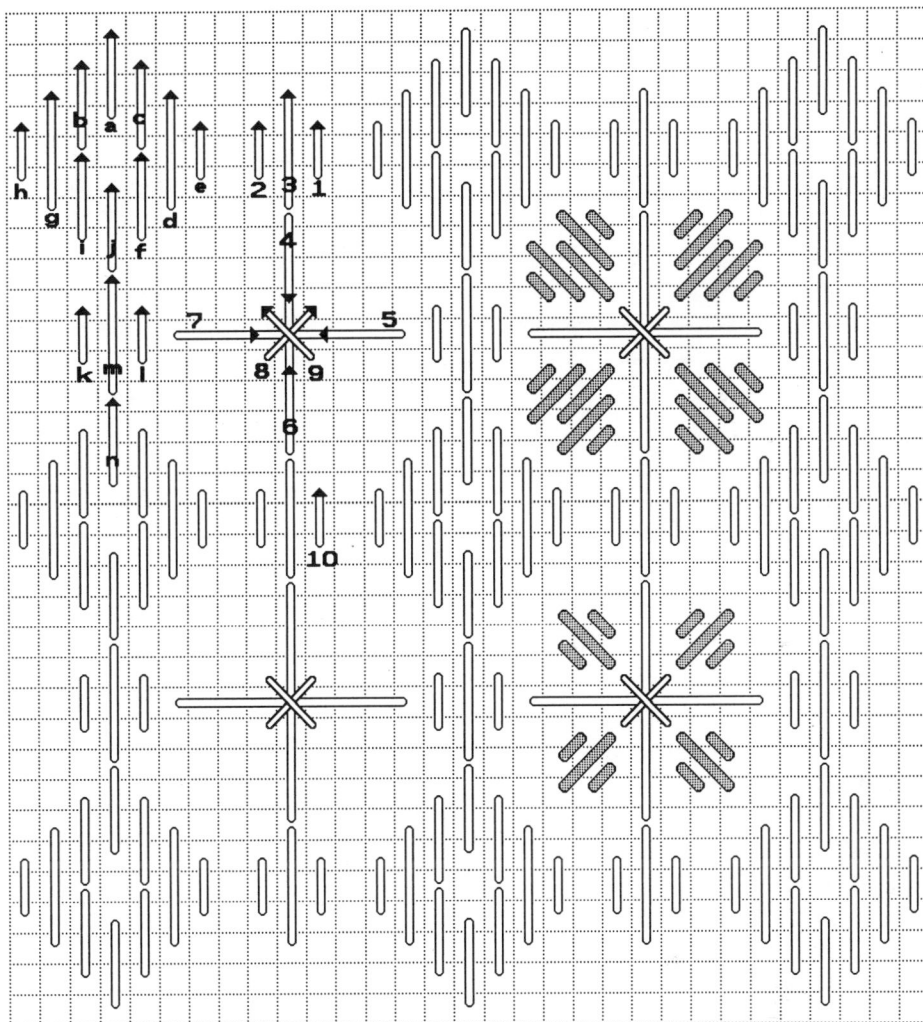

Corners are easy to turn, but there is an open hole between each vertical row so travel carefully. My solution is to alter the sequence of the last Enlarged Pavillion unit in anticipation of the change in the row direction. Use the counterclockwise path shown to the right instead of the "figure-8" path charted for the previous units. I have also added a clever "pivot" (stitches K-N) that allows one to travel to the Hungarian unit without a thread showing in the open hole. Stitch K is what I call a "rollover" stitch over a single thread that will place the traveling thread behind the canvas thread instead of the hole.

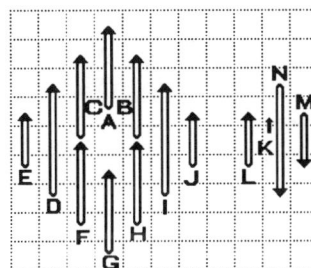

A stitch over one thread will sink and disappear so stitch N will lay smoothly on top of stitch K. Stitches L-M enable the thread to change direction, and the pivot is completed.

Step 2. I have provided two additional fillings to further embellish the large open area. Both are four-way clusters of two different satin stitch units. The small radiating squares are Mosaic stitches. The radiating heart shapes are Partial Scotch stitches. Work these groups in vertical rows. Lay the stitches from the outside in. Use a counterclockwise path, starting with the upper right cluster. End on the middle stitch of each unit to keep the traveling path to the next unit tidy and concealed.

CHAPTER 3 – OPEN PATTERNS WITH DIAGONAL STITCHES

The patterns in this chapter all have open networks composed of diagonal stitches. Secondary fillings may include a variety of treatments, but the main pattern (Step 1) will have repeated units of only diagonal stitches.

These patterns are among the most versatile since they compensate well inside any shape. A straight stitch over a single thread is unstable on canvas or linen, but any size diagonal stitch holds securely. Diagonal stitches also tend to make interesting four-way clusters, and a number of the patterns are composed of such arrangements. When used in alternating repeats, such clusters form exciting diamond lattices with large open areas that can be further embellished to form intricate composite patterns. Some of these are included to demonstrate such possibilities and to inspire you to play further.

1. Open Network of Mosaic and Tent Stitches. Diamond Lattice. Each diamond repeat in this pattern is formed with a single Mosaic unit that alternates in every direction with two Tent stitches. The stitches in the pattern are all placed upright rather than four-way. The usual sequence recommended is to lay all of the rows in one direction first. Then add the perpendicular rows to fill in the gaps.

Use the numbered sequence for the rows from upper left to lower right. Notice that the middle stitch of the Mosaic units is omitted in this sequence.

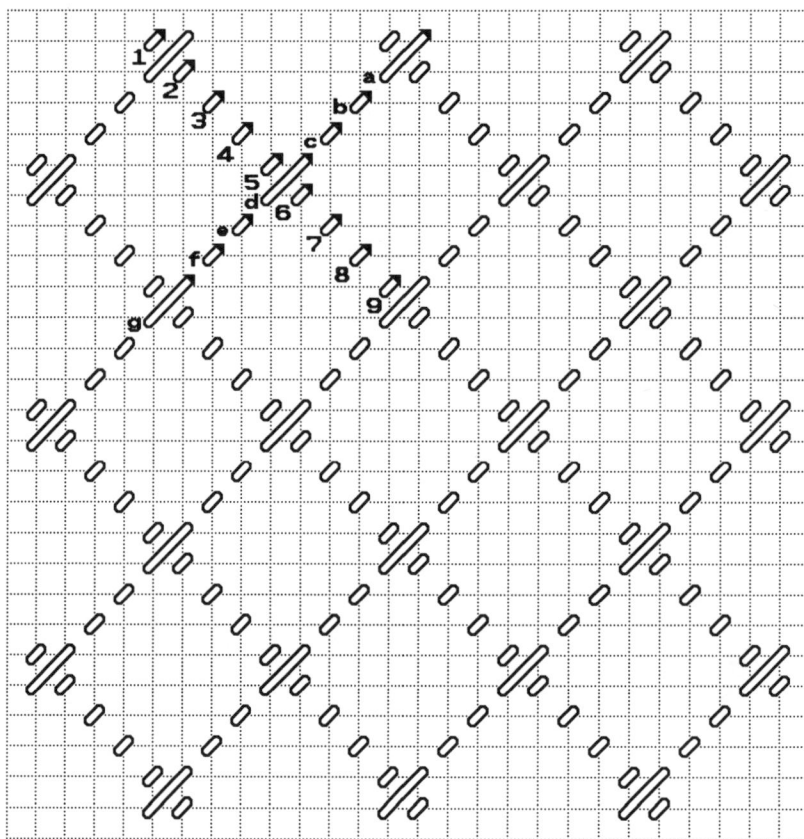

By adding these center stitches in the reverse rows (the lettered sequence), the pattern has a slightly stronger backing which is better for accommodating the thread tails. If the pattern is done in floss or silk, the middle stitch will look more uniform as well since it will spread out evenly over the previously laid side stitches.

This pattern also adapts well to a maze path treatment. Since the sequence is a back stitch path in every direction, it is possible to zigzag the rows in whatever direction is convenient.

42

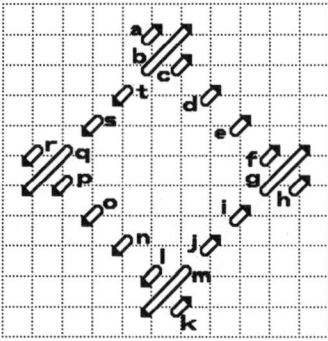

A sample zigzag path is shown to the left, and it shows the appropriate way to pivot in a Mosaic stitch. In this case the center Mosaic stitch is added in the normal sequential order unless floss is used. Then do the side stitches first and add the middle stitch last.

NOTE. All stitch units composed of parallel satin stitches look better in floss when the middle stitch is done last. This is the focal point of the symmetrical unit, and the long middle stitch will spread out evenly over the side stitches.

Stitches executed in sequential order tend to lean slightly towards the previous stitch so symmetrical units will appear slightly less uniform unless this alteration is made.

A smaller version of this pattern is shown to the right. There is only one Tent stitch between each Mosaic unit but the network is still a diamond lattice. Such scale adjustments are possible in simple open networks by adding or subtracting elements, so keep this in mind.

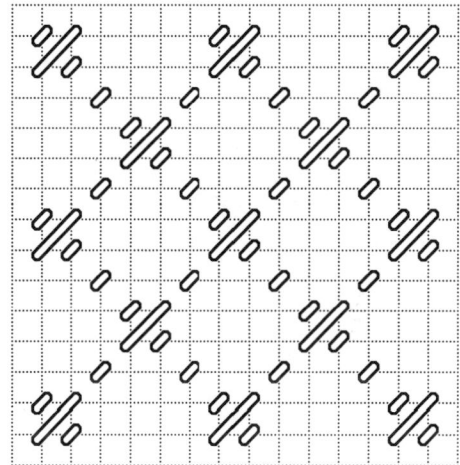

2. Open Woven Variation. The pattern below is an enlarged version of a stitch that I learned as Diagonal Woven stitch. Pairs of parallel stitches are arranged in horizontal rows.

Alternating rows place the pairs perpendicular to those of the previous row. The sinking holes of all the stitches are behind the stitches of adjacent rows on both sides so the pattern appears "woven." This pattern forms a natural triangle as shown, and it was used in the basket of *Strawberry Delight"* (Color Plate VIII). Its woven texture is perfect for the subject matter, and its natural shape combines well with the bold brown triangles.

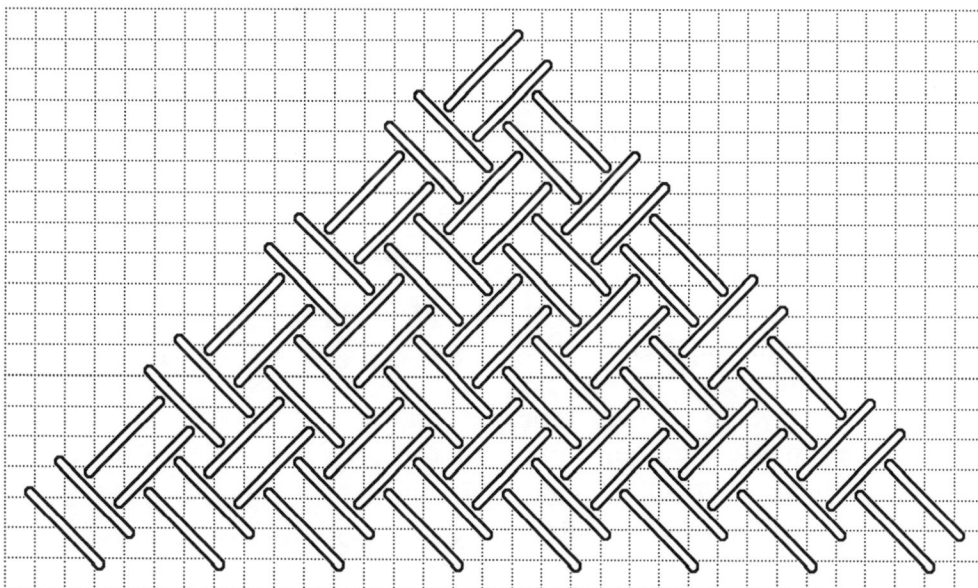

The criss-cross arrangement of the alternating rows makes this pattern easy to build as well. Stitches always come up in empty holes and sink smoothly behind the stitches of the previous row if the needle slants at an angle.

The traditional Diagonal Woven stitch uses a similar sequence and is shown to the right. Notice that this smaller version of the stitch has stitches that straddle two intersections whereas the enlarged version has stitches that straddle three threads. This adjustment is needed to provide the appropriate number of sinking holes for the pairs of stitches.

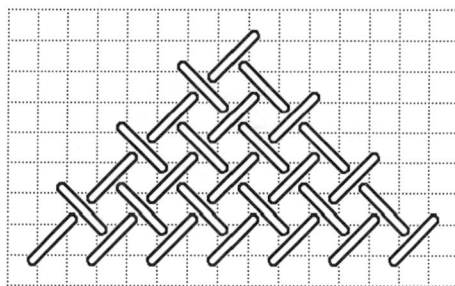

This pattern is slightly open. All threads are covered but canvas holes are visible. The enlarged pattern is more open and quite lacy in appearance in light shades.

3. **Open Networks of Reverse Mosaic.** This small stitch is called a "reverse" Mosaic because the normal order of "short-long-short" stitches is reversed to a "long-short-long" sequence. This stitch is not a box stitch like its parent Mosaic so it creates lovely negative spaces when arranged in an open pattern.

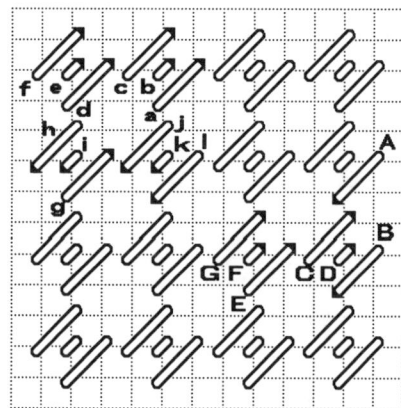

In the arrangement to the right, the open space could be filled with Mosaic units in a contrasting color to form a classic solid diaper pattern. However, when left empty the "square" space does not appear to be a square because of the indentations of the reverse units.

I like this stitch because it is easy to pivot within the sequence. The sequence suggested is one of horizontal paths, but I have shown two different changes of direction to clarify how the pivot is accomplished. Stitches are usually laid in sequential order, but on the units at the beginning of the rows, both side stitches are executed first to reverse the direction that stitches are laid. The transition is smooth from row to row, and a back stitch pull is maintained on both ends of every stitch.

Variation 1. This open arrangement uses Reverse Mosaic stitches in four-way clusters to form a square network. Two distinctive alternating open areas result, and the pattern is lovely by itself.

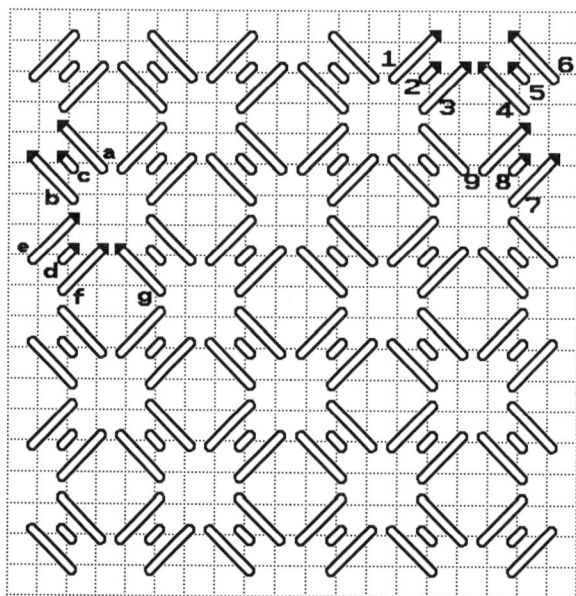

The sequence provided shows two different pivots that make the units turn corners gracefully. Unlike the previous pivots, all of the stitches remain upright throughout the sequence. The 1-9 sequence needs no adjustments since the traveling thread from 6-7 falls behind the dense part of both stitches. When stepping down on the left side, however, the traveling thread is best hidden by going from c-d so the middle stitch is done last in the final unit of the row and first in the first unit of the next row.

Variation 2. This pattern is also attractive when one unit is omitted in a nine-unit square. The pattern to the right could serve as a corner motif in a border or as one repeat of a large overall pattern. The bold middle open area can also accommodate a variety of additional fillings.

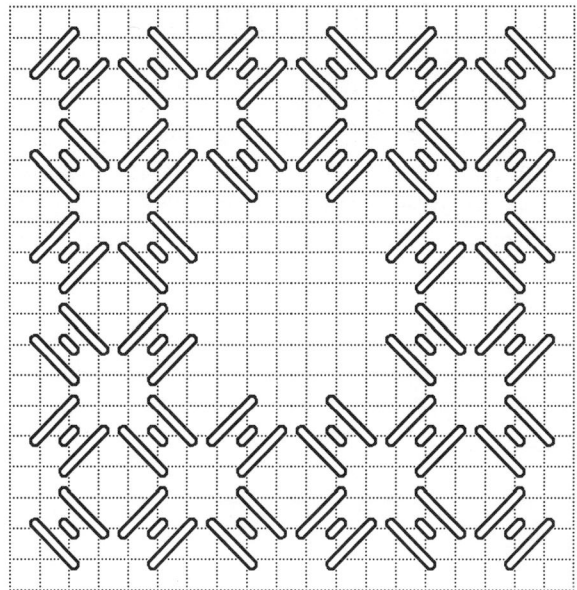

All of these Reverse Mosaic patterns are shown in the sampler on the inside back cover.

The next examples will use a similar concept of four-way clusters to form patterns. The first stitch explored is the Diagonal Hungarian. This stitch could be called an Enlarged Mosaic or a Partial Scotch unit, but its proportions more closely resemble an upright Hungarian – hence my choice of the name.

4. Open Networks of Diagonal Hungarian. Clusters of Four-way Diagonal Hungarian units create a cross shape that combines well in a checkerboard arrangement. The negative space between the units is large so a variety of other elements can be added to form interesting patterns. Two of my favorites are provided here, and a border using these clusters is also shown on page 124.

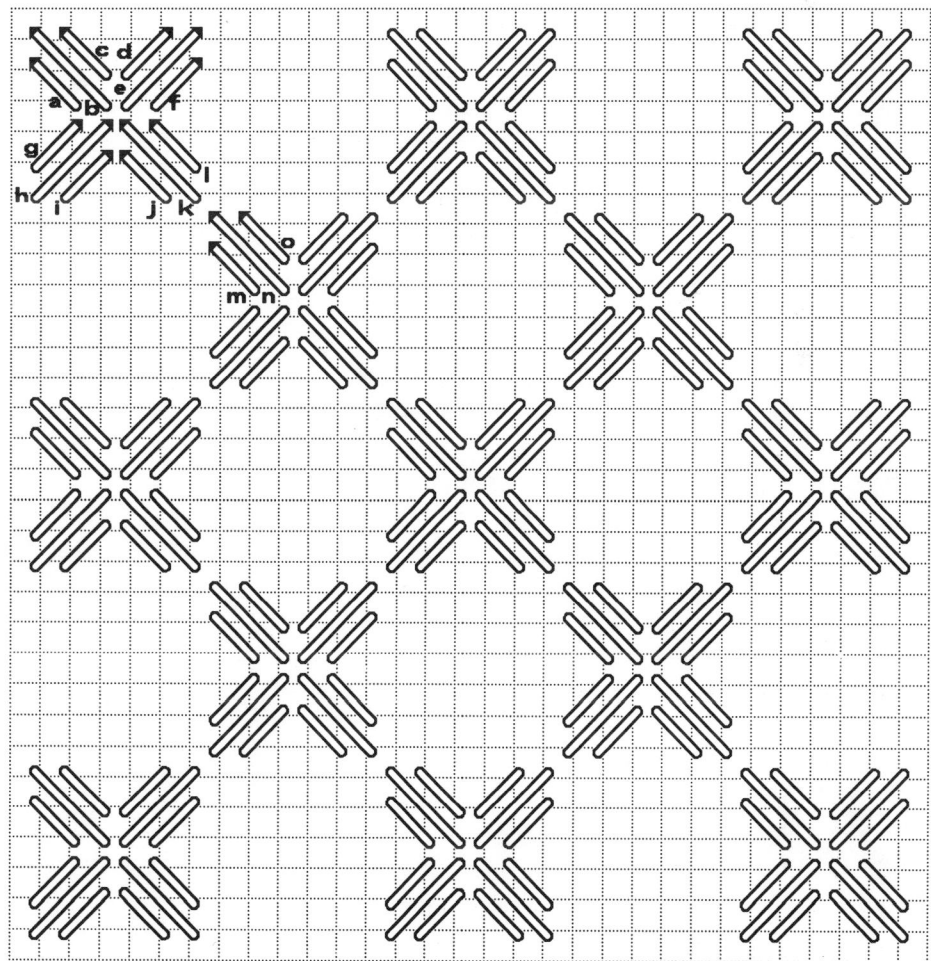

Execute this open arrangement in diagonal rows as shown in the lettered sequence in the upper left corner. Each unit is stitched in sequential order from left to right, but the d-f and g-i units are actually "side trips" off of the main diagonal path of the sequence which flows from upper left to lower right. All traveling threads are concealed, and this sequence is very efficient and easy to remember.

45

Variation 1. This variation adds what appears to be a diagonal couching pattern to the open Diagonal Hungarian arrangement, but it is actually an addition of a large Double Cross. Upright Crosses are also added to the centers of the Four-way Diagonal Hungarian units.

This pattern is shown in the sampler on the inside front cover. A #5 rose perle is used for the Diagonal Hungarian units. A star green metallic is used for the foundation crosses of the Double Crosses, and a medium dark green in #8 perle is used for both sets of Upright Crosses. The patterning is bold, and the large crosses form diamond "outlines" that frame in the Diagonal Hungarian clusters in an attractive way.

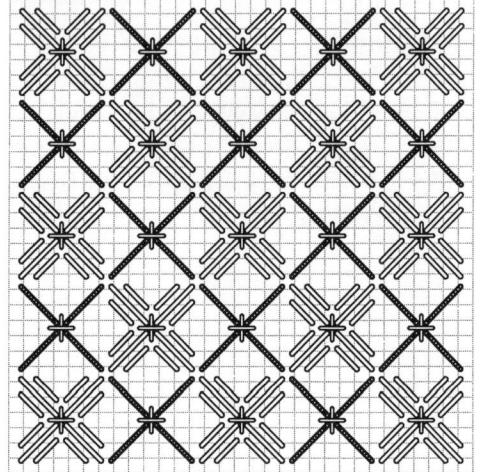

Sequences. In the composite pattern the Diagonal Hungarian pattern is done first. as Step 1. Then the large crosses are executed as Step 2. The cleanest way to do these is to treat them as eyelets and to add them in a radiating path. A lettered sequence is shown to the right that shows how to execute these units in zigzag rows. With four stitches in each "mock cross" it is easy to adjust the o r d e r o f t h e progression to end on a convenient stitch for traveling to the next unit. One can travel counterclockwise or clockwise in the sequence, and this is determined by the location of the next "mock cross."

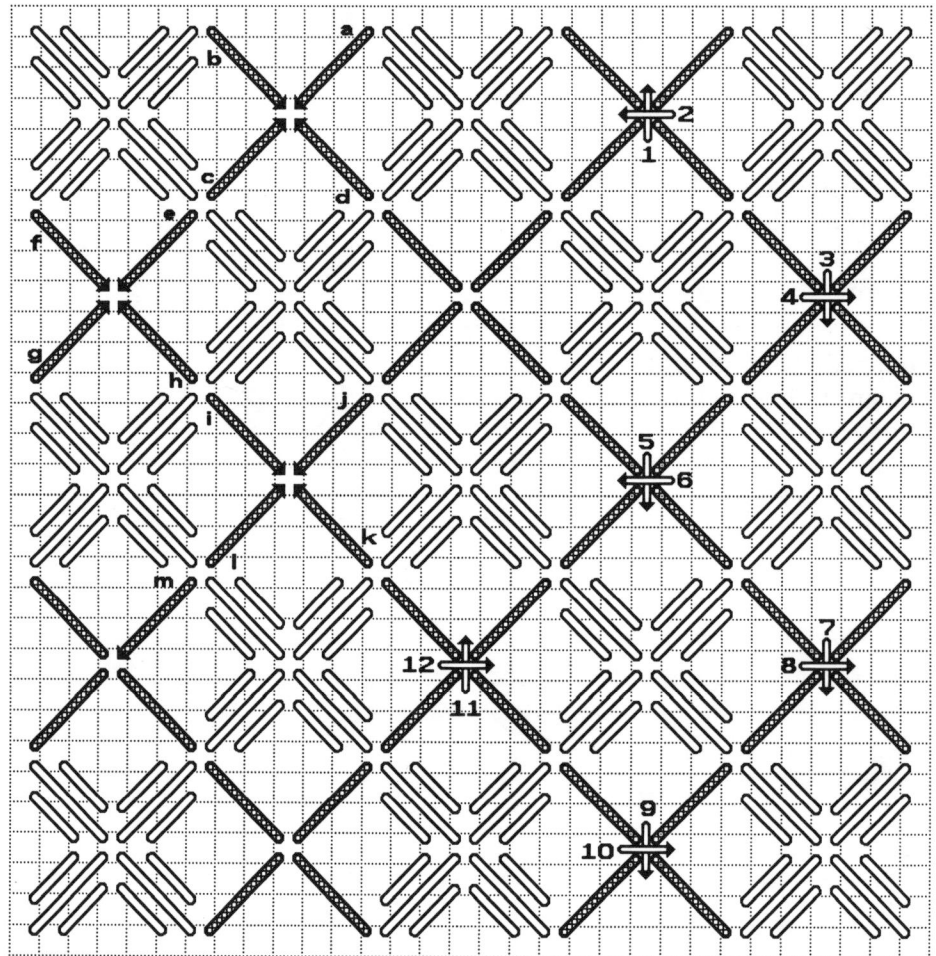

NOTE. From now on this concept of dividing a cross into four eyelet stitches will be referred to as the "eyelet method."

Step 3 adds the Upright Crosses for the large Double Cross units. The numbered path above shows an appropriate zigzag sequence. Notice how the direction of the top cross is laid away from the direction of the next unit to keep every stitch snugly wrapped. After the first unit, the vertical stitches are laid downhill because this forces the traveling thread to fall behind the spokes

46

of the "mock cross." The angle is still adequate to maintain a back stitch pull on both ends of the stitches so the alteration also honors other priorities as well.

Step 4 adds the Upright Crosses in the centers of the Diagonal Hungarian units. I used the same thread for both sets of Upright Crosses, but it is not practical to combine the two groups into one sequence. Use a diagonal path to add these units and make the same adjustments prescribed for the Step 3 sequence.

Variation 2. The second variation is similar to the first one but somewhat more elaborate. At first glance, the open areas seem to have both a square lattice and a diamond lattice arranged between the clusters of Four-way Diagonal Hungarian units. The bold upright stitches form the square lattice and the diagonal units of Double Tent create the illusion of a diamond lattice, so neither arrangement is a couching pattern.

After the Diagonal Hungarian network is completed, proceed in the following order:

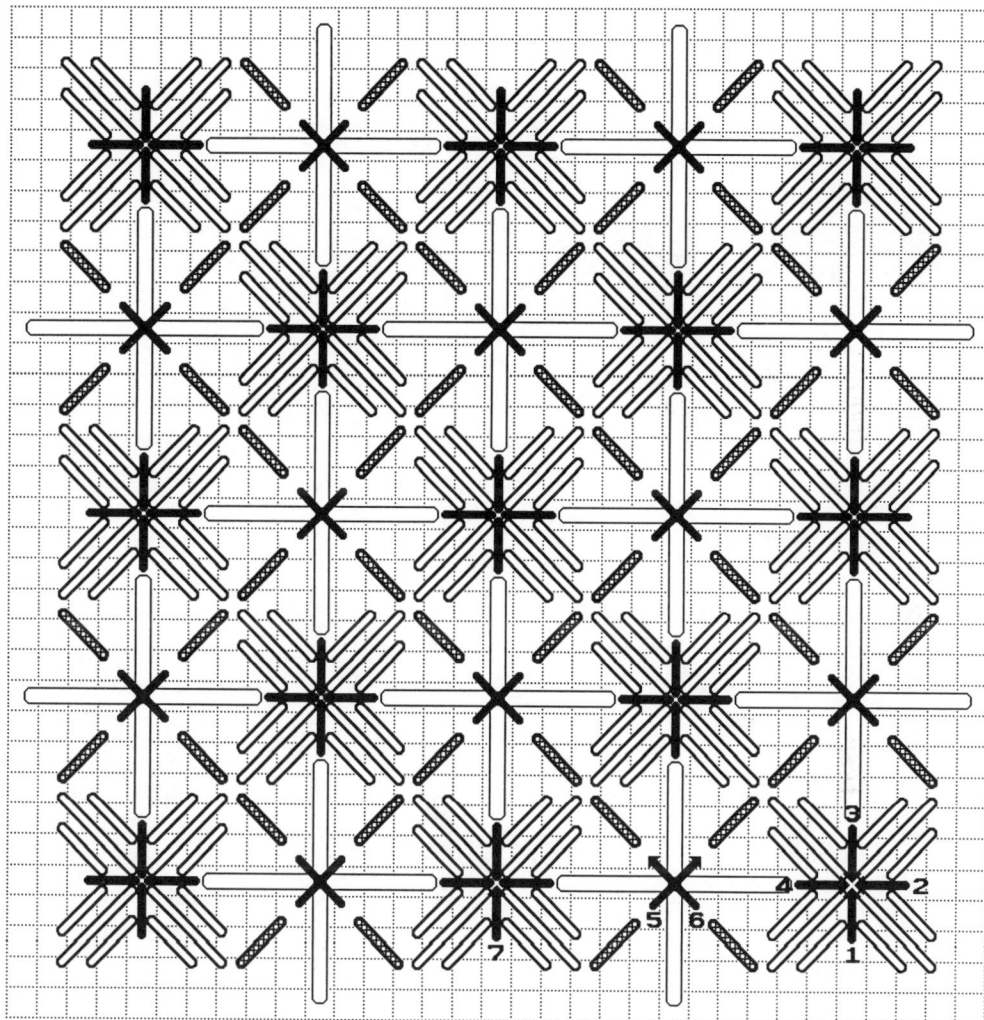

Step 2. Add the bold upright stitches in radiating paths of "eyelet" stitches, as done in the previous pattern. (These are also "mock crosses.")

Step 3. Add the Double Tent stitches in diagonal rows of back stitches, and travel by weaving through the backing of the Diagonal Hungarian clusters.

Step 4. Combine the crosses that straddle the Step 2 stitches with the Algerian Eye units that embellish the Diagonal Hungarian clusters. These can be executed in either horizontal or vertical paths. (A right to left sequence is numbered above.) If two different colors are preferred, use a separate diagonal path to add each group of accent stitches.

This pattern is on the same sampler as Variation 1. In between the two patterns is an elaborate border that uses Diagonal Hungarian clusters too. The directions for this border are located on pages 122-124.

5. Open Networks of Reverse Diagonal Hungarian Units. If one can have a Reverse Mosaic stitch, one can also have a Reverse Diagonal Hungarian stitch. To the right I have arranged the slightly larger unit in an overall open pattern with rotated Mosaic units in the in-between rows.

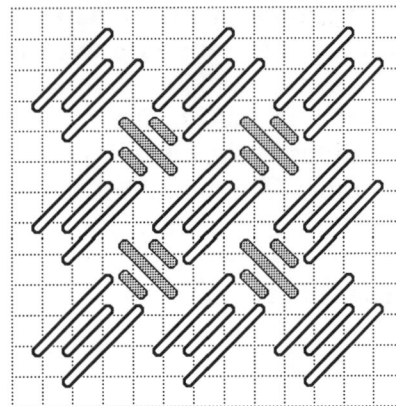

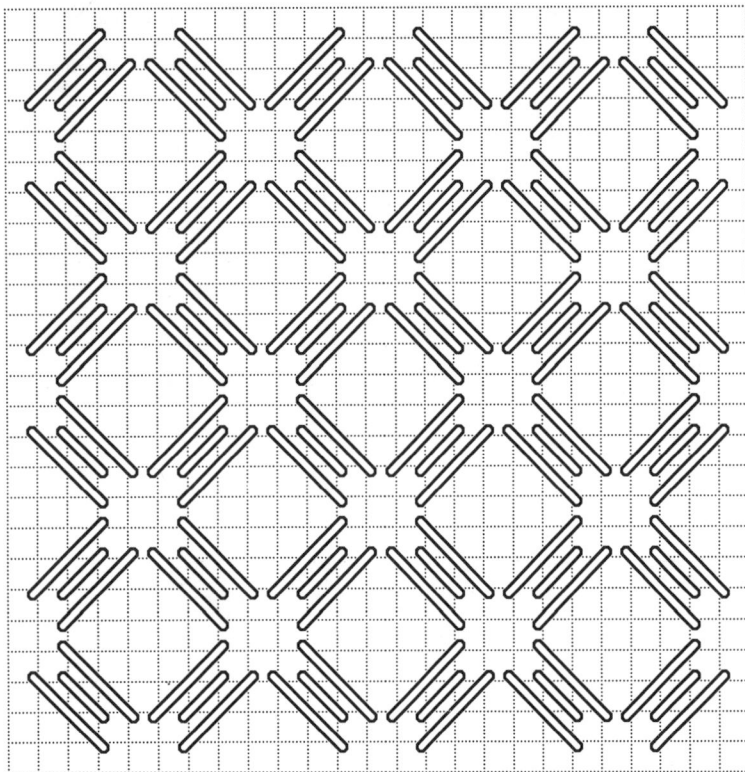

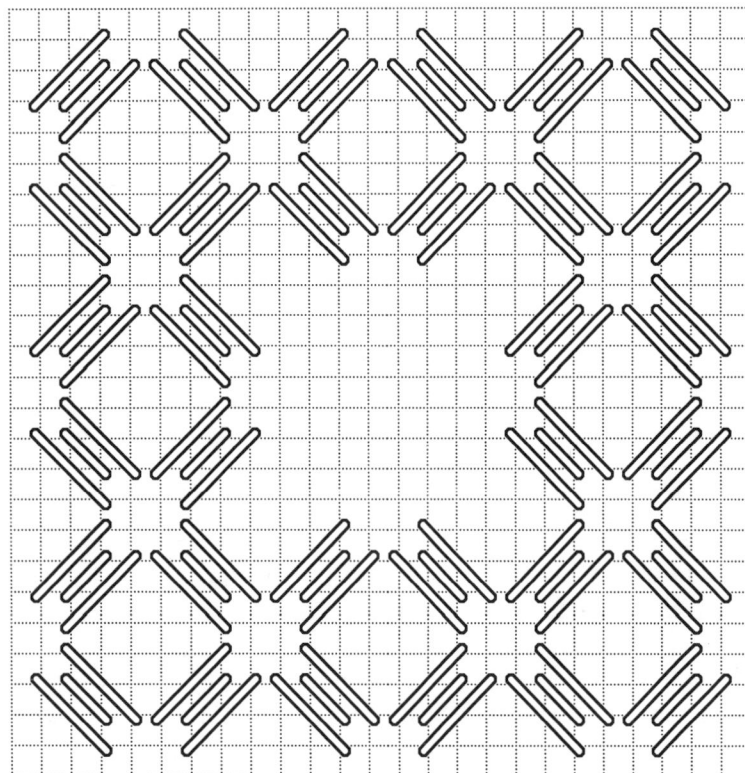

The open space between units is a rectangle, and these units are arranged with the same spacing as the Open Woven Variation on page 43. If flip-flop units of these Reverse Diagonal Hungarian stitches were added between the rows shown above, a similar but solid version of that pattern would result.

Variations 1 and 2. To the left are two open patterns of Reverse Diagonal Hungarian units arranged in four-way clusters. Their appearance is similar to the Reverse Mosaic patterns on pages 44-45. The scale is larger and the diamond shaped negative space is bigger, but the visual impact is similar because the shapes of the units are related, and the small square in the center of the clusters is identical.

The next series of patterns are additional examples of open networks of Reverse Mosaic. They did not follow the original section on this stitch because the sequence for laying out the main network is different due to the irregular arrangements in the patterns. The method of executing the Diagonal Hungarian and Reverse Hungarian variations is more closely related, so these patterns were inserted first.

This concept of "irregular arrangements" is another way to vary a stitch or pattern, so three different examples are featured.

6. Variations 1 and 2 of Open Patterns with Cluster Rows of Reverse Mosaic. The same main network of Reverse Mosaic is used for both of these variations, they will be considered together. The two patterns have vertical rows of contiguous four-way units of Reverse Mosaic, but there are two open threads between each parallel row.

This is a logical spacing for a stripe, so the first example to the right shows exactly that. Because of the spread out arrangement, it is best to execute the Reverse Mosaic units in vertical paths, as numbered to the left. Use a different thread for every pair of cluster rows.

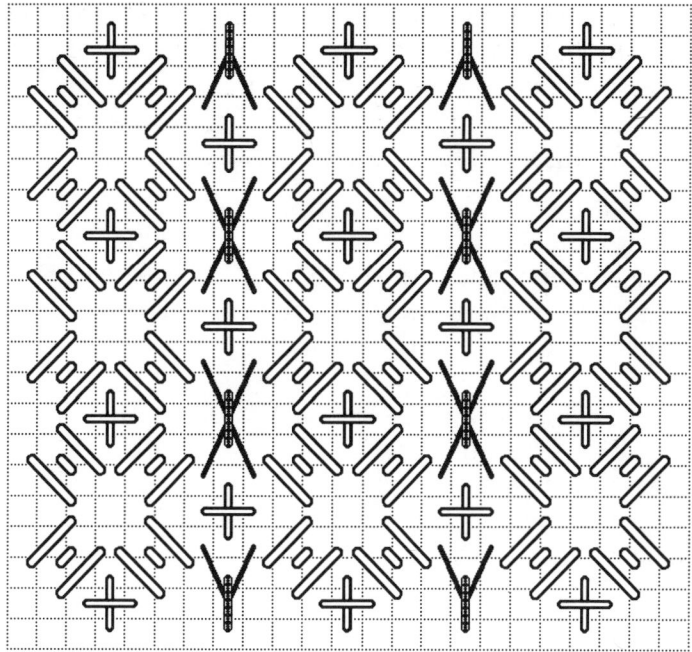

Units of Tied Oblong Cross alternate with units of Upright Cross in the open area, and additional Upright Crosses are added to the diamond centers of the four-way Reverse Mosaic units.

Add the Upright Cross units in diagonal paths as Step 2 since they will automatically conceal the traveling threads.

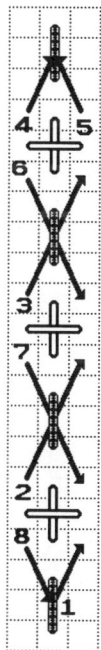

Add the Oblong Cross units in vertical rows as Step 3, using the running stitch sequence shown to the left. The traveling threads fall behind the Upright Cross units, so they are concealed.

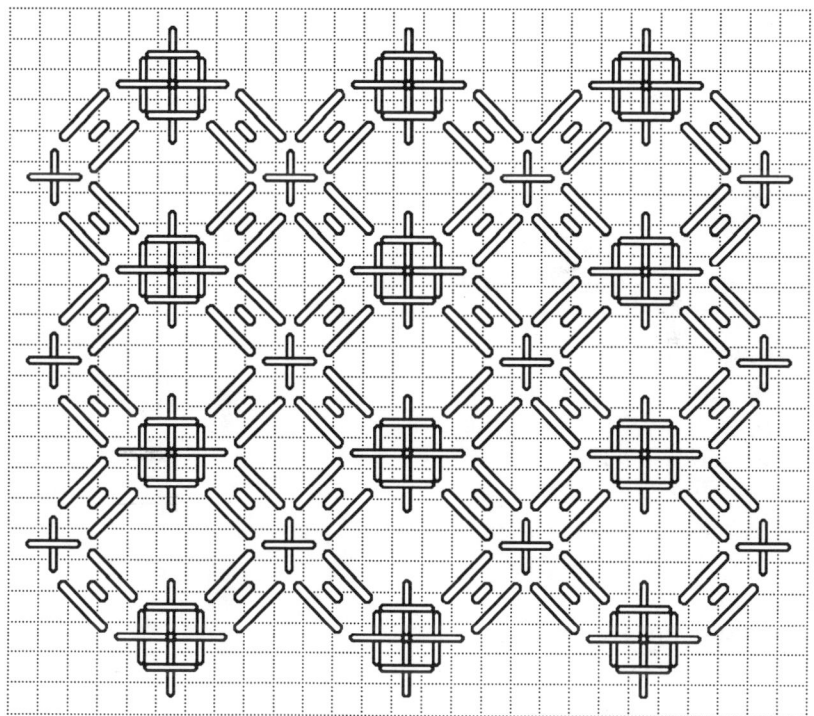

The second pattern to the right above is an allover pattern with the same main network of Four-way Reverse Mosaic clusters. The clusters of Upright Crosses create a bridge between the separated rows of Four-way Reverse Mosaic, so the pattern is no longer a stripe.

These two patterns are shown in the sampler on the inside back cover. The second pattern shows the main network in pink with the additional groups of Upright Crosses also in pink. Tied Oblong Crosses are added in between the Upright Cross clusters, but the pattern is still an allover repeat. These crosses are placed differently but can be executed in the same way. Add the tiedown stitches as a row of back stitches after the crosses are completed. The chart to the right shows the placement of the Oblong Cross units along with a sequence for the diagonal rows of Upright Cross clusters combined with the individual Upright Cross units. Ending on a side stitch in the cluster forces the traveling thread to fall behind the unit of Reverse Mosaic between the two segments, so this is the best path.

NOTE. The placements in this pattern create attractive oval shapes because the Upright Cross fillings are two different sizes. The next pattern will create circles instead of ovals since the units between the Reverse Mosaic clusters are all identical.

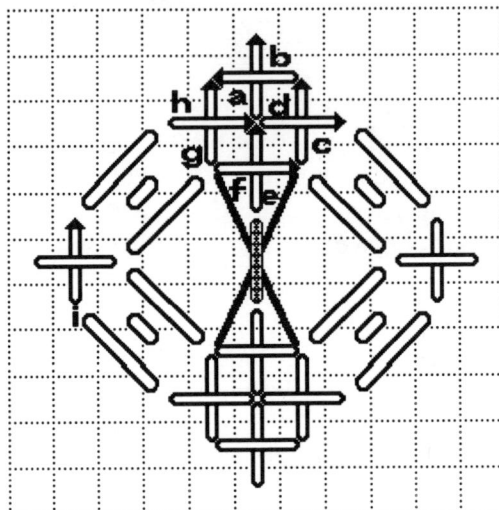

Variation 3. The pattern to the right has two open threads between every cluster of Reverse Mosaic units. Instead of a cluster of Upright Crosses between the units, a Double Straight Cross is substitute.

In the upper left corner there is one unit of Two-way Tied Diagonal Oblong Crosses, shown with a recommended sequence. These units are added to the example shown in the sampler on the inside back cover. They are arranged as an alternating filling, leaving the in-between areas unfilled. I often use this kind of partial filling in open patterning, especially when the negative space is interesting. The pattern is still an allover repeat, but the repeats are more spread out.

7. Open Patterns with Chain Link Stitch. The next series of patterns will all have a Step 1 network of Chain Link stitch, which derives its name from its oval shape. It is actually a variation of Dotted Scotch, and its proportions are the same as the Diagonal Hungarian units except that the center intersection is no longer covered. With this added open area, these patterns are particularly pretty on a dark canvas, and the examples shown in the sampler on the inside rear cover are directly under the patterns that were just discussed. The plain rose pattern shows the Chain Link units arranged in four-way clusters, and the clusters are arranged in a checkerboard of alternating groups.

Sequence. The ideal way to execute this pattern is to do all of the diagonal rows in one direction first, using a back stitch sequence to keep all the stitches snugly wrapped. Then add the perpendicular rows, using the same back stitch sequence. This method does require traveling long distances between rows so an outline must surround the filling to make such traveling efficient in a finished design.

An alternative sequence provided in the overall chart to the right shows a lettered back stitch sequence for diagonal rows that travel in an upper right to lower left direction.

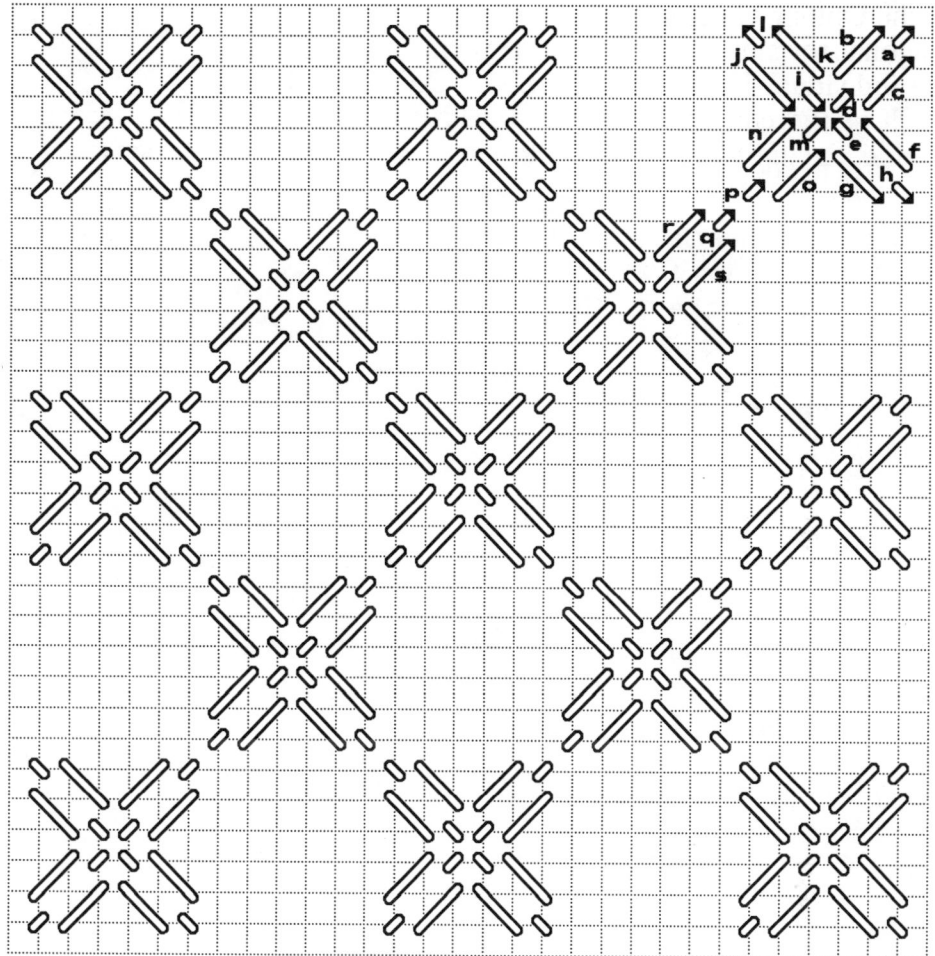

This sequence, however, has "side trips" that add the upper left and lower right units in the four-way cluster (stitches e-l). It is possible to use this path on canvas since the pivots on stitches g-h and k-l will not slip through the sized canvas thread. However, such a maneuver would be dangerous on linen and is not recommended.

If preferred, a combined sequence can be used that would eliminate these somewhat questionable pivots. Instead of traveling to a new parallel row after completing each diagonal row, it is possible to take a back stitch in the outline to end the row. Then weave back to the center of the first cluster and begin a new direction here. I often use this maze path approach in my work since it does avoid having to travel extensively in an outline. Lattice patterns usually make such zigzag rows practical, and as long as one keeps the stitches snugly wrapped and consistent, any "short cuts" are not obvious. In this particular pattern, the open area inside each oval is a canvas intersection rather than a hole, so any weaving will not show.

Because of the limited ability to maneuver in open patterning, I am trying to show you as many ways to shift directions as possible. Doing so within the pattern is usually better than having to weave in the backing of the surrounding area to travel to new entry points. Since most of my first doodles of each pattern are sample squares rather than actual fillings in a design, I seldom have the luxury of a built-in outline for traveling. However, in the color plates you will notice how often such an outline is strategically used in my finished pieces to provide convenient surrounding areas that allow the mobility needed.

Variation 1. The chart to the right shows the same checkerboard arrangement of Four-way Chain Link units. This time units of large Tied Oblong Crosses with radiating Upright Crosses have been added to the open diamond areas to form an attractive alternating repeat. Add these additional elements in two colors. Do vertical rows of Oblong Crosses first, using the sequence concept on page 49.

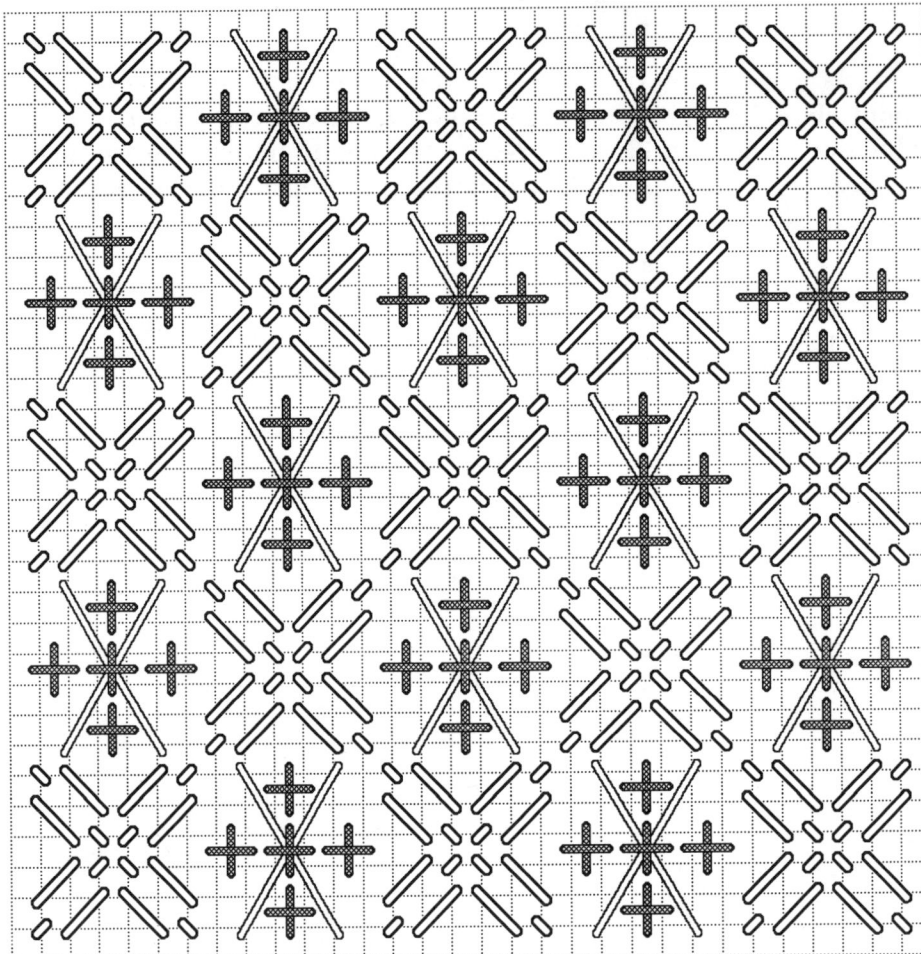

NOTE. Splitting the Oblong Cross sequence into two trips cleverly forces these threads to fall behind the Chain Link clusters. A more traditional cross sequence would not have hidden the travel paths.

**VARIATION 2
CHAIN LINK CLUSTERS**

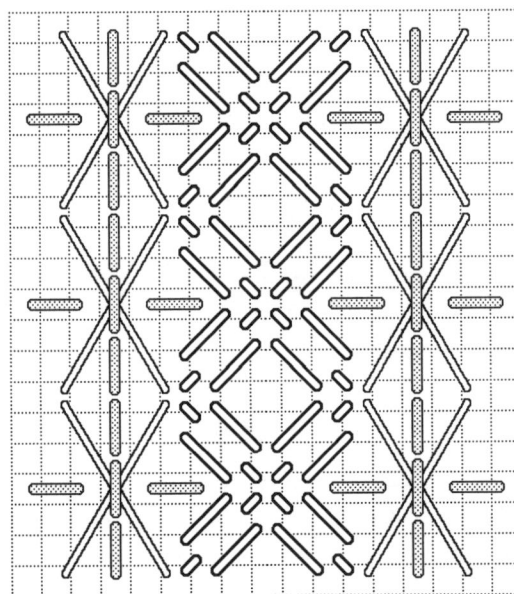

OBLONG CROSS SEQUENCE

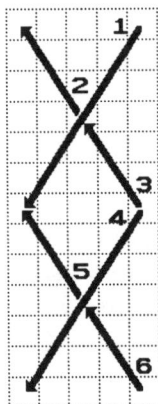

Variation 2. This variation is shown to the right and is a stripe. The center row has contiguous units of Four-way Chain Link clusters. Due to this arrangement, it is best to work the right sides of the clusters in one vertical path and the left sides of the clusters in a second vertical path (Step 1). If perle cotton is used, a long thread can be split, using one end to stitch one side and the other end to add the second side.

Step 2. Oblong Cross Sequence. This time an even more creative solution had to be used to add the Oblong Crosses. By splitting the second stitch into two stitches rather than the usual single one,

I was able to keep the traveling threads concealed. Since there is a top cross that will overlap this "broken stitch," the crosses will look normal in the final presentation so any tampering with a traditional sequence will not be obvious.

NOTE. The use of layered stitches often allows one to alter a sequence for a necessary purpose without changing its usual appearance once it is completed. Such combination stitches also enable one to add additional accents of color to patterns since they can be done in a separate sequence. Such versatility is a definite advantage in designing open patterns, so I use a lot of composite stitches in my patterning.

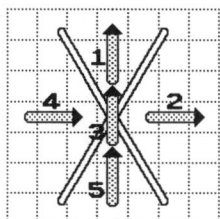

Step 3. The Brick tiedown stitches are combined with the radiating Brick stitches. Use the numbered sequence to the left, and work these stitches in vertical rows. Both sequences conceal the traveling threads well.

8. Open Pattern with Alternating Units of Tent Frame and Partial Dotted Scotch with Diagonal Rows of Tent Outline. This square network is shown below and is a simple combination, but it can be a very effective stripe. It was used in *Twickenham* (Color Plate XIII) in the background area.

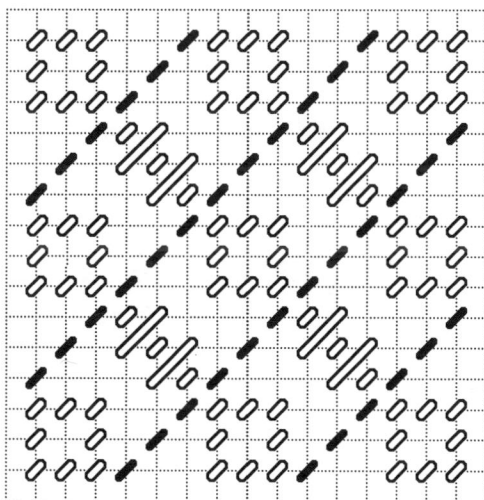

The converging lines of the four-way arrangement and the intense sapphire metallic make this pattern a dramatic focal point in the geometric design.

The name *Twickenham* was suggested by a friend who thought the design resembled an English garden. The outlines suggest the formal paths of the garden and I suppose the stripes suggest carefully planned rows of flowers.

This pattern connects best if the alternating units are stitched in diagonal paths from upper right to lower left. A lettered sequence is shown in the sequence chart to the right. It is efficient to have each "framed" Tent Outline sequence end in the lower left corner. Traveling from this point to the Partial Dotted Scotch unit minimizes the risk of having any threads show in the open areas. Any other stitch has an open hole beyond it so stitch h is the ideal exit stitch.

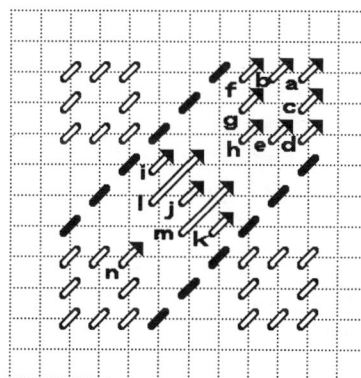

NOTE. A bead could be added to the center stitch of each Partial Dotted Scotch unit, if desired.

Once all of the Step 1 sequence is completed, add the diagonal rows of Tent Outline in back stitch paths to complete the pattern (Step 2).

9. Open Networks of Flip-Flop Units of Partial Dotted Scotch. Because of all the long and short stitches in its composition, the Partial Dotted Scotch is an interesting stitch to exploit on an open canvas. Its indentations make it particularly striking on a dark ground, and I like to use it in Flip-flop clusters as an outline. Like Flip-flop Hungarian, it creates a similar rickrack edge. On the inside front cover, I used an outline of these stitches to form an alternating open network of round and cross shapes that are similar to those in the adjacent border of Flip-flop Hungarian. However, the edges are not smooth in this pattern.

To the right is the overall chart of the arrangement shown on the sampler. These rows of outline stitches should be executed in sequential order like the units of Diagonal Hungarian on page 122. Use horizontal paths to connect the outlines, and make side trips off of the main path to add the in-between units.

When making a side trip, it is possible to alter the normal sequential order to allow a more graceful return to the main path. The inset on the left below provides an example of one detour to illustrate this concept.

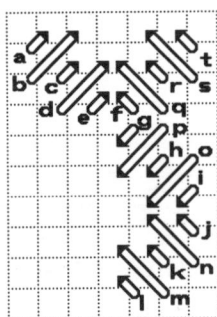

By doing the Tent stitches first and then returning to the starting point on the larger Double Tent stitches, both units of the side trip can be added efficiently with no extra effort. If a sequential order is used, it would be necessary to weave back to the main path after the side trip is completed.

Variation 1. The pattern shown to the right shows the original network with additional clusters of Four-way Partial Dotted Scotch units added to the open areas.

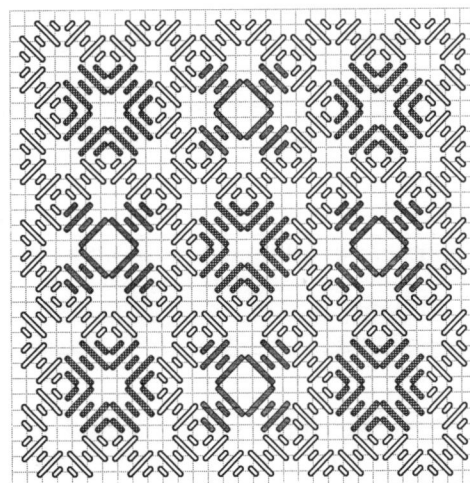

In the sampler on the inside front cover these clusters are done in two different colors to further identify the two different negative spaces with their separate fillings. Notice that the filling in the circle shapes has left off the inside Tent stitch of each unit, leaving a larger diamond outline in the middle of each cluster. **This example shows that contrasting elements inside open areas do not always have to be different stitches. Units of the same stitch in contrasting colors can be equally attractive.**

Variation 2. The next combination shows the same open network with two different composite stitch fillings inside the alternating shapes. This example is also on the same sampler below the other two. Inside the circle shape I combined a Double Cross with radiating Brick stitches. In the "X" or cross shape I added a cluster of five Upright Cross units with radiating diagonal Double Tent stitches.

Any combination of colors and/or values may be used for these accent fillings. No numbered sequences are needed since these stitches have all been used in earlier composite stitches. To refresh your memory the "eyelet method" works best to execute both sets of radiating lines and the foundation cross of the Double Crosses. Avoid traveling over open holes on entries and exits.

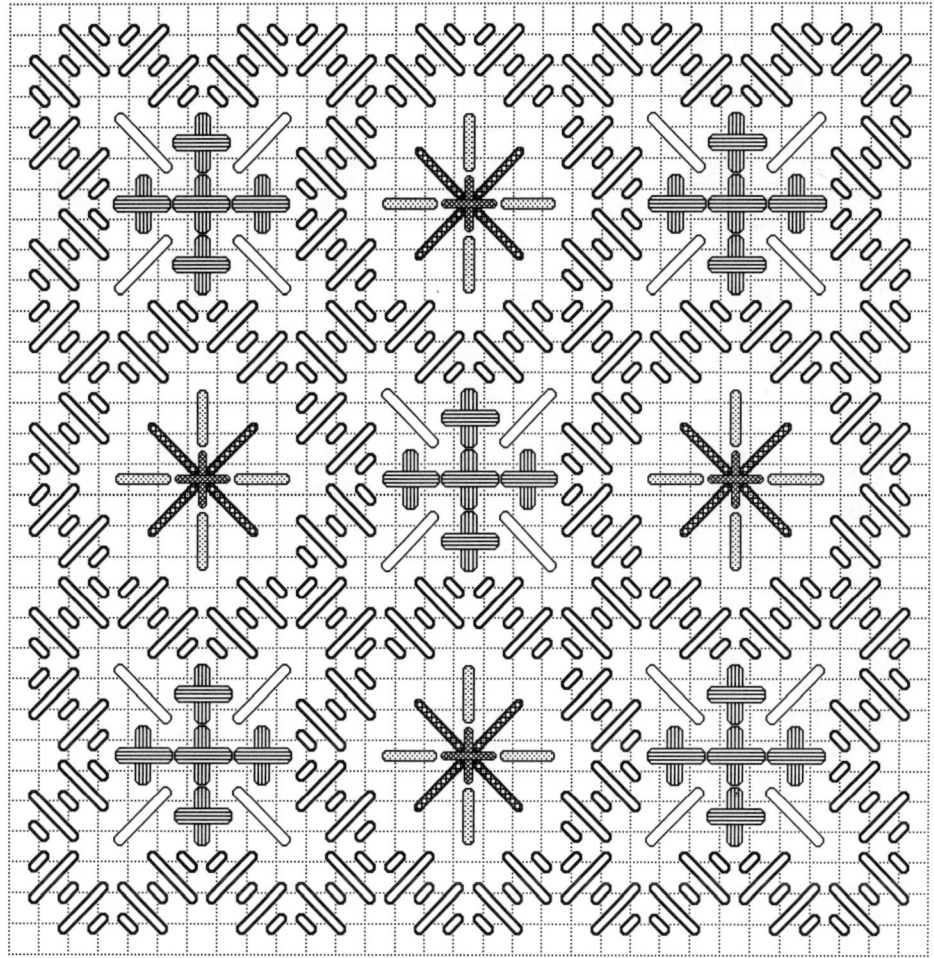

Add the Upright Cross clusters in clockwise or counterclockwise paths. To travel to spread out open areas, weave through the Partial Dotted Scotch outlines.

10. Open Network of Flip-flop Long Diagonal Stitches. These two open patterns are actually variations that were inspired by another composite pattern. When I stitched *Hummer Huddle* (Color Plate VI), I used the caning pattern listed on page 102 in the side sections of the border. After the design was completed, I thought the circle area behind the birds needed to be embellished but I wanted a soft background pattern. I decided to stitch a sample of just the diagonal stitches of the caning pattern to see if they would make an attractive pattern. The resulting negative space of open diamonds was a nice surprise, and the scale of the arrangement balanced well with the other areas in the design.

Instead of choosing darning rows for such an open area, however, a combination of alternating running and back stitches is used that forces the traveling threads to fall behind a canvas thread rather than a hole. It is somewhat unorthodox to use an alternating sequence when stitches do not join in solid rows; however, if concealing the traveling threads is the first priority, such measures override other considerations. If the sequence is used consistently throughout the pattern, all of the parallel stitches will have the same tension and look. It will not be that obvious that the perpendicular stitches are slightly different in appearance because they will all match each other.

55

The chart to the right shows the sequence for two rows. Notice that the traveling path in the downhill row is horizontal whereas the path for the uphill row is vertical. I could have reversed the direction of stitch 7 and made all of the traveling paths parallel, but there were two reasons for the change. First it is easy to find the starting point for stitch 7, as charted, since it is close to a perpendicular stitch of the previous row. The likelihood of a misplaced stitch is far less than it would be if one had to count over to the other side. In addition, the alternating directions of the paths of the rows make it easy to restart the pattern consistently if the stitching is interrupted. By merely checking the backing, one can begin in the correct direction if there is a lapse of time between stitching sessions.

Since backgrounds are seldom completed in one sitting, this is a consideration that justifies the manipulation of the sequence.

Variation 1. The pattern to the right uses the same arrangement of flip-flop diagonal stitches. The in-between staggered rows of stitches are removed, however, leaving only the aligned rows.

This pattern is used for the outside background area of *Flurry of Butterflies* (Color Plate VII). Because this variation produces a subtle stripe, it is arranged in four-way quadrants so it miters at the midpoint of every side. It is a very open pattern, so traveling between rows must occur

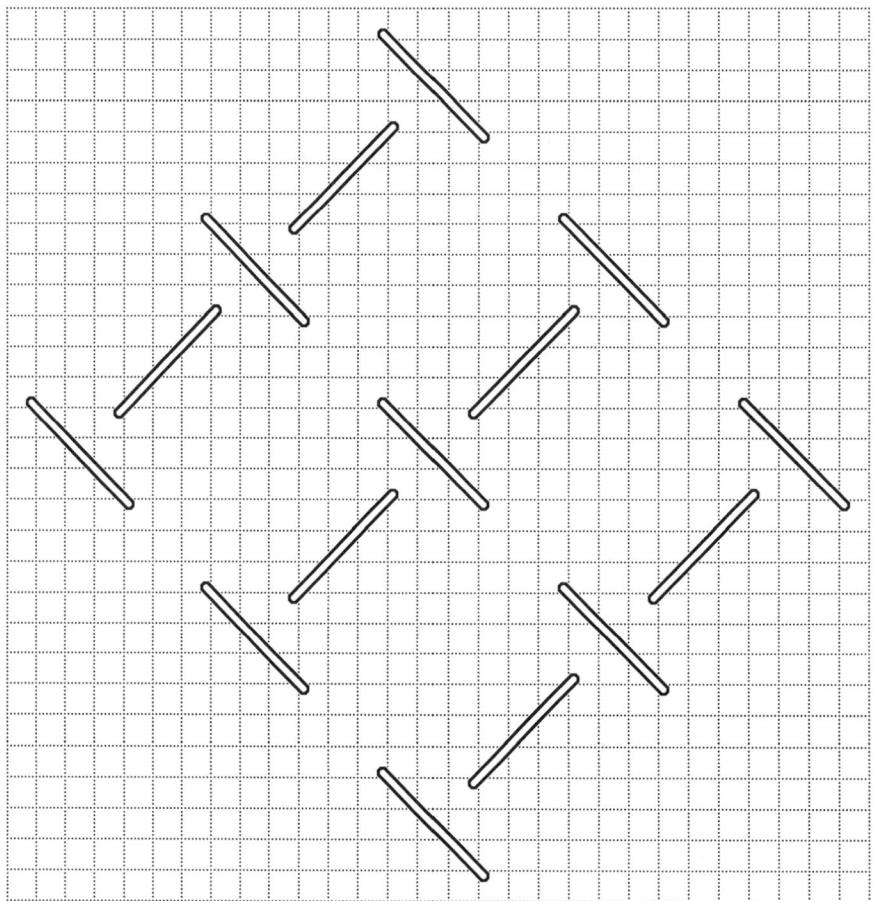

56

either in the inner outline of the Imari plate or in the selvedge area of the canvas beyond the edge of the design.

11. Open Networks of Four-Way Units of Hot Wheels. The core stitch of these patterns is one of my variations of Partial Scotch units. The shape reminds me of the miniature cars my two sons used to collect so I couldn't resist the name.

If I had used this stitch in simple adjacent four-way clusters, the negative space would have been too similar to that of some of the other four-way diagonal arrangements previously shown. Therefore the clusters in the pattern to the right are separated by small clusters of Four-way Tent units. The presence of so many Tent stitches in this combination gives it a delicate texture.

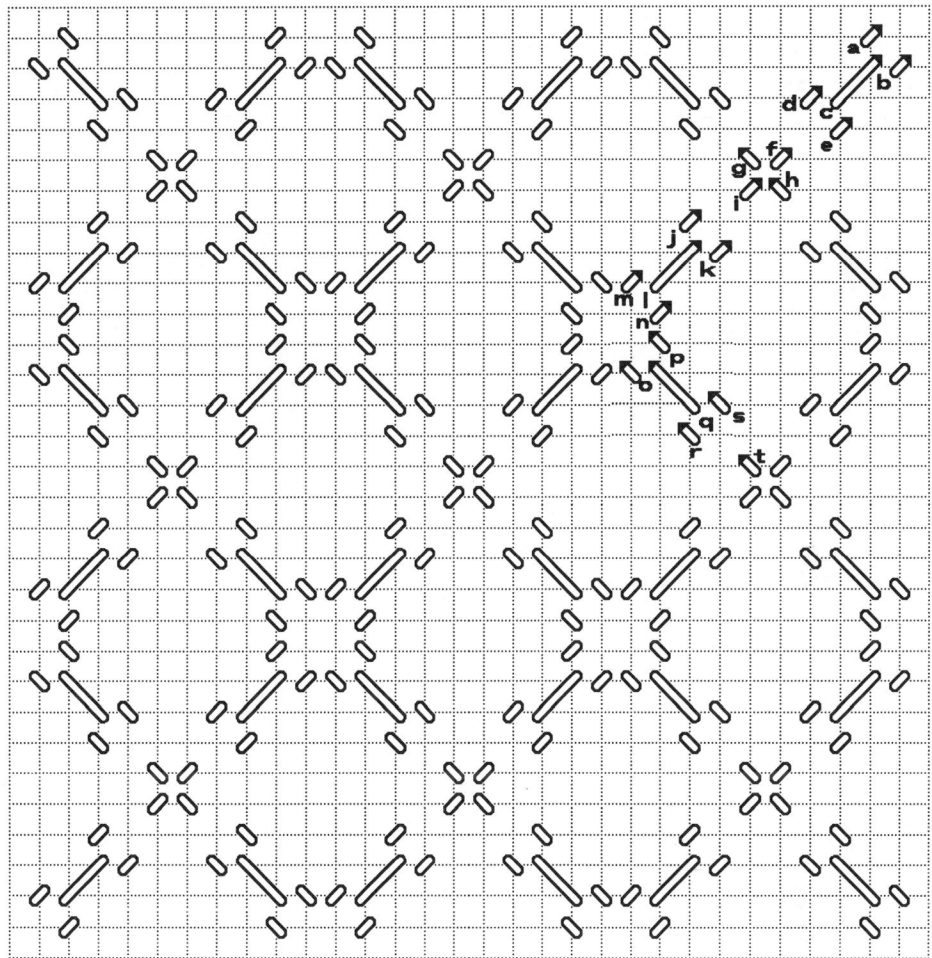

As an open network, the pattern suggests overlapping flower petals. The lettered sequence provided outlines a diagonal zigzag path to connect the spread out units. When a pattern is going to have additional elements, the sequence would not have to avoid the open areas, but this one is consistent and works for the open network as presented.

NOTE. This pattern should be in the chapter of combination networks since it has alternating clusters of two different stitch clusters. All of the stitches are diagonal, however, and this pattern is the parent of the Enlarged Hot Wheels network that follows, so I kept the two examples together.

On the next page there is a larger version of this pattern, but the center units have been eliminated. The bold inside negative space could make an attractive centerpiece for either a geometric design or an unusual corner motif for a border. An example of this medallion is in the sampler on the inside front cover, and I added the same four-way filling shown to the oval shapes along the outside edge.

Add the radiating stitches of the Enlarged Cross as Step 2. Do these with the "eyelet method," and travel behind the clusters of Four-way Tent units. Add the five Upright crosses in a

57

contrasting color in a sensible clockwise path that will carry the thread behind the Tent clusters to the adjacent ovals.

VARIATION 1 - SINGLE REPEAT PATTERN OF ALTERNATING FOUR-WAY CLUSTERS OF HOT WHEELS AND TENT STITCHES

12. Open Networks of Four-way Clusters of Enlarged Hot Wheels. The next two patterns are examples of diamond lattices with main networks of Four-way Enlarged Hot Wheels. Each stitch of this diagonal unit is twice the size of those of the parent stitch, so the unit is bolder but has the same general composition. In the checkerboard arrangement shown on the next page, the open areas form large diamonds and small squares. The two shapes can accommodate a wide variety of inner fillings. I have provided one intricate composite pattern on page 60.

MAIN NETWORK OF FOUR-WAY ENLARGED HOT WHEELS

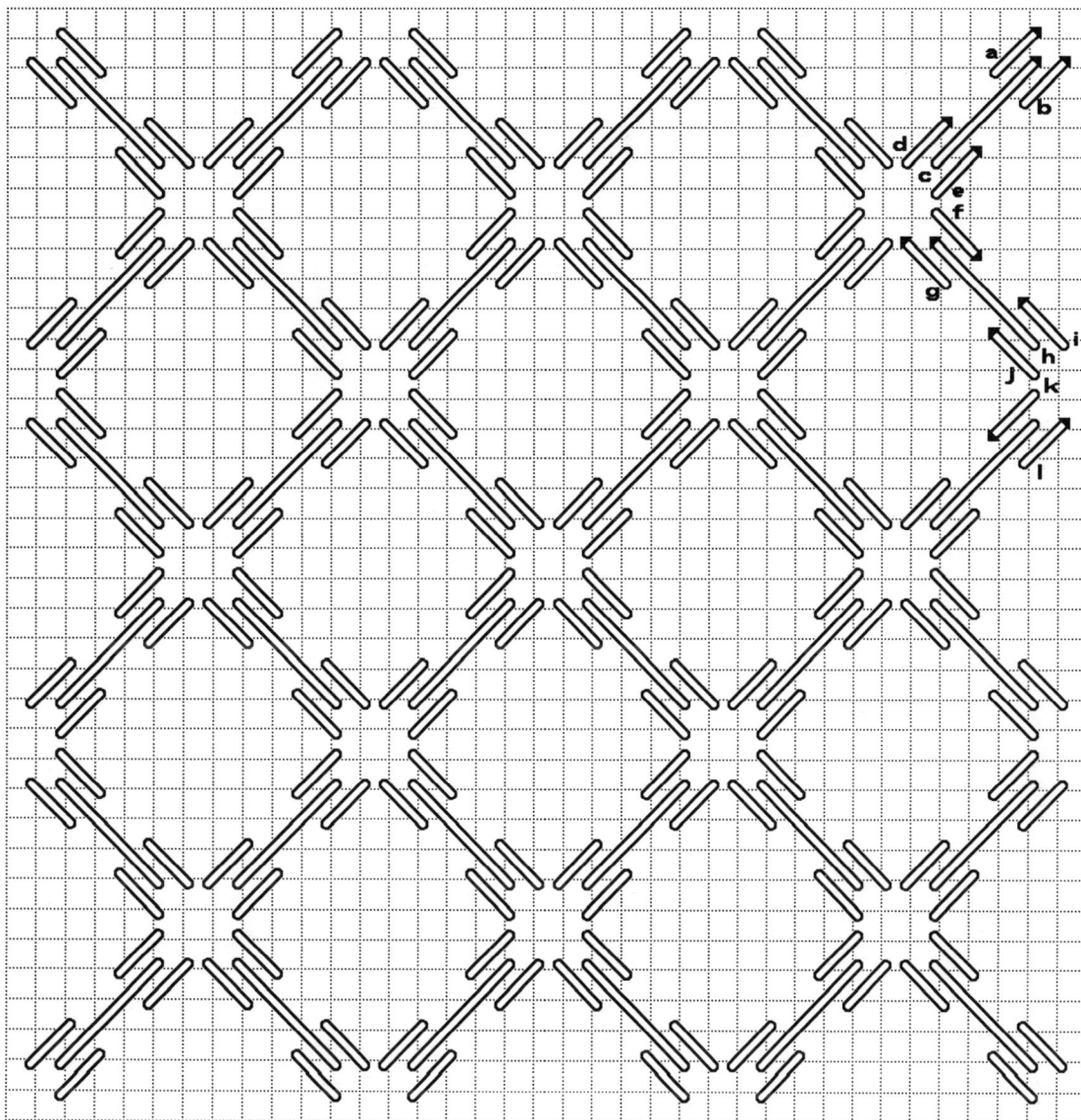

The lettered sequence suggested is a zigzag vertical path that uses a back stitch progression. Each time a corner is turned, there is a pivot stitch on the entry stitch of the next unit. This entry stitch is a running stitch, and the back stitch rhythm is resumed on the second stitch of each unit.

The composite pattern presented on the next page has two different additional fillings, which alternate in the arrangement. Along the sides of the sample square some elements of the Hungarian accent are eliminated, and the pattern becomes a single large repeat. This pattern and the open network presented above are both in the sampler on the front inside cover (to the right and below the example of the previous pattern).

COMPOSITE PATTERN - MAIN NETWORK OF FOUR-WAY ENLARGED HOT WHEELS ACCENT FILLINGS OF CROSS STITCHES, FOUR-WAY UNITS OF HUNGARIAN, UPRIGHT CROSSES AND TENT CLUSTERS

This pattern looks intricate but builds step-by-step in an orderly manner once the main network is completed. A suggested order would be as follows:

Step 2. Add the Cross stitches in diagonal zigzag paths.

Step 3. Add the Four-way clusters of Upright Cross clusters in clockwise or counterclockwise paths, following the diamond lattice trail to travel to the next cluster.

Step 4. Add the Hungarian units in radiating paths around the clusters of Four-way Enlarged Hot Wheel units. Lay these stitches from the outside in to enable easy traveling on the diamond lattice.

Step 5. Add the Tent clusters in diagonal rows. Side trips can be made in the corners, if desired, by weaving through previously stitched areas.

These modified arrangements have been included to demonstrate the process of altering an allover pattern to either create a larger repeat (which can be used as a center "medallion" or a corner motif in a border) or a stripe (which can be used as a border as well as a filling). Simple changes of color or value as well as changes in the physical layout can be used to produce variations, so possibilities are endless.

13. Open Networks with Clusters of Four-way Extended Diagonal Hungarian Units. The stitch that forms the base of the next series of patterns is one from my doodle cloth of Hungarian stitches. By extending the middle stitch of a Diagonal Hungarian unit, I formed this interesting offspring, which creates exciting open networks when it is used as a four-way cluster.

To the right is an overall chart of the main network of the variations that follow. A sequence is provided that works the units in horizontal rows of flip-flop units. As the sequence progresses, the order of doing the three stitches alternates because neighboring units meet on the extended stitches when they lean towards each other, but they join at the side stitches when they lean away from each other. Therefore it is necessary to change the order of each group of stitches in anticipation of the position of the next group.

To turn the corner at the end of each row, I did not execute stitch r first because it was needed to get me back to the center in order to pivot and start the next row. Stitch u was done last in the next group because it was needed to get back to group v-x.

Once corners have been turned, the alternating sequence can be resumed, so additional changes only occur when the row directions shift. These units are not symmetrical like Diagonal Hungarian, Chain Link and Hot Wheels; therefore the negative space around the cluster forms petal shapes with directional changes rather than uniform "non-directional" shapes like the others.

The open areas of this pattern seem to suggest a repeat of overlapping flower petals. When I noticed this, I decided to use the pattern as a border around the sampler on the back cover. Notice how the color treatments of the corner motifs make them look like whole flowers. I repeated this motif in the center band as a way of unifying the design. This border pattern and the variation used around *Santa Sampler* (Color Plate III) are included on pages 128-130 of the border chapter.

Variation 1. Open Network of Extended Diagonal Hungarian Combined with Cross Stitches and Upright Cross units. This pattern is used in the corners of the border of *Hummer Huddle* (Color Plate VI). It is an ideal choice since it compensates easily inside the slanted lines. I used a star green metallic for the Crosses and the Upright Crosses, so a combined sequence is used.

Step 2. Add the alternating units of Upright Cross and Cross stitches in diagonal paths. Always cross away from the direction to which you will be traveling on the top cross of both stitches to keep the stitches snugly wrapped.

Variation 2. Open Network of the Variation 1 Pattern with the Addition of Four-way Units of Tied Oblong Crosses. The pattern shown below is identical to the one to the right, but the open areas are filled with Tied Oblong Crosses. The placement of these units in a four-way position reinforces the fact that the open spaces are different and makes them more individual.

There are examples of these first two patterns in the sampler on the inside front cover. All of the examples appear again in the bottom doodle cloth of Color Plate XIV.

Use the "eyelet method" to add these units because there is no other way to conceal the traveling threads.

Several repeats of this sequence of radiating "split" stitches is applied to the Tied Oblong Cross cluster shown below. The traveling thread should carry behind the dense part of the Extended Hungarian units.

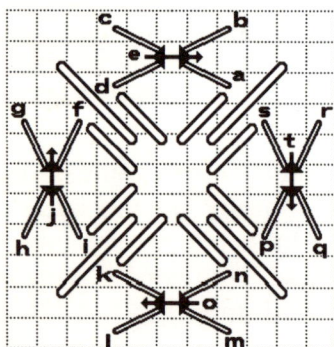

62

COLOR PLATE II

Br-r-r-r-rdbath

COLOR PLATE III

Santa Sampler

COLOR PLATE IV

Just Plain Folks

COLOR PLATE V

Underwater Ballet

COLOR PLATE VI
Hummer Huddle

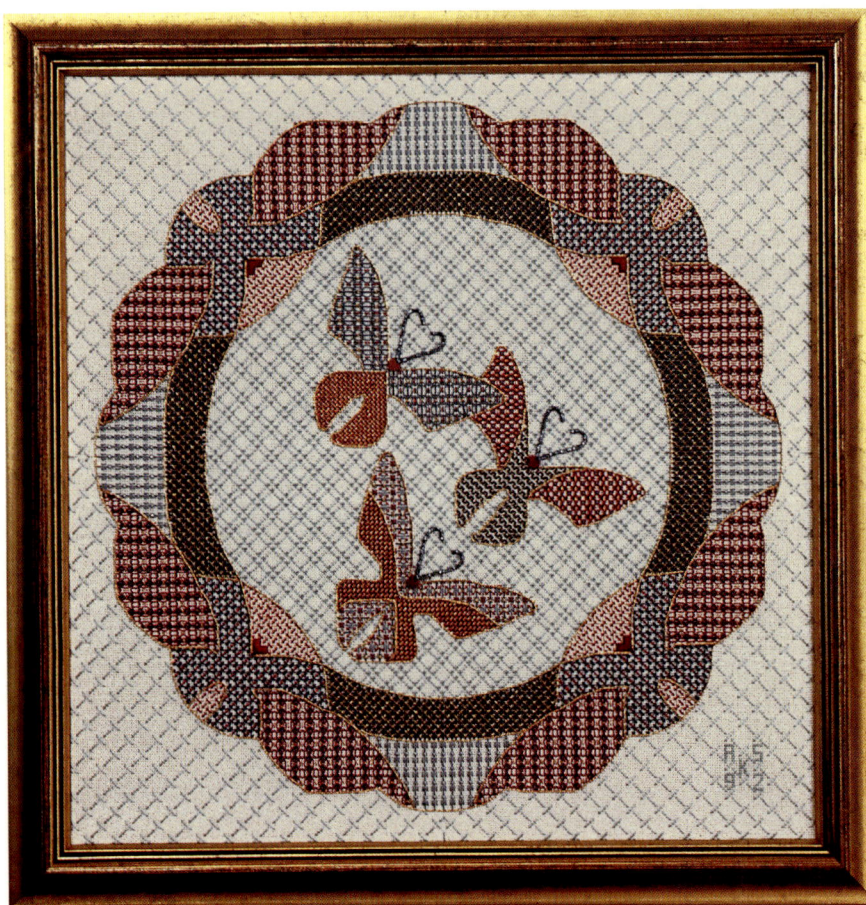

COLOR PLATE VII
Flurry of Butterflies

COLOR PLATE VIII
Strawberry Delight

COLOR PLATE IX
Dresden Heart

COLOR PLATE X
Oriental Butterfly

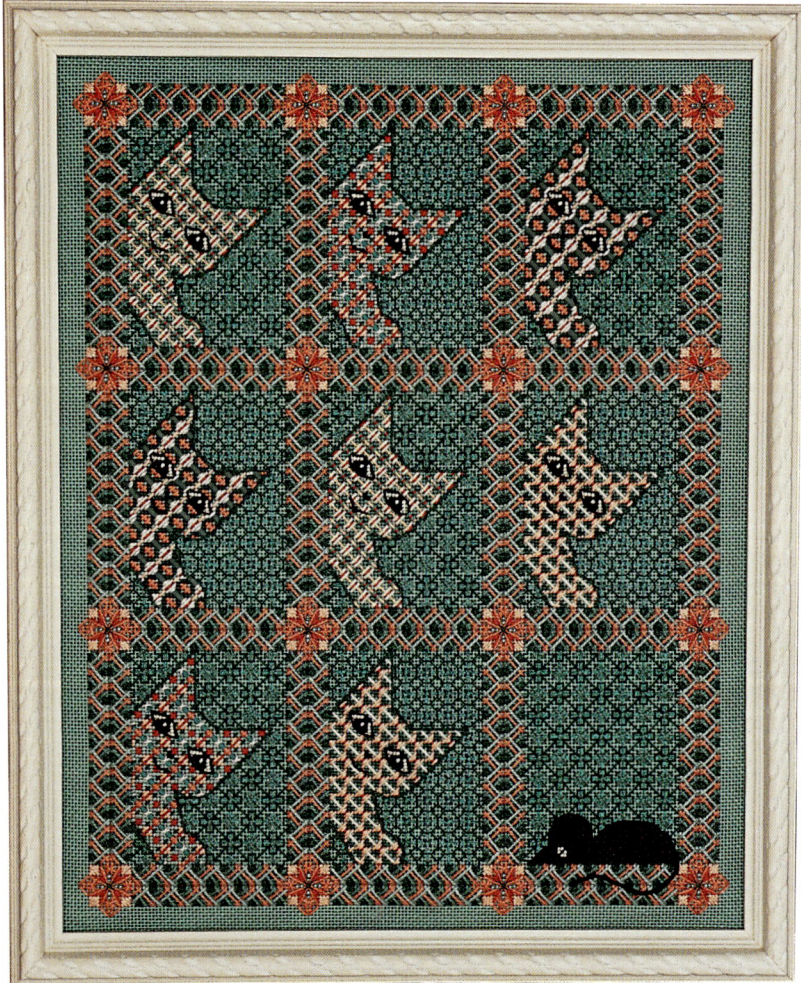

COLOR PLATE XI
Tease Time

COLOR PLATE XII
Hungarian Hootenanny

COLOR PLATE XIII
Twickenham

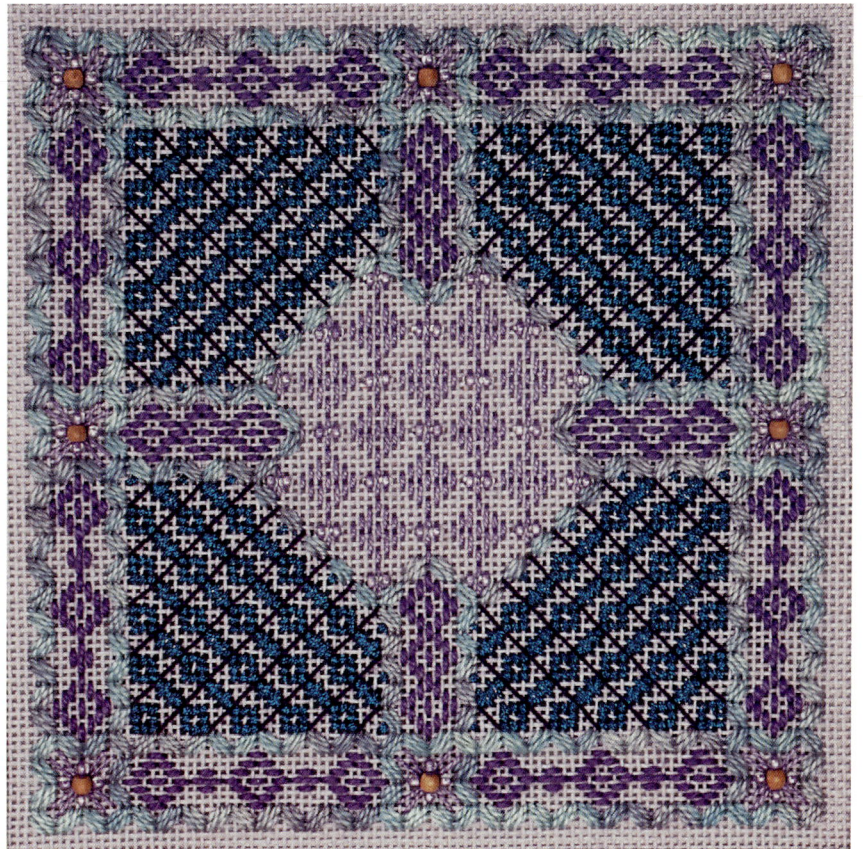

COLOR PLATE XIV

Doodle Cloth 1 (Top) - Open Networks of Partial Pavillion and Zigzag Paths
Doodle Cloth 2 (Bottom) - Open Networks of Four-way Extended Diagonal Hungarian

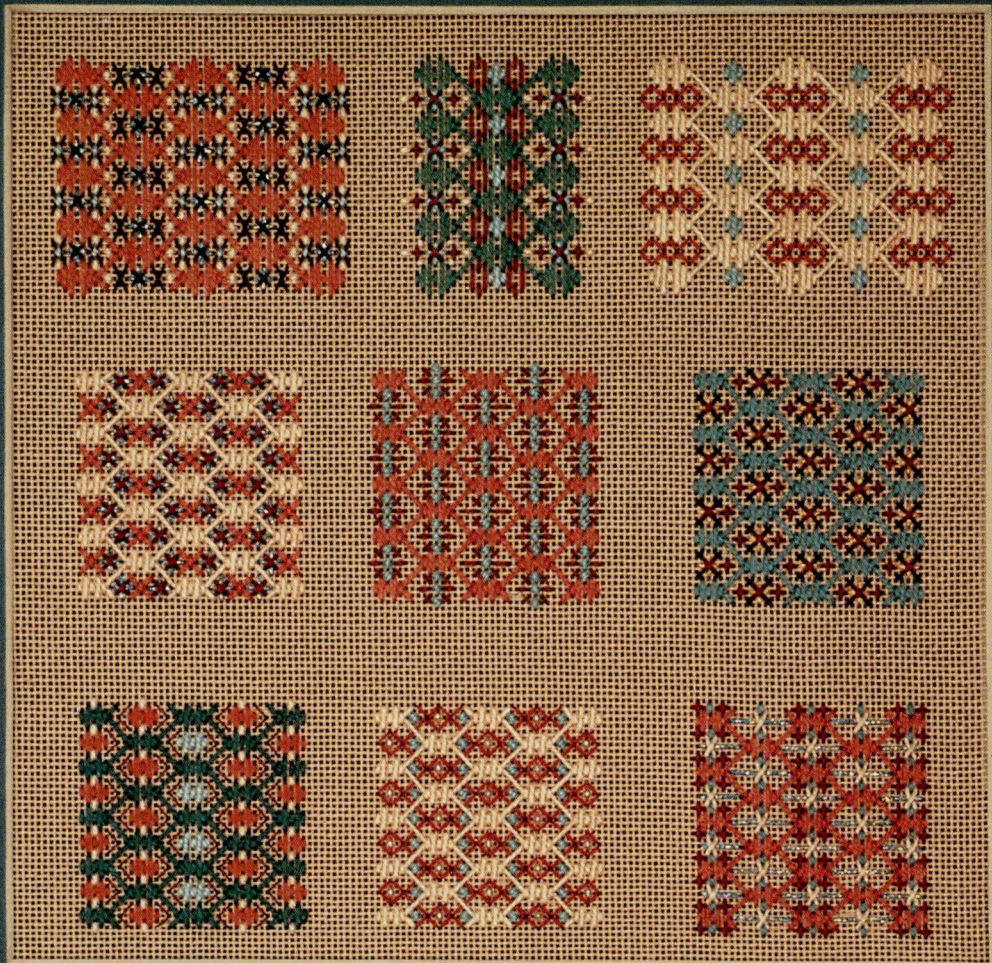

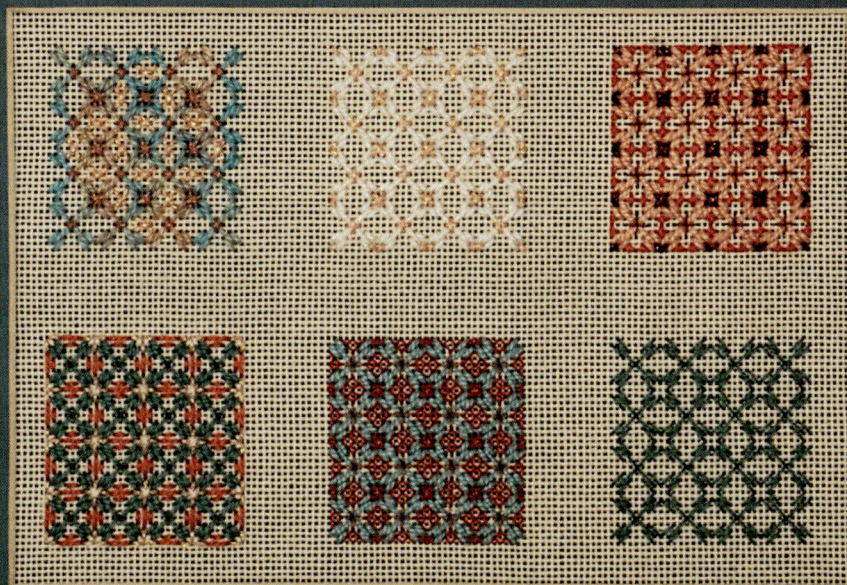

Variation 3. Open Network of Four-way Clusters of Extended Diagonal Hungarian Units Combined with Overlays of Double Straight Cross and Additional Accents of Four-way Hungarian Units. The use of the layered Double Straight Cross units makes this variation quite three-dimensional. Add these units as Step 2 either in one thread or two contrasting threads in separate sequences.

Add the Four-way Hungarian units as Step 3. They are easy to place since the center stitches share holes with the Double Straight Cross units on both sides.

This example is in the lower left corner of the doodle cloth in Color Plate XIV.

Variation 4. Open Network of Four-way Clusters of Extended Diagonal Hungarian Units Combined with Four-way Brick Stitch Clusters, Smyrna Crosses, and Blackwork Diamonds. This pattern is dramatic, and the dark blackwork appears to be behind the main network.

Step 2. Add the Smyrna Crosses in diagonal paths.

Step 3. Add the Four-way Brick stitches. The outside sinking holes of these radiating stitches will share holes with the blackwork motifs.

Step 4. Use the sequence chart to the left to add the blackwork diamonds in vertical paths.

NOTE. Since the blackwork filling is symmetrical inside the four-way open areas, they now appear to be identical instead of four-way.

63

Variation 5. Open Network of Four-way Clusters of Extended Diagonal Hungarian Units Combined with Four-way Brick Stitch Clusters, Smyrna Crosses, and Pairs of Upright Cross Units. This example has all of the elements of Variation 4, but pairs of Upright Cross units have replaced the blackwork diamonds. The pattern is more open, and the four-way arrangement of the Upright Cross filling forms rings or circles around the Brick clusters. Add the Upright Crosses in vertical and horizontal rows to conceal the traveling paths.

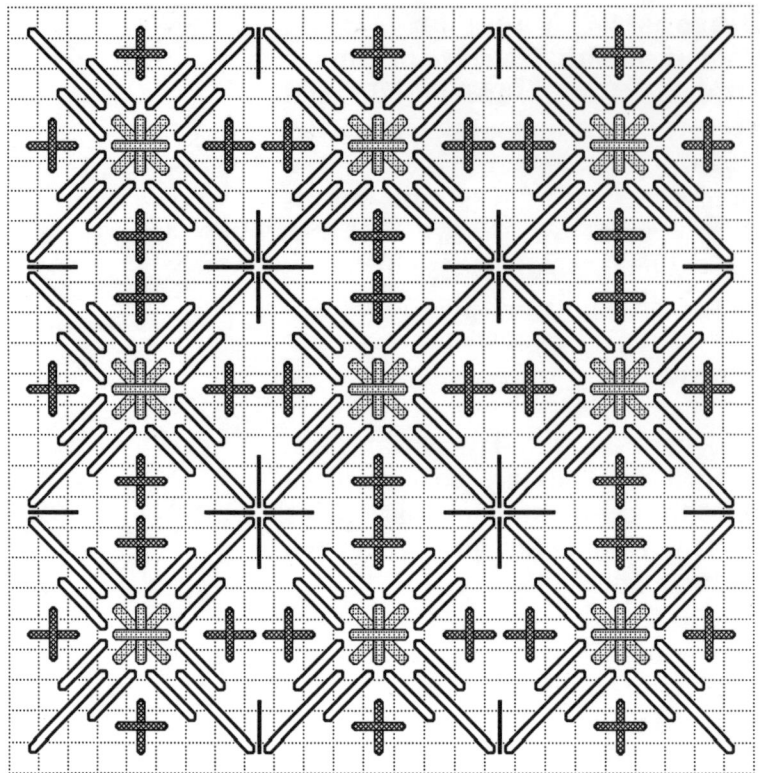

This final variation appears in the upper right corner of the doodle cloth, and the previous example is in the middle of the bottom section. The color treatments used in the doodle cloth samples are quite different, and they reveal how important color and value are in making the details of a pattern more prominent. Even subtle changes in these characteristics can change the dominance of the patterns dramatically. Changes in the texture and weight of the threads used is a third variable, so hopefully I have demonstrated the endless potential for variation that is available in a single pattern.

14. Open Networks of Nobuko Stitches. This stitch is an unpublished one as far as I know so I have featured an example of a solid overall pattern in the chart to the right. I learned this stitch in a class twelve years ago from a New England teacher who could not identify its origin. Five years later when I was sharing the stitch in a class on the West Coast, I learned that there was a Japanese lady with the same name who used to teach in Southern California. Today stitches "travel" farther and wider in a shorter amount of time with the extensive network of seminars available, and I was delighted to solve this mystery.

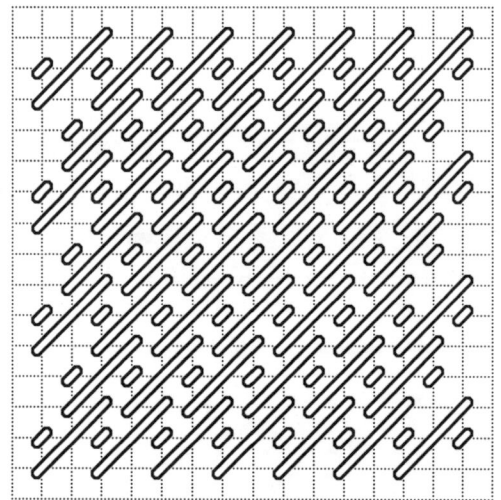

The stitch makes a wonderful grounding, and each row has an alternating sequence of a Tent stitch followed by a long diagonal stitch that straddles three intersections.

Notice that in successive rows the short stitches of the previous rows share holes with the long stitches of the surrounding rows. This "clue" or observation will make it much easier to find the starting point when adding new rows. The pattern forms a subtle stripe with slanted lines rather than strong diagonals, and it compensates well in irregular shapes. It has fast become a basic staple in my stitch palette, and it should become one of the classic diagonal stitches.

64

The first series of open patterns that use this stitch have a main network of offset Mirrored Nobuko units, which are variations. I have rotated and mirrored the original stitch units in this pattern to make the parallelogram shapes fit the page better.

Repeats of offset stitches generally create a slanted line rather than a diagonal, and this allover pattern forms a rhomboidal parallelogram. Such an unusual geometric shape can be interesting in a design, so I usually stitch my samples in these configurations to remind me of this potential.

Step 1.   Execute these stitches in sequential order, using either oblique or diagonal paths. In this shape the oblique paths are more efficient since there are only four rows in the offset direction whereas there are eleven rows in the diagonal direction.

Use the same weight thread throughout the variations that follow since all the additional fillings will be diagonal stitches. (Note the one exception in Variation 2).

Variation 1. Open Network of Offset Mirrored Nobuko Rows with Accent Fillings of Hungarian and Chain Link. This pattern produces a vivid diagonal stripe since the color changes occur between the short rows of the pattern.

Step 2. Add the Hungarian stitches in diagonal paths.

Step 3. Add the Chain Link units in diagonal paths.

This is almost a solid pattern, but there is a canvas "peekaboo" inside each of the Chain Link units.

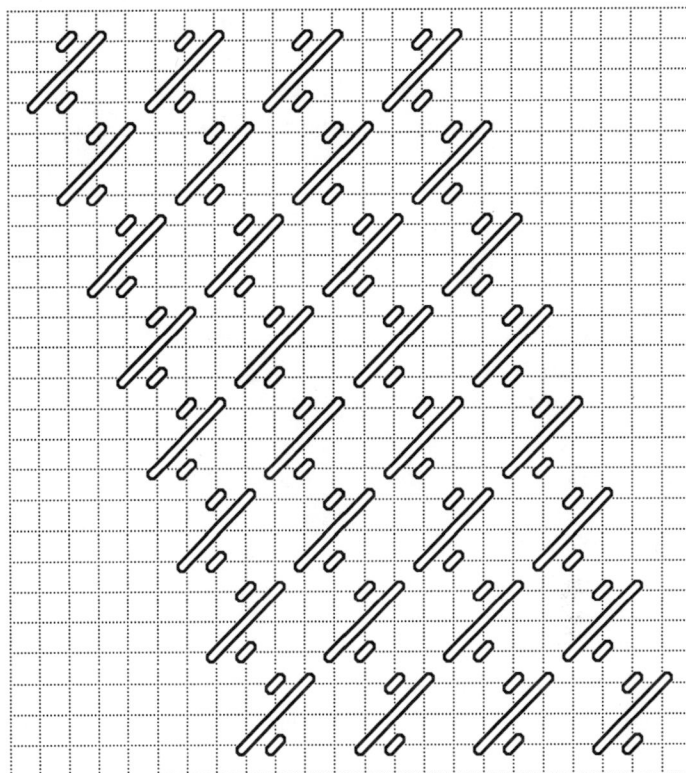

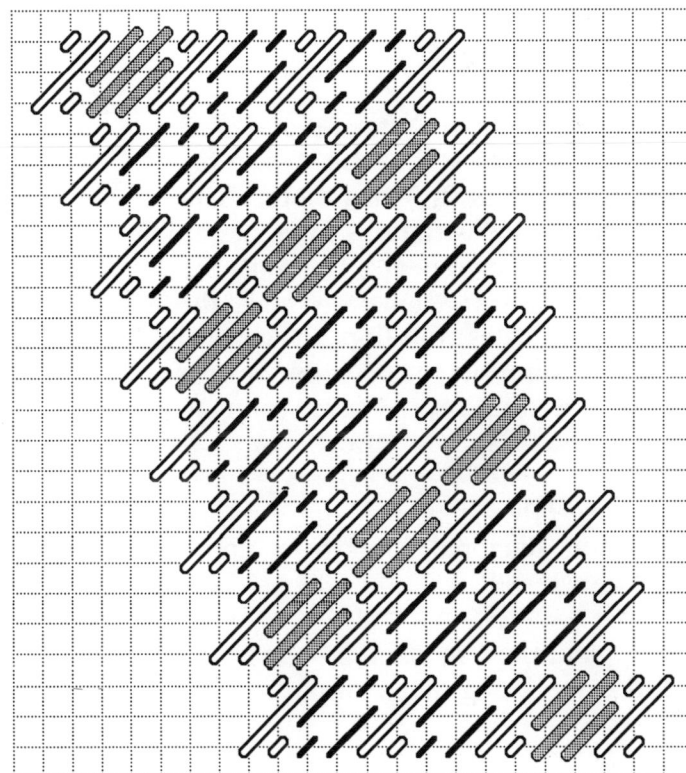

Variation 2. Open Network of Offset Mirrored Nobuko Rows with Accents of Tied Diagonal Oblong Crosses in Two Colors. This pattern appears to form an oblique stripe when the alternating rows of Tied Oblong Crosses are done in a contrasting thread.

Step 2. Add the Tied Oblong Crosses in oblique rows in whole units. Use a light weight thread for these layered stitches, and a different color or value is also recommended. Lay the crosses so that the traveling is done at the top or bottom of the stitches rather than at the sides where exposures are likely.

I used an alternating sequence which keeps all the stitches snugly wrapped, and one repeat of this is shown in the overall chart to the right.

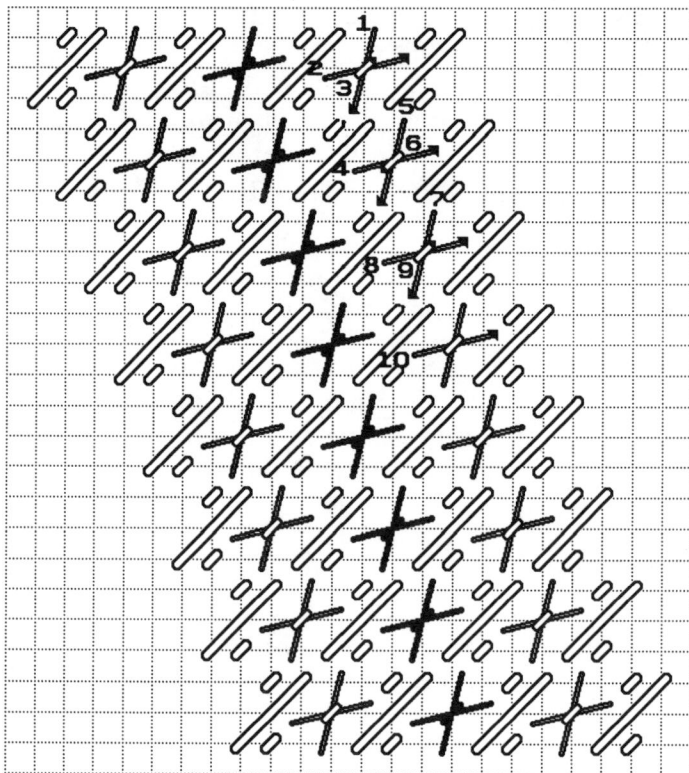

Variation 3. Open Network of Offset Mirrored Nobuko Rows with Accents of Chain Link Units in Two Colors. This time I used color variations to create an alternating diaper repeat. The units are shaded to form triangles, and the isosceles triangles flip-flop in vertical repeats. Adjacent repeats would mirror this pattern and reverse the color to continue the "diapered" effect.

Step 2. Add the Chain Link units in one color, using diagonal paths from upper right to lower left.

Step 3. Add the Chain Link units in the second color, using diagonal paths.

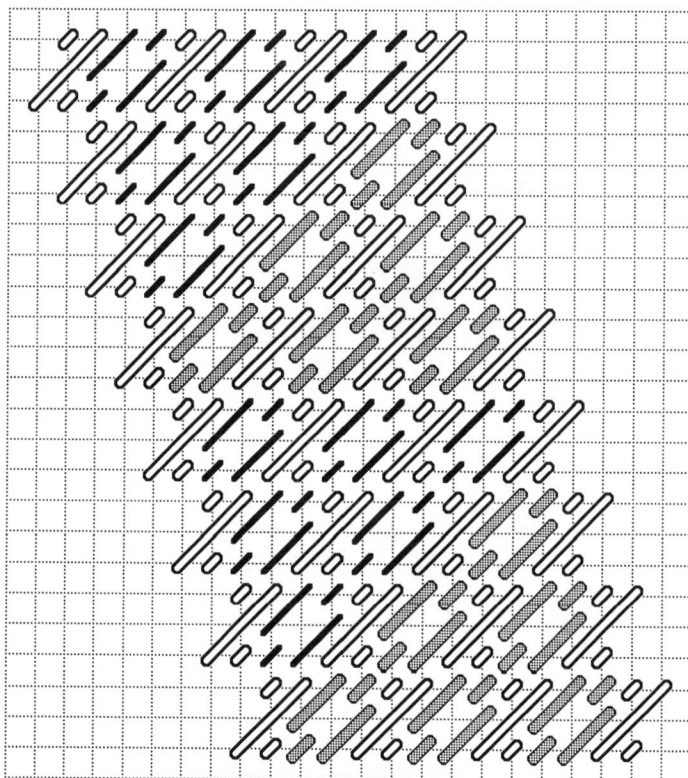

66

Variation 4. Network of Offset Mirrored Nobuko Rows with Accents of Reverse Mosaic and Double Tent. This pattern is a solid one, but I included it to illustrate that all patterns with only diagonal stitches can form a traditional solid pattern.

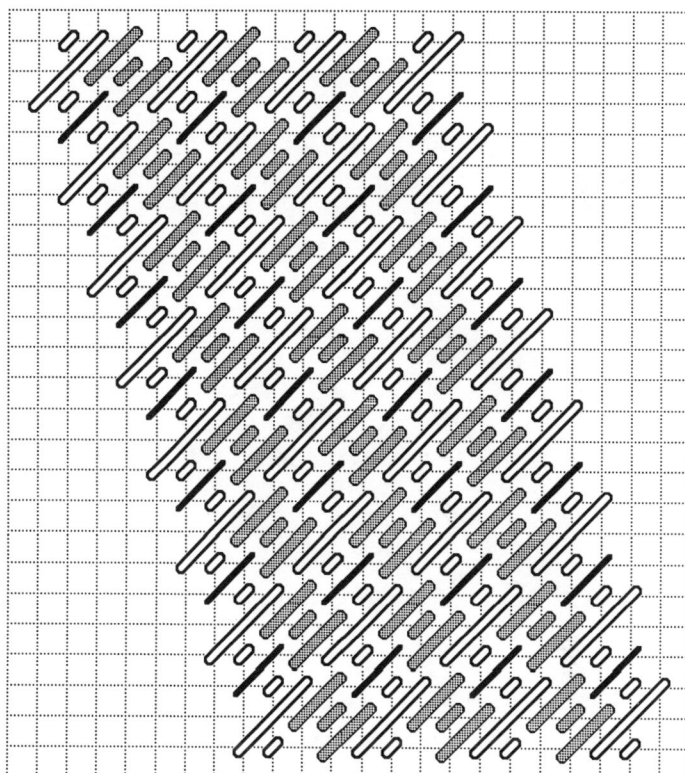

If the Nobuko network is stitched in a dark color, the pattern will be a definite stripe. However, if this network is done in a pale color, the pattern will appear to be an allover one because the diagonal lines of the Nobuko stitches will not be dominant.

Step 2. Lay the Reverse Mosaic units in oblique paths.

Step 3. Add the Double Tent stitches in diagonal paths.

Open Network of Oblique Rows of Flip-flop Nobuko Units. The next series of patterns will all have the same main network of flip-flop oblique rows of Nobuko. The "horizontal" oblique rows have units that are rotated 90° in alternating rows. This placement forms interesting large and small "circles" when adjacent rows are completed. These shapes are actually squares, however; once they are filled, they will appear that way.

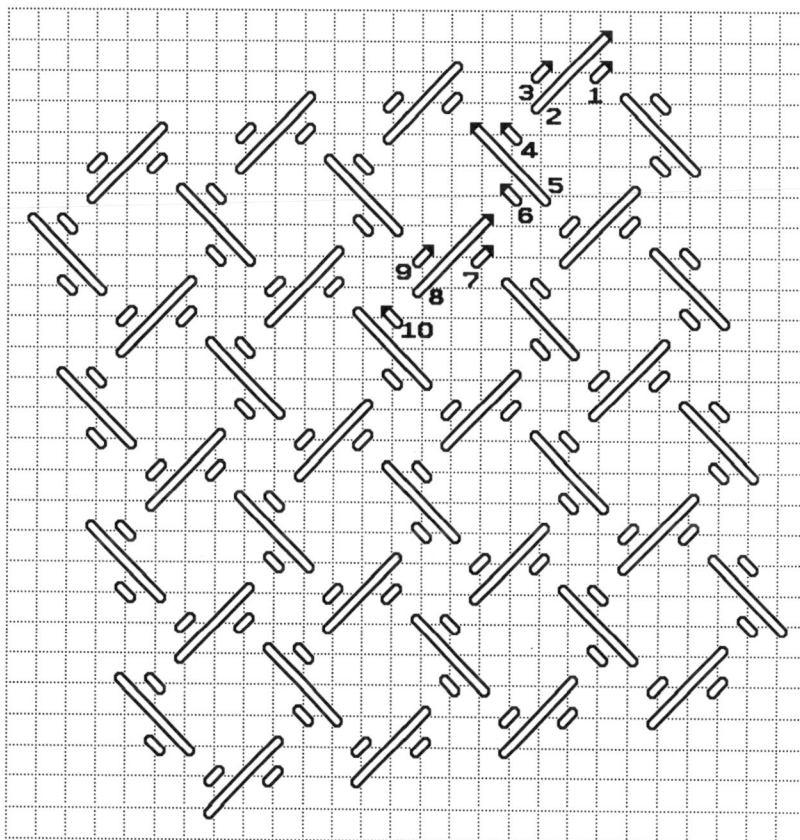

Such illusions are common with canvas stitches that have indentations. The repeats of this pattern are oblique in both directions so the overall shape is a parallelogram.

Sequence. Work the units in "vertical" oblique rows, using a right-to-left sequence for each unit. The traveling threads will automatically be concealed.

67

Variation 5. Open Network of Flip-flop Nobuko with Accents of Mosaic Stitches. This pattern is featured as a border, but it could be an allover pattern if the Mosaic units were added to every four-way cluster of Flip-flop Nobuko units. Add the Mosaic units in oblique paths from top to bottom as Step 2.

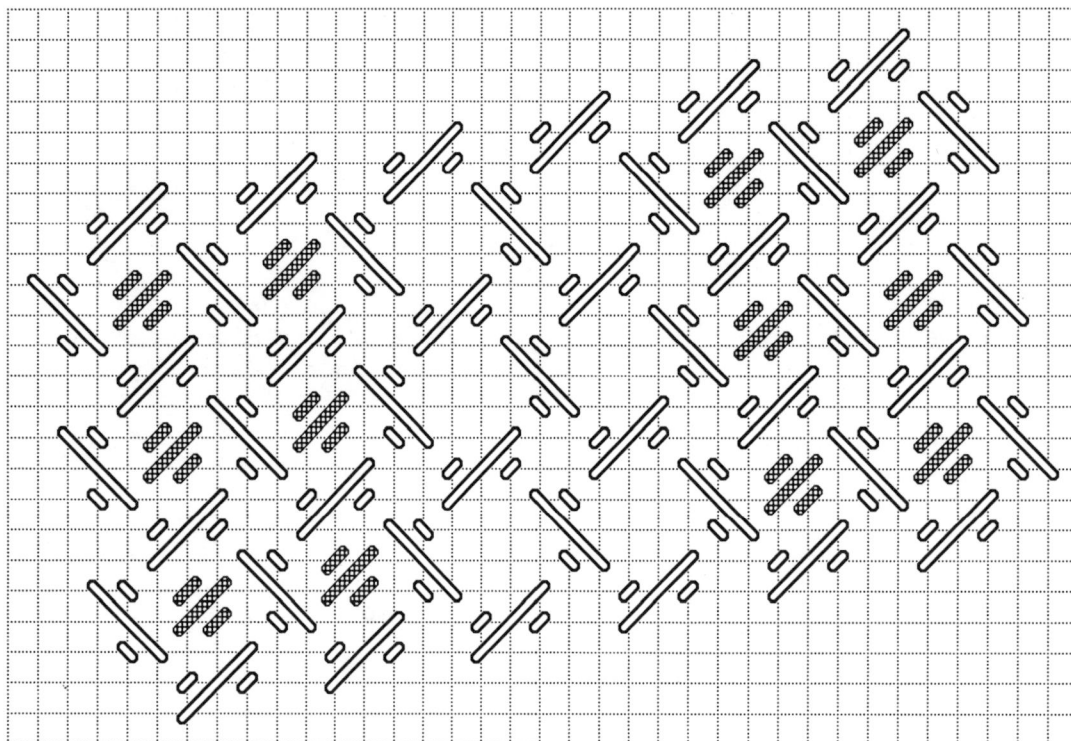

Variation 6. Open Network of Flip-flop Nobuko with Accents of Mirrored Partial Mosaic Units. This pattern is still quite open, and the mirrored stitches create an interesting bow tie or spool shape inside the circles.

Add these diagonal stitches in oblique "horizontal" paths. Work the stitches "downhill" in the right-to-left rows and "uphill" in the left-to-right rows. Otherwise they will not wrap snugly.

This variation will also be Steps 1 and 2 of the next and final pattern of the series. It is a solid pattern that forms a true diaper.

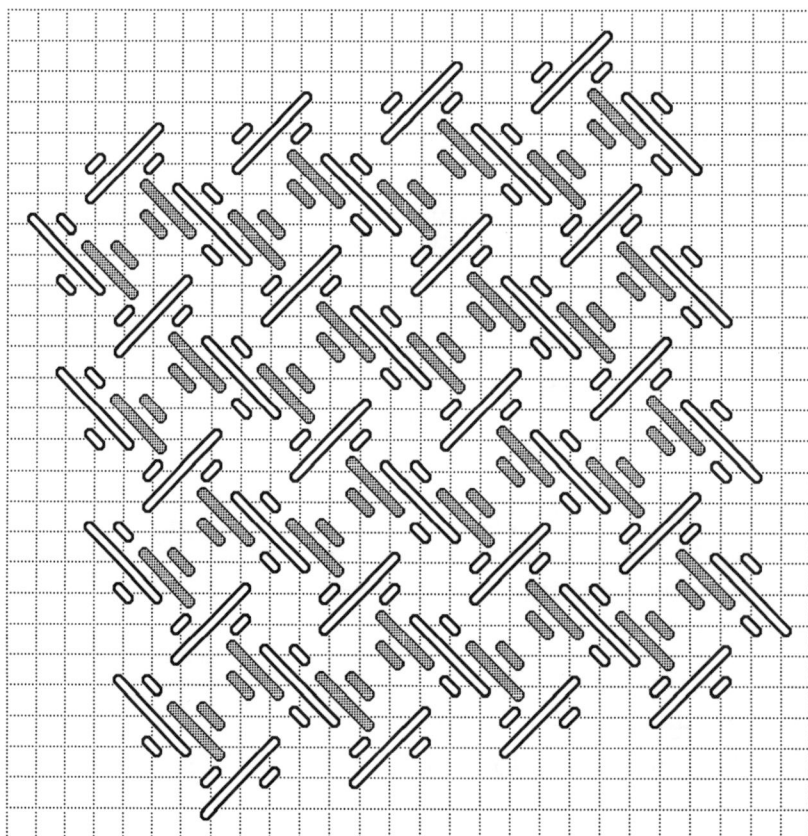

Variation 7. Open Network of Flip-flop Nobuko with Accents of Mirrored Partial Mosaic Units in Two Colors, and Mosaic Stitches.

Step 3. Add the second group of Mirrored Partial Mosaic stitches in "vertical" oblique paths. Use a different value of the same color used in the Step 2 units.

Step 4. Add the Mosaic stitches to the remaining small squares in either horizontal or vertical oblique rows.

NOTE. All of these pattern samples have an interesting jagged or sawtooth edge that makes them attractive as isolated geometric shapes. They also maneuver well in irregular shapes except for Variation 2 which has the Diagonal Oblong Crosses.

This chapter features patterns with open networks that are produced with combinations of two different styles of stitches. Such combination networks tend to form larger scale patterns because there are two different units that form each repeat. The availability of larger negative spaces allows more intricate patterning to be added to the main network so the potential for variations is greater as well.

Some of the stitches used have been explored in earlier chapters as single stitch networks or filling stitches, so I will refer you back to these chapters for sequence information, if needed.

1. Open Pattern with a Diamond Lattice Composed of Alternating Clusters of Four-Way Hot Wheels and Double Cross Units.

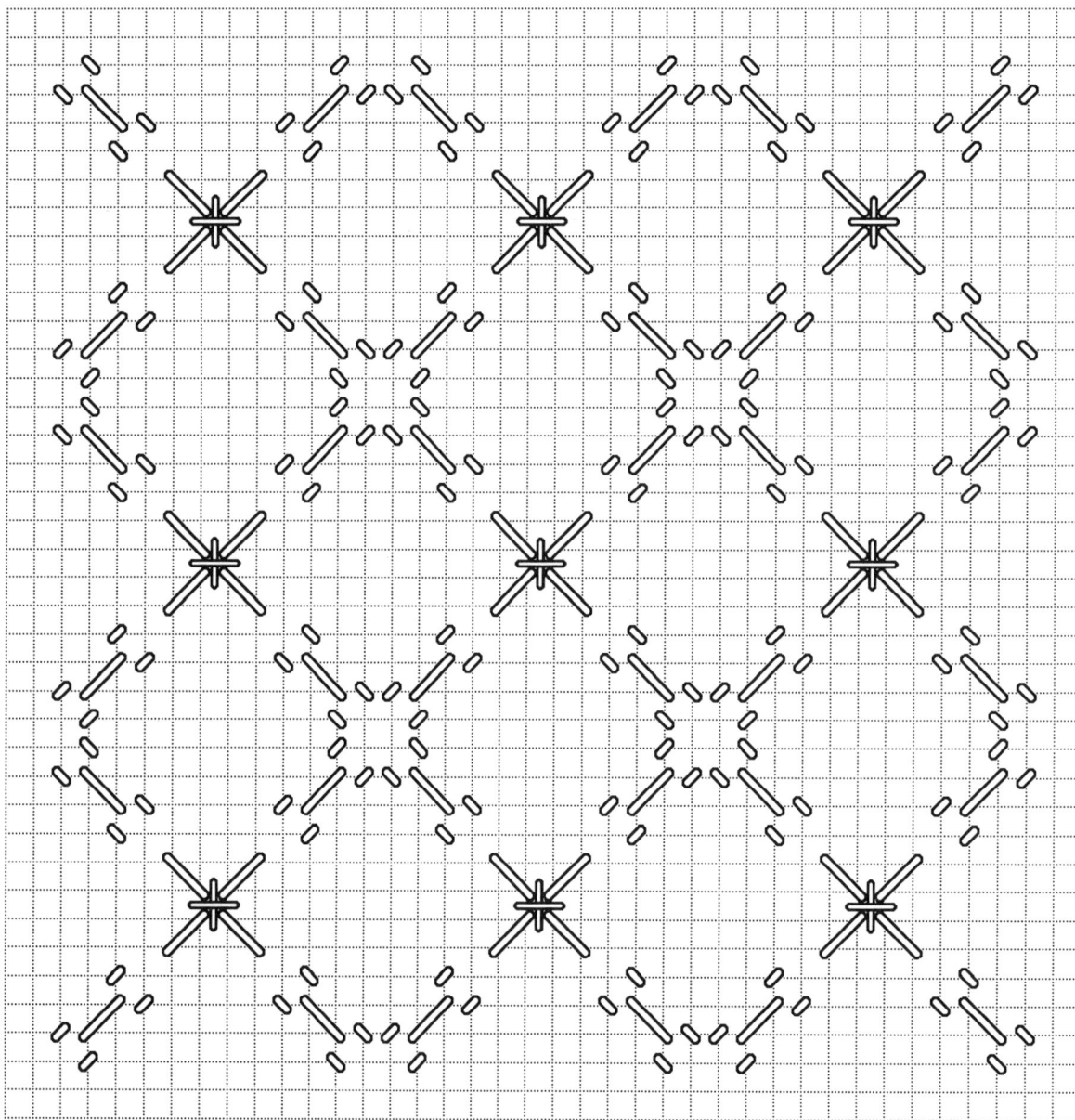

This pattern is spread out, so it is more efficient to execute the outlines with zigzag rows. Work the clusters of Hot Wheels in back stitches, as shown on page 57. Add the Double Cross units in two separate sequences. The first path should add just one foundation cross; either one can be done first since the top cross will cover any inconsistency. The second sequence, which travels in the opposing direction, will add the second foundation cross and the top Upright Cross. Splitting the sequence in this way is another method to manipulate this stitch so that no "eyelet method" has to be used.

Variation 1. Open Pattern of Alternating Clusters of Four-Way Hot Wheels and Double Cross Units. Additional Elements Include Four-Way Ray Variations, Four-Way Tied Oblong Crosses and Beaded Brick Stitches.

This composite pattern is elegant, especially if the Brick stitches are beaded. Lay the Hot Wheel-Tied Double Cross diamond network first as Step 1, but read Step 4 before proceeding.

Step 2. Add the Ray Variation units in radiating paths from the outside in (except for the first group which wraps better if stitched from the inside out). Connect the clusters in either vertical or horizontal rows. Lay the long stitch first, and then add the two side stitches in each group. Visually these stitches form a square lattice after they are completed.

Step 3. Add the Tied Oblong Cross units in between the Ray stitches. These must be done with the "eyelet method" to conceal the traveling paths.

Step 4. Add the Brick stitches and bead them. It is also logical to combine this step with the Step 1 outline since the Brick stitches are in the middle of the four-way clusters of Hot Wheels. Use the same thread for both steps but change the value or color of the bead.

There is an example of this pattern in the sampler on the inside front cover. Even though I used a light green #8 perle for Step 1, I added pink beads with the green thread as part of the Step 1 sequence.

Variation 2. Addition of Four-way Satin Stitch Clusters. Four of the Tied Oblong Cross units in this overall pattern have been replaced by a bold satin stitch unit in my sample on the inside front cover. It suggests a flower shape and creates a focal point.

A detailed view of this alternative filling is shown in the chart to the right. The substitution converts the overall pattern shown in Variation 1 to one large repeat instead.

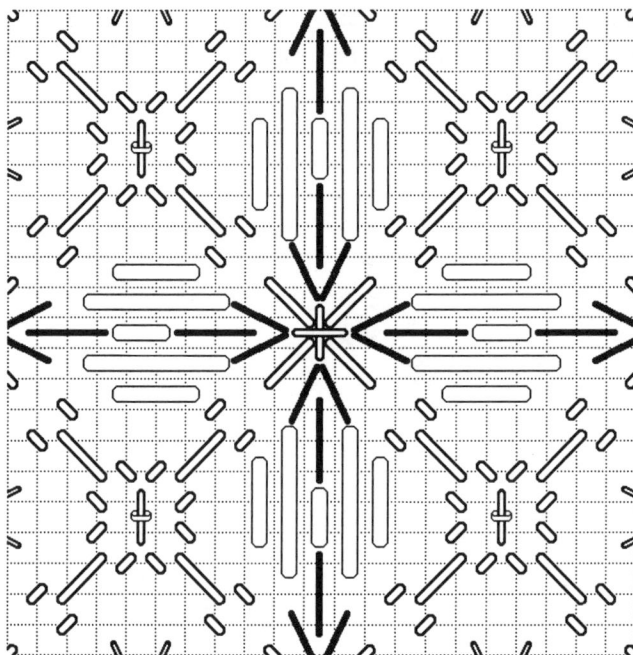

2. Open Network of Four-way Clusters of Diagonal Hungarian Units Arranged Around a Center Unit of Smyrna Cross. This pattern of square repeats forms a diamond lattice. As the pattern repeats, each "spoke" of every radiating cluster is also a part of the adjacent cluster. When units merge like this, the pattern repeat has what is called "overlapping" elements. Merging or compressing independent parts of a pattern repeat is another way to create a pattern variation.

Step 1. Sequence. A lettered sequence is shown in the upper right corner of the overall chart to the right. The main path is one of diagonal rows, but the sides of the Diagonal

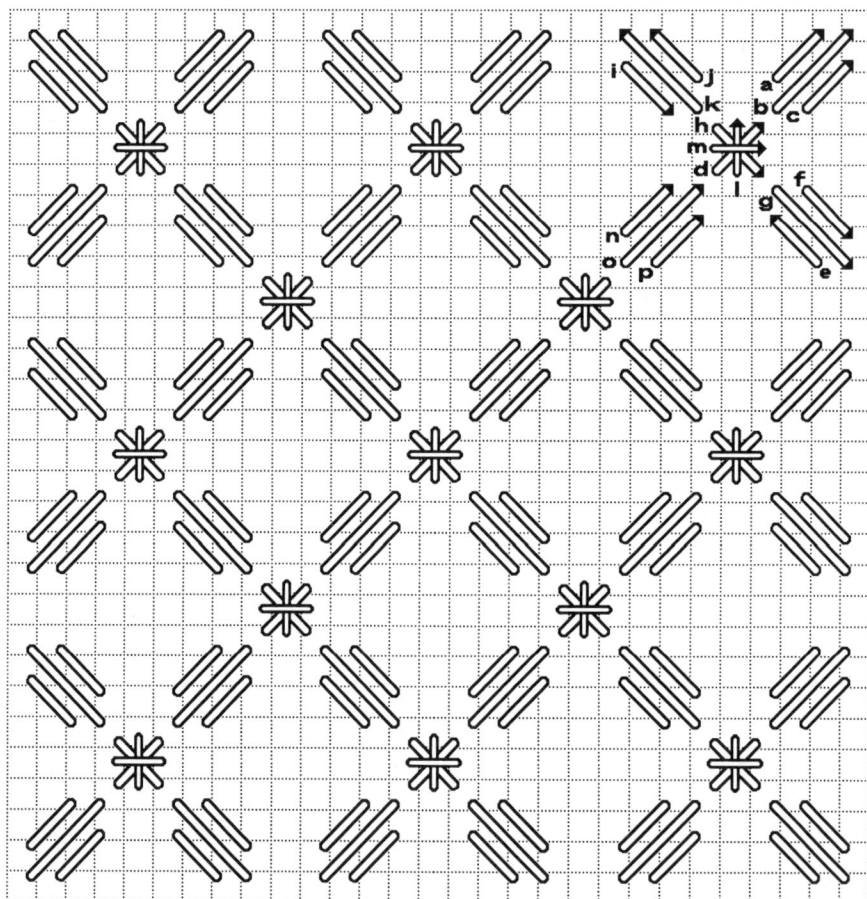

Hungarian clusters are added as side trips. To accomplish this efficiently, the Smyrna Cross sequence is done in segments to allow the thread to travel gracefully to the extended areas. A pivot takes place in both of the side trip units to enable the thread to return to the main path. If both side stitches are added in the first row, other rows will only have a single side trip so merely skip these stitches and continue with the sequence as lettered.

The alternative to doing these side trips is to work separate diagonal rows to connect these units. The use of the side trip concept is far more efficient since long journeys in the backing can be avoided, but any manipulations must be consistent and keep all stitches snugly wrapped. Open areas around all of the Step 1 stitches must remain uncluttered as well.

An example of this open pattern is featured in the lower left corner of the sampler on the inside front cover, and it is surrounded by the three variations that follow.

Variation 1. Composite Pattern Combining a Main Network of Four-way Diagonal Hungarian and Smyrna Cross with Alternating units of Double Straight Cross and Blackwork Stars. This pattern appears to be totally blackwork since the alternating elements are done in the same thread. The blackwork stars are actually combined with Double Straight Cross units to form a secondary allover pattern. Two compatible networks have been combined, but each could be used as a separate single pattern as well.

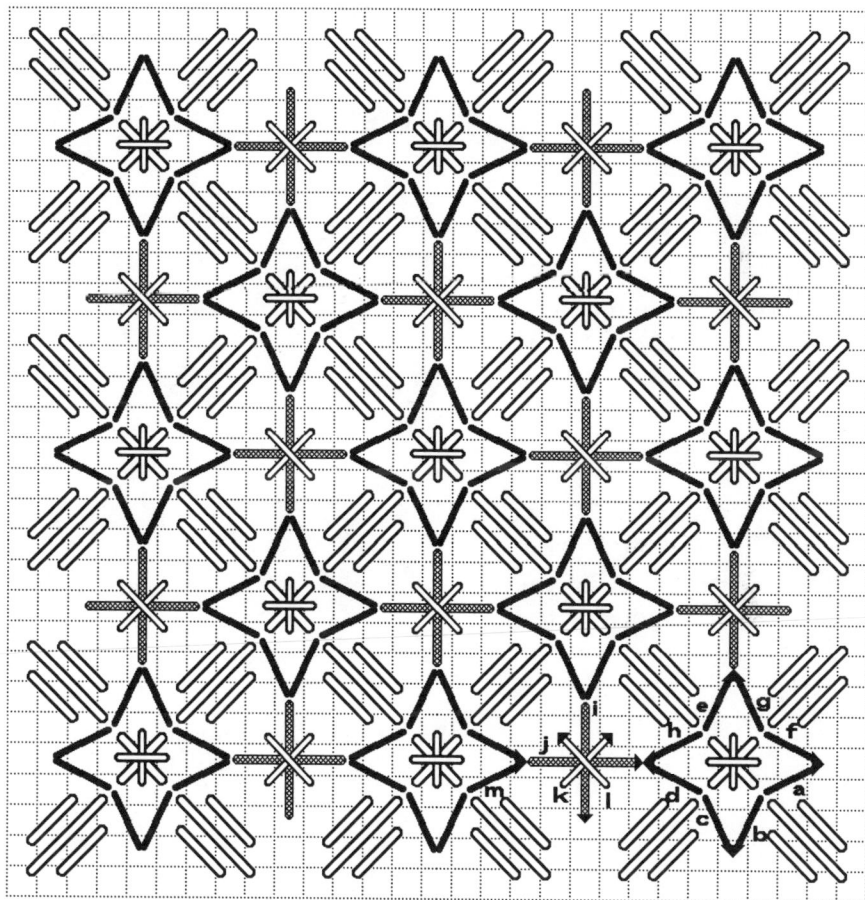

Step 2. The star and diamond units are added with a combined sequence in horizontal paths, as shown in the lettered sequence in the lower right corner of the overall chart above. The diamonds are actually a bridge between the stars, and they conceal the traveling threads in an attractive ornamental way. Stitches a-d of the blackwork stars are an alternating sequence of back stitches and running stitches. Stitches e-h represent a double running stitch side trip that eventually rejoins the main path or outline.

Variation 2. Composite Pattern Combining a Main Network of Four-way Diagonal Hungarian and Smyrna Cross with Accents of Double Straight Cross Units, Upright Cross Clusters, and Cross Stitches with a Border of Four-way Tent Clusters. This pattern is very dense so canvas exposure is minimal. The arrangement, as shown on the next page, is also a single repeat. Two separate overall patterns could be created if only the Double Straight Cross units or the combination cluster of Cross stitch and Four-way Tent stitches were used throughout the pattern. A row of several repeats of the medallion, however, could make a handsome border with a zigzag edge so I want you to keep seeing these possibilities within a single pattern.

Step 2. When a pattern is this dense, I usually add the stitches that are closest to the main network first since they will add further density to this area. The Upright Cross units surround the Smyrna Cross units so add these first in diagonal paths from upper right to lower left. Use a clockwise sequence for each cluster.

Step 3. Add the Double Straight Cross units in either one or two colors. Add the foundation stitches, using the eyelet method, and travel vertically or horizontally from unit to unit. (No shortcuts please, or threads will show!)

Step 4. Add the Cross stitches. These units form a ring of stitches along the outer edge. The stitches are close to each other and traveling between units is convenient since the Diagonal Hungarian units will conceal the traveling paths. Make sure the tension on the Cross stitches remains consistent as the travel direction shifts.

VARIATION 2 - OVERALL PATTERN

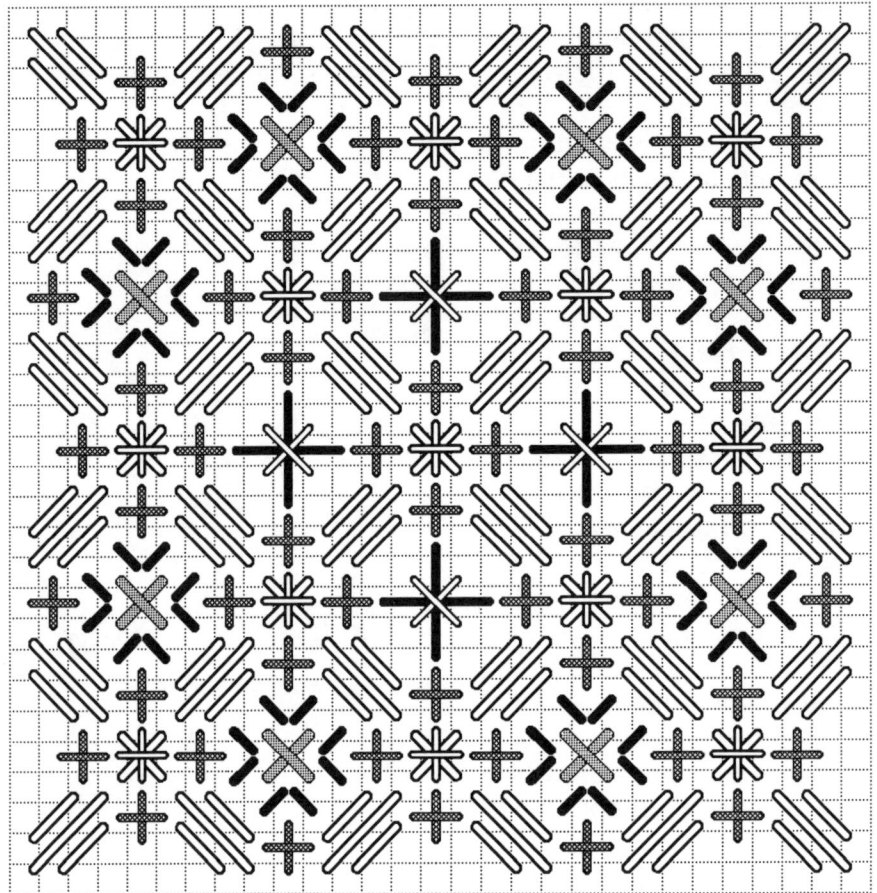

Step 5. Add the radiating pairs of Tent stitches around the Cross stitches. Work these from the outside in so that they pivot correctly.

Variation 3. Composite Pattern Combining a Main Network of Four-way Diagonal Hungarian and Smyrna Cross with Accents of Upright Gobelin Clusters, Upright Cross Clusters, and Diamond Blackwork Petals. This pattern is actually an allover arrangement, but only one repeat is shown in the sample, so it appears to be a medallion or corner motif. The overall chart for the sample appears on the next page.

Three separate accents form the large repeat after the main network is completed. These accents are also spread out so it will be necessary to weave through the backing of the Step 1 main network to get to the new locations. The Upright Cross clusters should be added as Step 2 in clockwise or counterclockwise paths.

Add the radiating Upright Gobelin stitches as Step 3, and work these from the outside in. Plan the sequence in anticipation of the next cluster so that you end on an appropriate stitch.

Step 4. Add the blackwork diamonds, using the numbered sequence shown in the lower right corner of the overall chart to the right. Since the diamonds surround the Smyrna Cross units, they should be worked from the middle out each time.

Plan the starting and ending points of each group in anticipation of the next cluster. The example shown uses a clockwise path. When a counterclockwise path is needed, the left side of the top diamond should be done first and the right side should follow to enable the traveling thread to travel correctly to the next diamond outline.

I planned the sequence shown to make the traveling path carry behind the Smyrna Cross rather than behind the Diagonal Hungarian unit. Other sequences are possible, but I find this one the most flexible in adapting to the traveling needs required.

Variation 4. Composite Pattern Combining a Main Network of Four-way Diagonal Hungarian and Smyrna Cross with Accents of Four-way Tent Clusters, Four-way Ray Variation, and Four-way Upright Clusters. This final variation is shown in the sampler on the inside back cover. It is also combined there with a border that is discussed on pages 126-127, so only the inside pattern is covered here. Like the previous pattern, this variation has a large repeat, so only a single repeat of the overall pattern is shown on the next page. It has a similar large diamond arrangement, and three separate fillings are combined. All of these surround the Smyrna Cross units, leaving bold four-way open areas in between.

No numbered sequences should be needed for this arrangement. Add the Four-way Tent stitches first as Step 2 since they fill in the area around the Smyrna Crosses that form the large diamond.

Then add the Upright Cross clusters around only the four corner units of the diamond shape as Step 3.

Add the Ray Variation units as Step 4 to complete the pattern.

Since the Step 1 network is done in green and the secondary elements are done in shades of red and pink, this geometric combination tends to suggest flowers climbing a trellis.

The theme of flowers is continued in the fancy border that accompanies this pattern in the sampler. I added some small tulips to the blackwork outline.

Many four-way clusters can be used to suggest flowers, and many of the fillings I have used are from a doodle cloth of flower shapes that I developed. I continue to add new possibilities, and some of these can be seen in *Blue Oriental Lantern* (Color Plate I).

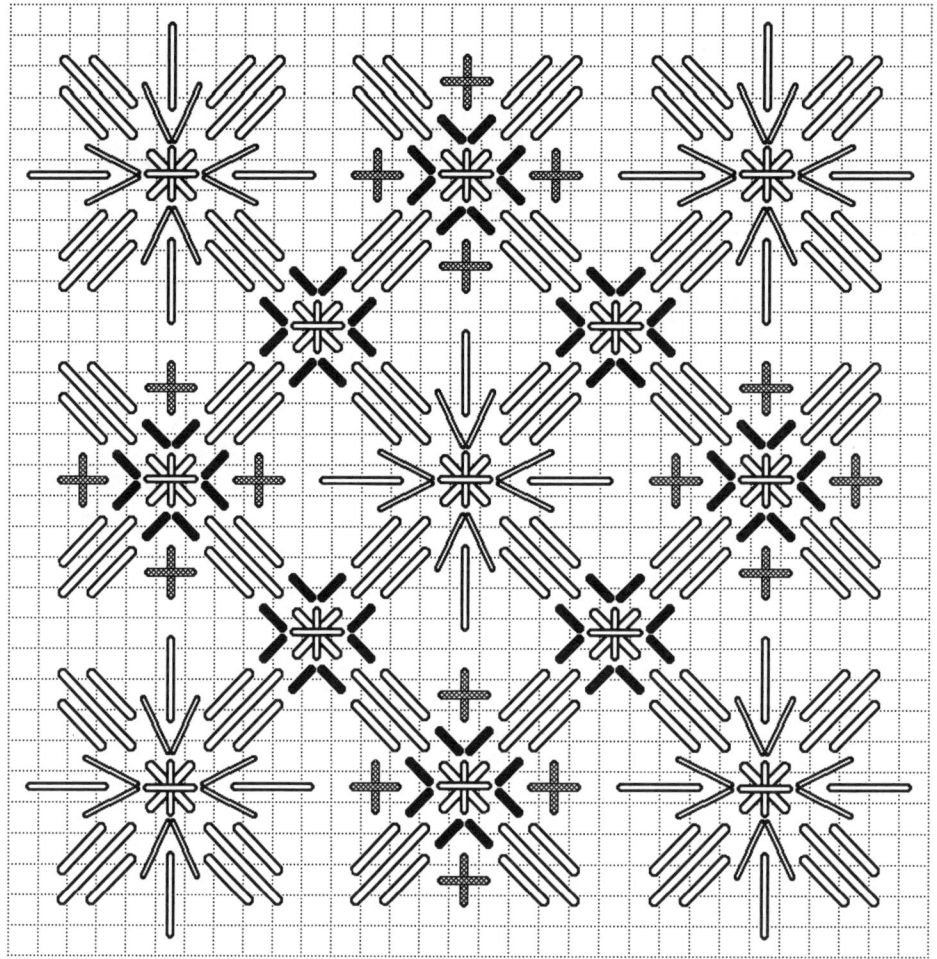

3. Open Networks with Alternating Units of Double Crosses and Diagonal Oblong Cross Units. The next series of patterns have a bold main network that is a diamond lattice. Units of Double Cross are connected by four-way arrangements of Diagonal Oblong Crosses. The open areas are large jagged diamonds, and I will be showing four composite patterns that build from this open network.

A small segment of the open network is shown to the right with a split sequence that connects the pattern units with zigzag diagonal rows. The presence of crosses in a pattern gives one great flexibility to readjust a stitch direction and to change sequence paths as needed, so I often plan crosses as "strategic elements" in a pattern to connect units conveniently.

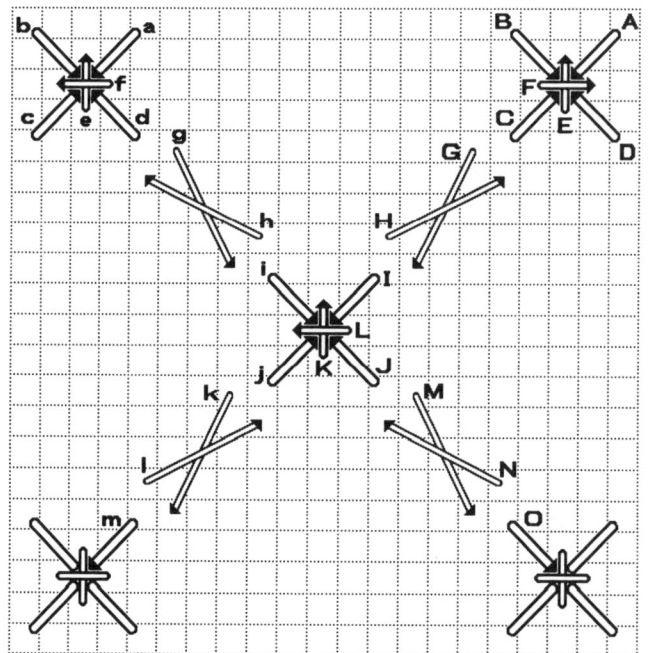

76

However, in this arrangement, the Oblong Crosses are not tied, so it is important to leave the "more horizontal" stitch on top throughout the pattern. The first variation shown below uses these "untied" units, but the other three patterns add a tiedown stitch. These four variations are the four large squares in the upper right corner of the sampler on the inside back cover. Because this pattern is so open, I also used a heavy thread called velour for the main network of three of the examples shown.

Variation 1. Open Network of Alternating Units of Double Crosses and Diagonal Oblong Crosses Combined with Enlarged Double Crosses. This combination creates the illusion of two separate diamond lattice patterns, and the Step 2 filling appears to be behind the Step 1 network. It is actually side-by-side, but the spaces or "broken lines" around the Oblong Crosses are not that obvious so there is an illusion of layers at viewing distance.

VARIATION 1

Step 2. Add the Enlarged Double Crosses, using the "eyelet method" to conceal the traveling paths. A heavier thread can also be used for this step since no other elements will be added.

77

Variation 2. Open Network of Alternating Units of Double Crosses and Tied Diagonal Oblong Cross Units Combined with Enlarged Double Crosses and Four-way Clusters of Hungarian. This pattern combines Variation 1 with an addition of radiating Hungarian stitches around the Enlarged Double Cross units. The Oblong Crosses are tied in a contrasting color in the sample, and the same thread is used for the top crosses of the Double Crosses, so Step 1 is divided into two separate sequences. I also did the Enlarged Double Crosses in two colors. Only a sequence for the Hungarian clusters is needed, and I provided one repeat of a diagonal path on the overall chart below. Add these as the final step.

VARIATION 2 - OVERALL PATTERN

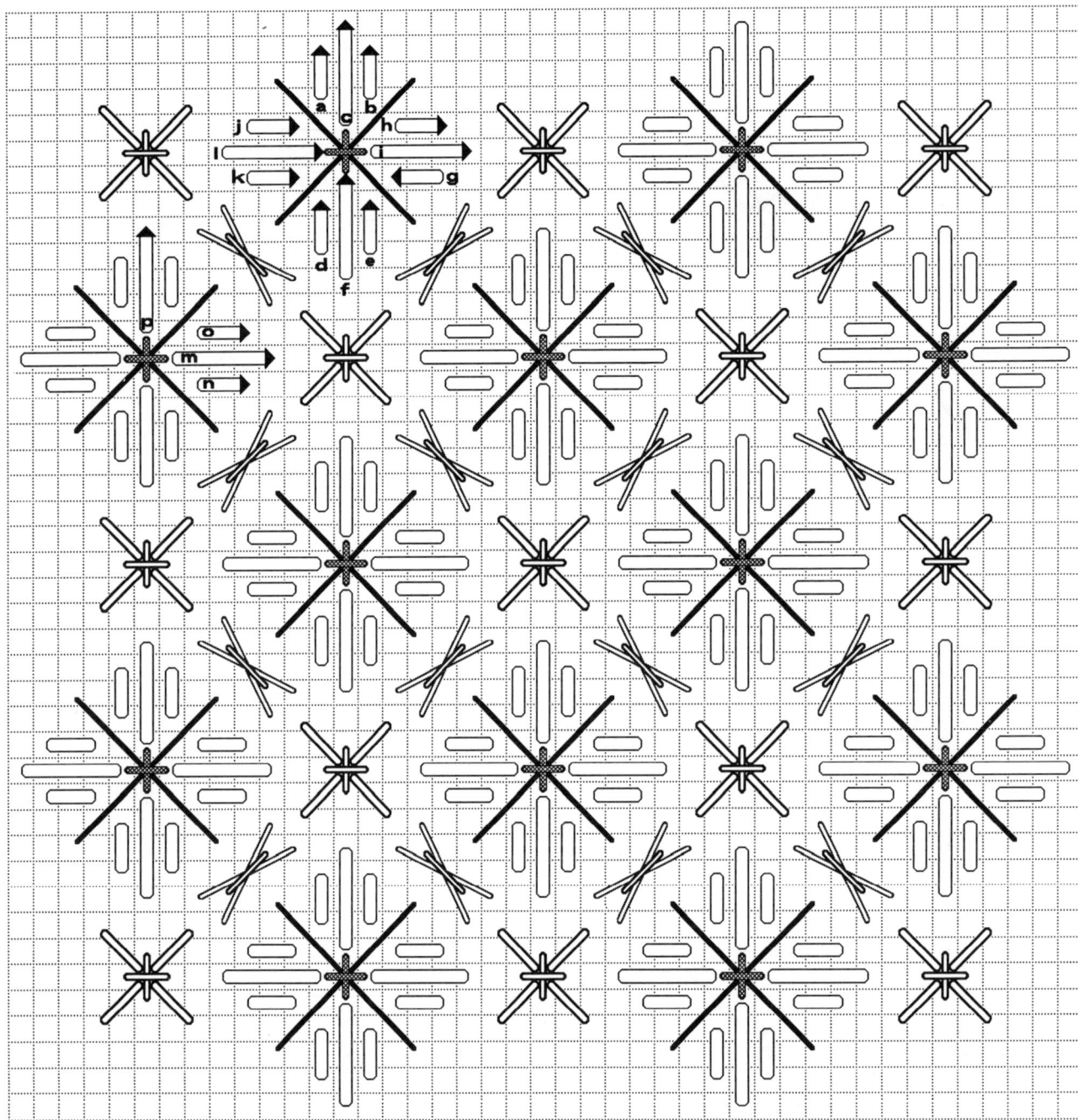

NOTE. The Hungarian sequence is determined by two priorities. First, the best pivot stitch is the long center stitch since it is closest to the center of the Enlarged Double Cross; therefore it is done

78

last in the first cluster. However, the path from l-m is best concealed if m is the first stitch of the next cluster, so the center stitch is done first to start this cluster. Use the side stitches of the Hungarian units to change the stitch direction, as needed, throughout the sequence. Keep the stitches snugly wrapped, and anticipate the next cluster when choosing the order of doing the units in each cluster. All traveling should be done diagonally.

Variation 3. Open Network of Alternating Units of Double Crosses and Tied Diagonal Oblong Cross Units Combined with Enlarged Double Crosses, Upright Cross Clusters and Brick Stitch Chevrons. This is a dense pattern that is dramatic. Like Variation 2 it is a network of Variation 1 with two additional accents.

VARIATION 3 - OVERALL PATTERN

Once the Variation 1 network is completed, add the Upright Cross clusters in diagonal paths. Then add the Brick stitch chevrons, using the sequence of diagonal paths shown in the lower right corner of the overall chart on the previous page. Since each chevron has 5 stitches, the chart numbers only the first stitch of each group and the direction of that stitch. Work the stitches in sequential order and pivot to add the next group. Notice that I worked the two groups on the right side of the Enlarged Double Cross first. Then a "return trip" is used to add the two groups on the left side. This works better in this pattern than trying to do each four-way cluster in a radiating path.

Variation 4. Open Network of Alternating Units of Double Crosses and Tied Diagonal Oblong Cross Units Combined with Blackwork Stars, Four-way Gobelin Clusters, and Upright Crosses.

VARIATION 4 - OVERALL PATTERN

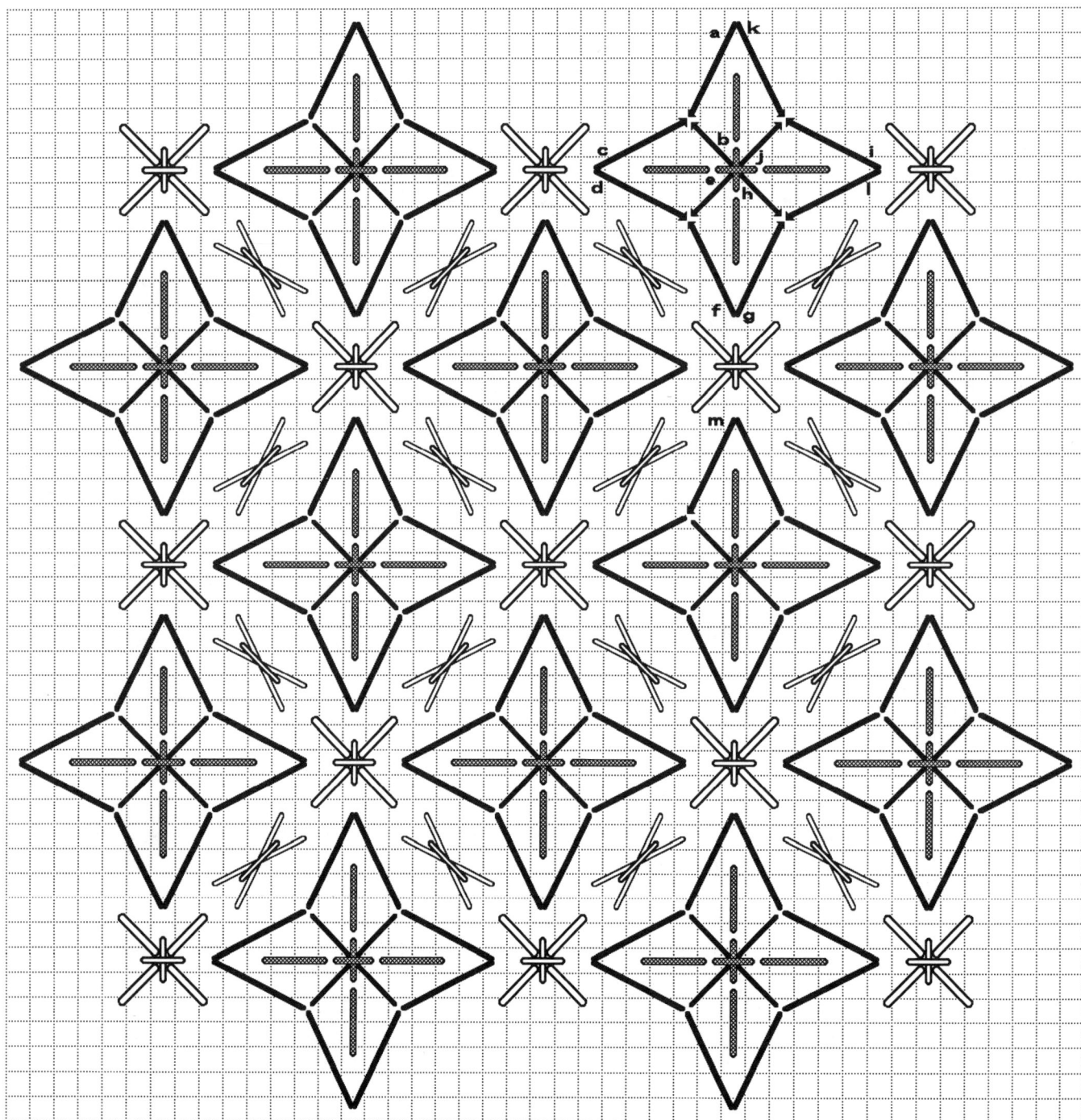

This variation starts with just the original Step 1 network. Then the large diamonds are filled with blackwork stars as Step 2. A sequence for these vertical paths is provided as part of the overall chart on the previous page. The inside diagonal stitches are added as side trips. The left side of each star is executed in a combination of running and back stitches, and the right side is stitched with a double running path.

Steps 3 and 4. After the isolated blackwork motifs are completed, add the inside accent stitches in a combined sequence. Vertical or horizontal paths are recommended, and no sequence should be needed.

4.   Open Network of Partial Pavillion Units and Zigzag Paths of Long Diagonal Stitches. At a first glance this arrangement looks like a Herringbone network, but it is not since the zigzag paths do not cross each other. They meet in shared holes and are overlapped by the sides of the Partial Pavillion units.

An unusual sequence is used to execute this open pattern, and several repeats are shown in the overall chart to the right. One part of the Partial Pavillion unit is done in the downhill row of the sequence, and the other half is added in the uphill row. Since it is not possible to both sink and come up in the same hole, the Pavillion segments are used to divert the thread so it can return to the same hole again.

The long stitch turns the best angle after stitch A so it becomes stitch B. It is important to keep the sinking hole of A open for the return entry.

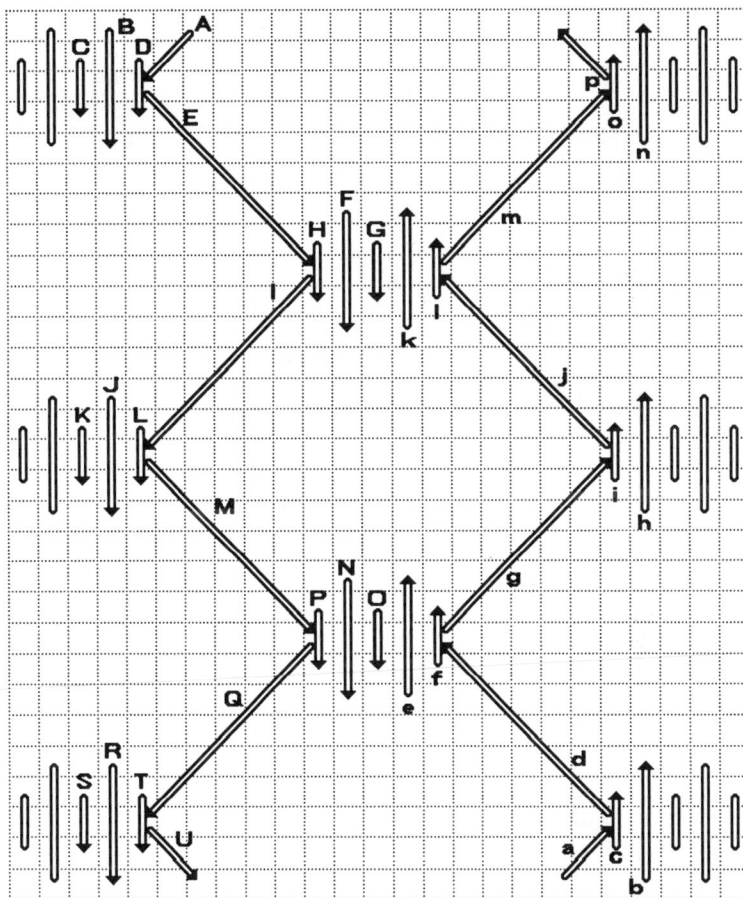

Laying these "side trip" stitches in a downhill direction also keeps the sinking hole of stitch A open. When stitch D is taken, keep it loose. Hold back the thread on top until the needle reenters the hole and then tighten it. On the uphill zigzag rows, there are only two stitches on the side trips, but again the long stitch is executed first.

The diagonal stitches in the pattern straddle 6 intersections so the open areas created are large. This open network is too bold to use by itself, but I developed a number of variations that use this foundation, or a smaller scale version, as a main network. The first of these has a blackwork filling and is shown on the next page. The blackwork pattern is in the design on the cover of my *Heart of Blackwork* book, but it was not included in the patterns covered. Since it is the "parent stitch" of the variations that follow, I have included it here as Variation 1.

81

Variation 1. Open Network of Partial Pavillion Units and Zigzag Paths of Long Diagonal Stitches Combined with a Beaded Brick Stitch and a Blackwork Filling. The blackwork outline in each open area is designed to reinforce the "bow tie" shape. The mirrored chevron shapes leave a small diamond center, and the beaded Brick stitch is actually a functional measure to enable the thread to pivot before it travels to the next repeat. Execute the main network, as shown in the overall pattern below, as Step 1. Then use the blackwork sequence provided below to add the blackwork fillings in vertical paths.

Blackwork Sequence. The lettered sequence shown uses a combination of back stitches and running stitches to execute the outline. The paths are manipulated to make M be the final stitch since it is an ideal exit stitch. I could not plan a sequence that would totally conceal the traveling path, so there is a thread in the open holes at the top and bottom of the area, but the beaded stitch eliminates the visibility of this path inside the diamond outline. Since the other exposure is consistent throughout the pattern, it is acceptable. In my finished design, however, I camouflaged the visible threads with a backing fabric in the same color, so no peekaboos are obvious.

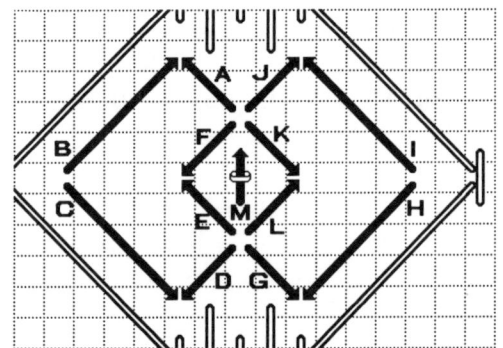

After doing this first pattern, I decided to do several variations on a doodle cloth, using a shorter diagonal stitch. A smaller scale pattern is more useful on canvas, and a number of attractive variations evolved that have diagonal stitches that straddle four intersections instead of six. This doodle cloth appears at the top of Color Plate XIV.

Variation 2. Open Network of Partial Pavillion Units and Zigzag Paths of Long Diagonal Stitches Combined with Upright Cross Clusters, Radiating Tent Clusters and Straight Gobelin Stitches. This pattern is in the middle of the doodle cloth. The strong vertical lines of the Upright Cross units make it appear to be a stripe, but it is not. Execute the "modified" main network shown below as Step 1 for this pattern and the next four variations.

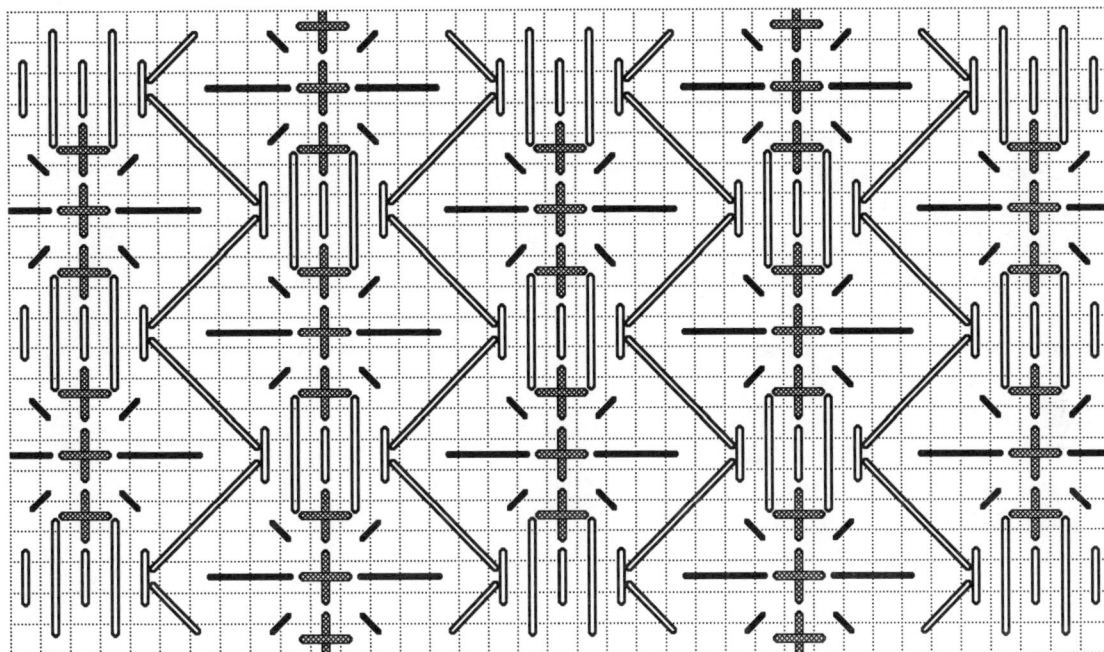

Step 2. Add the Upright Crosses in vertical rows to conceal the traveling threads.

Step 3. Add the radiating stitches in vertical rows as one sequence. Start with the upper right Tent stitch and work these in a counterclockwise path, laying the stitches from the outside towards the middle each time. The final stitch is the one at 3 o'clock, and no traveling threads will show between repeated segments.

The next four variations have the same Partial Pavillion main network as Variation 1, but a different canvas or blackwork filling is used in each "bow tie" repeat. The stitches used are simple familiar ones. Only a few of the sequences require special instructions, so only a single repeat of each filling is featured. Execute the same main network used for Variation 1 as Step 1, and then add the prescribed fillings to each open area, using vertical paths, to complete each pattern. Since the main network has mirrored zigzag paths, the open areas are staggered like the Partial Pavillion units.

Variation 3. Open Network of Partial Pavillion Units and Zigzag Paths of Long Diagonal Stitches Combined with Double Cross and Double Straight Cross Units. The staggered repeats in this pattern make the Double Straight Cross units form rings around the Partial Pavillion units. This is not obvious from the single repeat chart to the right, but look at the finished sample on the left side of the middle row of the doodle cloth. The Double Straight Cross stitches are done in two colors, but the

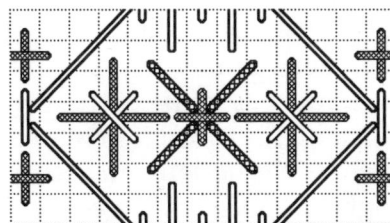

Double Crosses are in one color. Add the Double Crosses first as Step 2 since they are the center stitch. This pattern is dense so there is no need to use the "eyelet method" for these. Work them the usual way in vertical rows.

Add the pairs of Double Straight Crosses as Step 3. Both units of each repeat may be done together, but on my sample I actually executed these units with four vertical rows that combined the right units of one repeat with the left units of the adjacent areas. The traveling paths are shorter with this option, and fewer rows are always more efficient too.

Variation 4. Open Network of Partial Pavillion Units and Zigzag Paths of Long Diagonal Stitches Combined with Double Straight Cross, Upright Cross and Small Cross Stitches. This pattern is located on the right side of the middle row of doodles. I used the same thread for both the top cross of the Double Straight Cross units and the Upright Crosses to give me added flexibility in controlling the traveling threads.

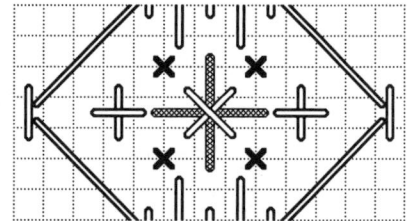

Step 2. Add the foundation crosses of the Double Straight Crosses, using a vertical path.

Step 3. Add the top cross of the Double Straight Cross with the Upright Cross units, again using vertical paths. Lay the underneath stitch of the center cross first, then add the right Upright Cross and travel directly to the left Upright Cross afterwards. End with the top cross of the center stitch. Adjust the direction of all the stitches to keep them snugly wrapped.

Step 4. Add the small crosses in a counterclockwise path. Begin with the upper right unit and end on the lower right stitch. Travel vertically to the next repeat.

Variation 5. Open Network of Partial Pavillion Units and Zigzag Paths of Long Diagonal Stitches Combined with Additional Partial Pavillion Units, Brick Stitches, and Blackwork Accents. This sample is located on the left side of the lower row of doodles. I used a contrasting color for the Partial Pavillion stitches in the middle row to suggest a stripe, and the bold Brick stitches are also eliminated in this row.

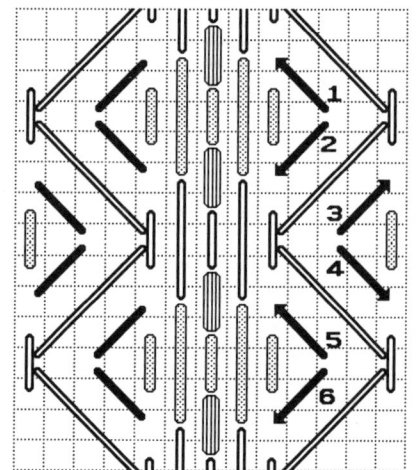

Step 2. Add the center Partial Pavillion stitches first in diagonal rows. Work these left to right each time.

Step 3. Add the Brick stitches in a vertical path.

Step 4. An unusual combination sequence is used for the pairs of blackwork stitches to keep both stitches snugly wrapped.

NOTE. When a combination path is used in continuous blackwork outlines, slight discrepancies in tension are not noticeable because all of the holes have two or more shared stitches. However, one must be totally consistent with two isolated stitches like these since one end of each stitch is by itself in a hole. By zigzagging the sequence, and adding the right stitches of one repeat with the left stitches of the adjacent repeat, I was able to keep both ends of every stitch snugly wrapped and to conceal the traveling paths as well. Even though stitches 2, 4 and 6 are running stitches the fact that they turn 90° makes them look as snugly wrapped as the back stitches. **"Deception" is necessary in needlework at times, and I believe in taking whatever measures are needed to get the most consistent look to my stitches.**

Variation 6. **Open Network of Partial Pavillion Units and Zigzag Paths of Long Diagonal Stitches Combined with Beaded Brick Stitches, Upright Crosses and a Blackwork Filling.** This pattern is located in the middle of the bottom row of doodles. The original pattern has a complete double running blackwork pattern underneath the canvas pattern, so one pattern is actually superimposed on top of the other pattern. I decided to be devious again, however, and show you how to add this blackwork after the Partial Pavillion network is completed.

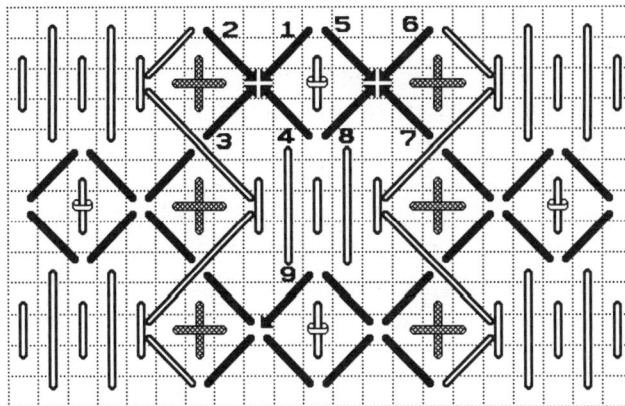

In my sample the blackwork stitches that pass under the long diagonal stitches straddle four intersections, but in the repeat above these stitches have been split into two short stitches that share the same hole under the canvas stitch, so they will look the same.

Step 2. This time the blackwork is done first because the traveling threads of the two canvas additions would interfere with the blackwork sequence if they were already stitched. Use the combination of alternating running stitches and back stitches numbered in the sequence above to execute this filling in vertical rows.

Step 3. Add the Beaded Brick stitches in vertical paths.

Step 4. Add the Upright Cross stitches in vertical rows. Since the right units of one repeat are between the left units of the adjacent stitches in a vertical alignment, it is more efficient to combine these aligned stitches in one vertical path. This strategy will also keep the area around the Beaded Brick stitches uncluttered as well.

Variation 7. **Open Network of Partial Pavillion Units and Zigzag Paths of Long Diagonal Stitches with Mock Couching, Tied Oblong Cross Units, Upright Crosses and Brick Stitches.**

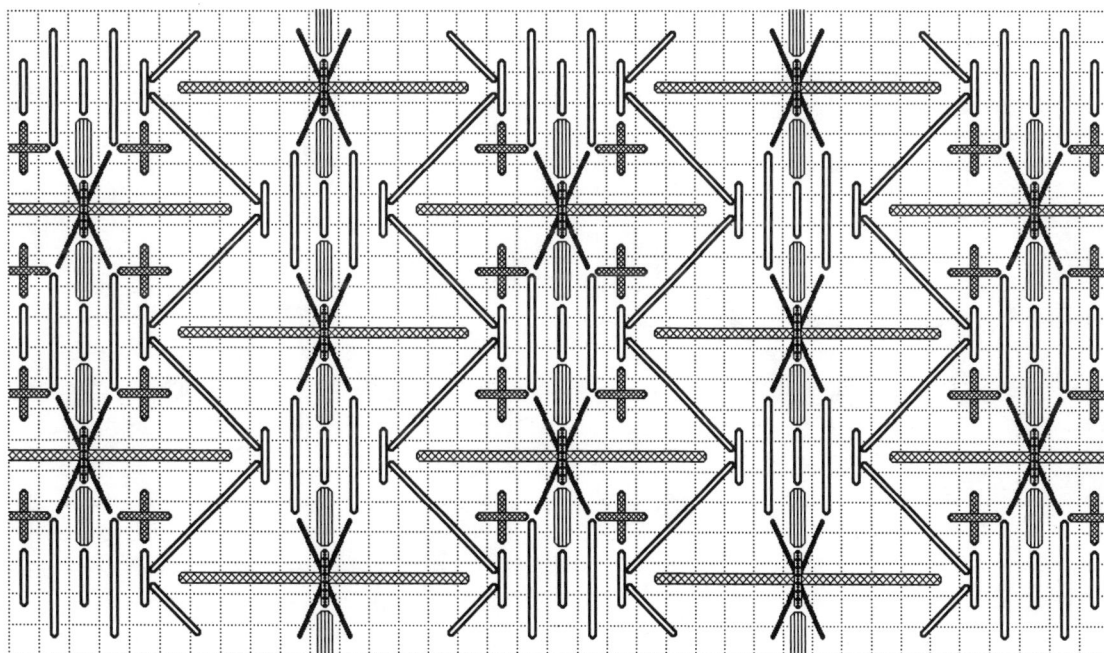

This pattern is located in the lower right corner of the doodle cloth. I am showing the complete width of the pattern in the overall chart on the previous page because I used two different treatments in the staggered rows to form a handsome stripe. This pattern also has "mock couching," so a bigger chart is needed to show this step. The doodle has two additional vertical repeats of the middle and side rows to form a square.

Step 2. Mock Couching. The long horizontal stitches behind the Tied Oblong Cross units appear to be tramé threads, but lay these as running stitch rows throughout the pattern as Step 2.

Step 3. Add the Tied Oblong Crosses in one color, using vertical paths. The tramé thread will conceal the traveling threads enough that there is no need to use the "eyelet method" for these stitches, so proceed with the traditional construction.

Step 4. Add the Upright Cross stitches to the middle and side rows. Stitch each pair of stitches in a left-to-right sequence all the way down each vertical row.

Step 5. Add the Brick stitches in a vertical path.

OPEN NETWORK OF ENLARGED PARTIAL PAVILLION AND LONG DIAGONAL STITCHES

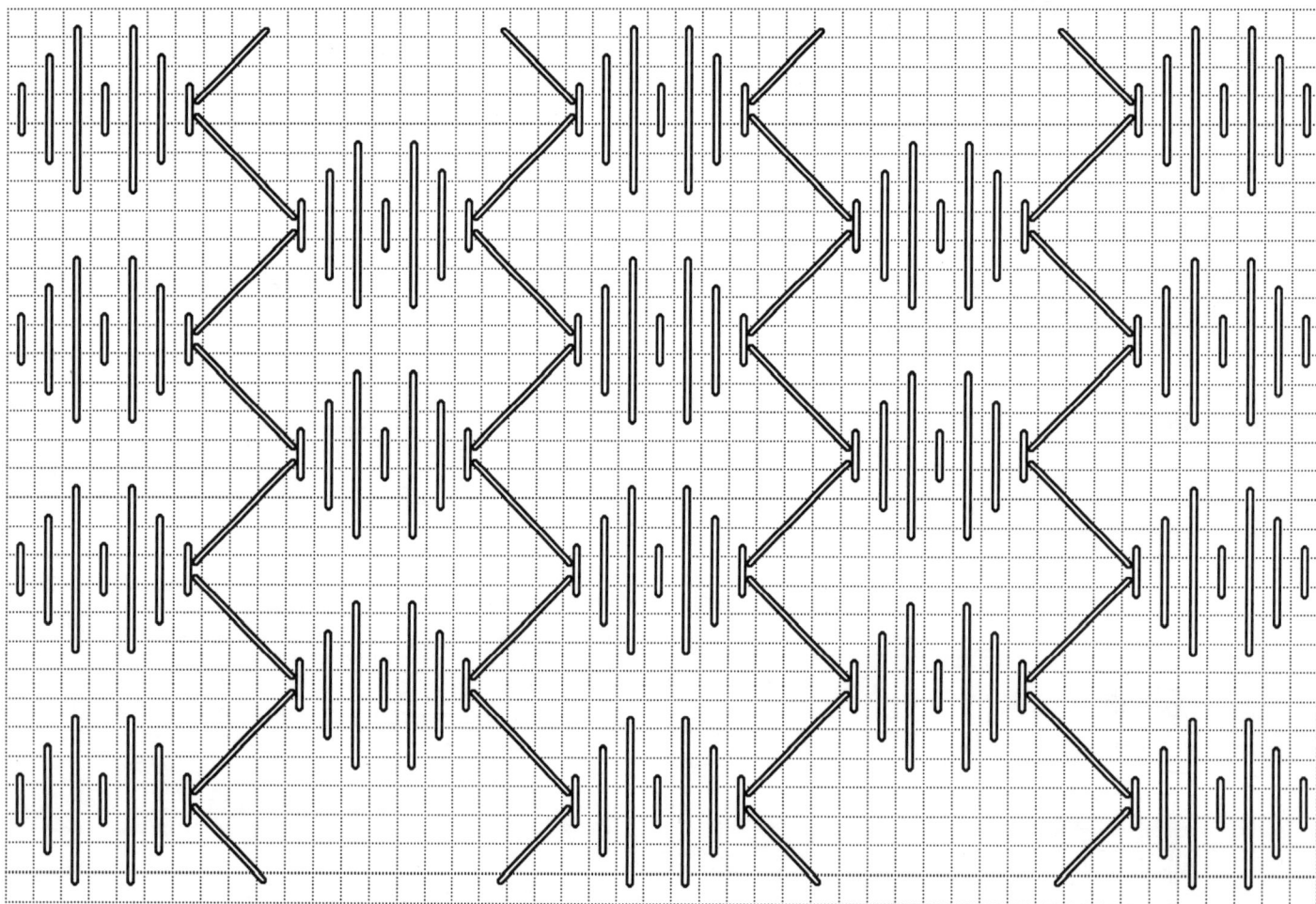

The next three variations all have a main network of Enlarged Partial Pavillion units combined with zigzag rows of Long Diagonal stitches that straddle four intersections. A sequence for the modified pattern is shown to the right. The larger Partial Pavillion stitches will make the main network bolder and the "bow tie" open areas will be wider. These three patterns are at the top of the doodle cloth. All three patterns have additional fillings that alternate in the staggered rows, so they appear as stripes. The two side examples are larger than the middle one, but only three rows will be shown in the charts that follow.

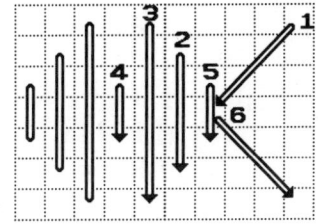

Variation 8. Open Network of Enlarged Partial Pavillion Units and Long Diagonal Stitches Combined with Hungarian Stitches and a Blackwork Filling. This pattern is simple but dramatic, and it is located in the upper right corner of the doodle cloth. The contrast between the sparsely filled open areas and the dense blackwork areas is quite different and something to consider when planning patterns. If you prefer to add additional accents around the Hungarian units, be my guest.

These two fillings are totally independent, so it does not matter which vertical row is done first. I have provided a sequence for the blackwork outline that uses a combination of alternating running and back stitches. The left half of the outline is done first, and then the right half is added. The traveling path from stitch 12 to stitch 13 will not show, and this priority determined my starting and ending points.

Add the Hungarian units in a left to right sequential order. Traveling is easy since there are no open holes between the elements, only exposed threads.

Variation 9. Open Network of Enlarged Partial Pavillion Units and Long Diagonal Stitches Combined with Hungarian Units, Upright Chain Link Stitches, Double Straight Crosses, Upright Crosses, and Radiating Tent and Brick Stitches. This pattern is located in the middle of the top row of doodles. It has a lot of elements, but they build nicely in sequential order.

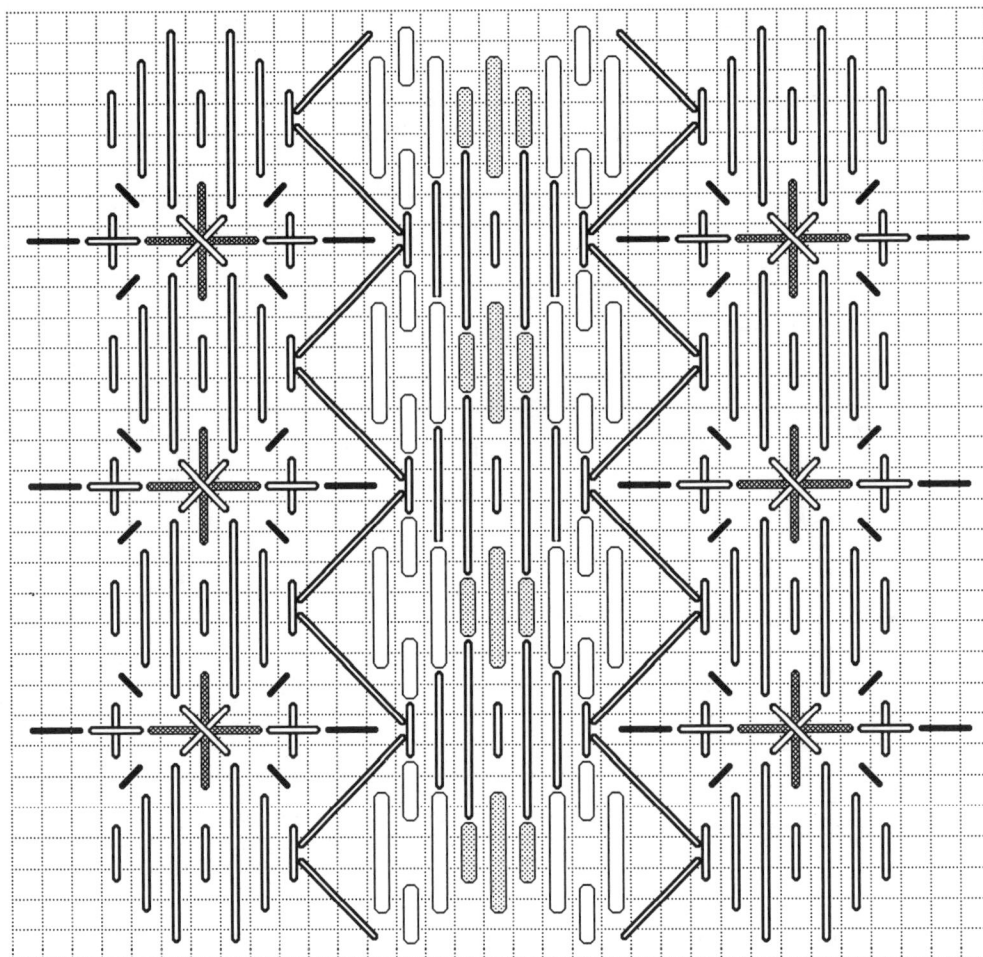

Step 2. Add the Hungarian stitches in the middle rows first since they are in the center.

Step 3. Add the Upright Chain Link stitches on both sides of the Hungarian units. Use two vertical sequences for these pairs. Stitch the units on the left side of the row in one vertical sequence, using back stitches from the top down. Repeat this sequence on the right side to complete the elements in the middle "bow ties."

Step 4. Add the Double Straight Cross units in two colors inside the other "bow tie" shapes. Work these in vertical rows, using the traditional sequence.

Step 5. Add the side units of Upright Cross. Work each pair together this time. Do the left unit first and then add the right unit and travel down to the next left unit. Adjust the top cross, as needed, to keep the stitches snugly wrapped.

Step 6. Add the radiating stitches in a counterclockwise path, starting with the upper right unit each time. Lay each stitch from the outside in.

Variation 10. Open Network of Enlarged Partial Pavillion Units and Long Diagonal Stitches Combined with Double Straight Crosses, Tied Oblong Crosses, Upright Crosses and Brick Stitches. This pattern is located in the upper left corner of the doodle cloth. The same basic fillings are added to all of the "bow tie" shapes. However, in the middle row the Tied Oblong Crosses are one-color units whereas those in the staggered rows are stitched in two colors. The Brick stitches are added to only the side rows for further distinction.

These subtle variations in the details still make a difference, but the stripe is less pronounced since the same colors are used for both treatments. I used the same color for the Brick stitches and the Upright Crosses. The same color is also used for the Brick tiedown stitch of the two-color Oblong Crosses and for the foundation cross of all of the Double Straight Cross units. Other combinations can also be very attractive, so please play and see what happens.

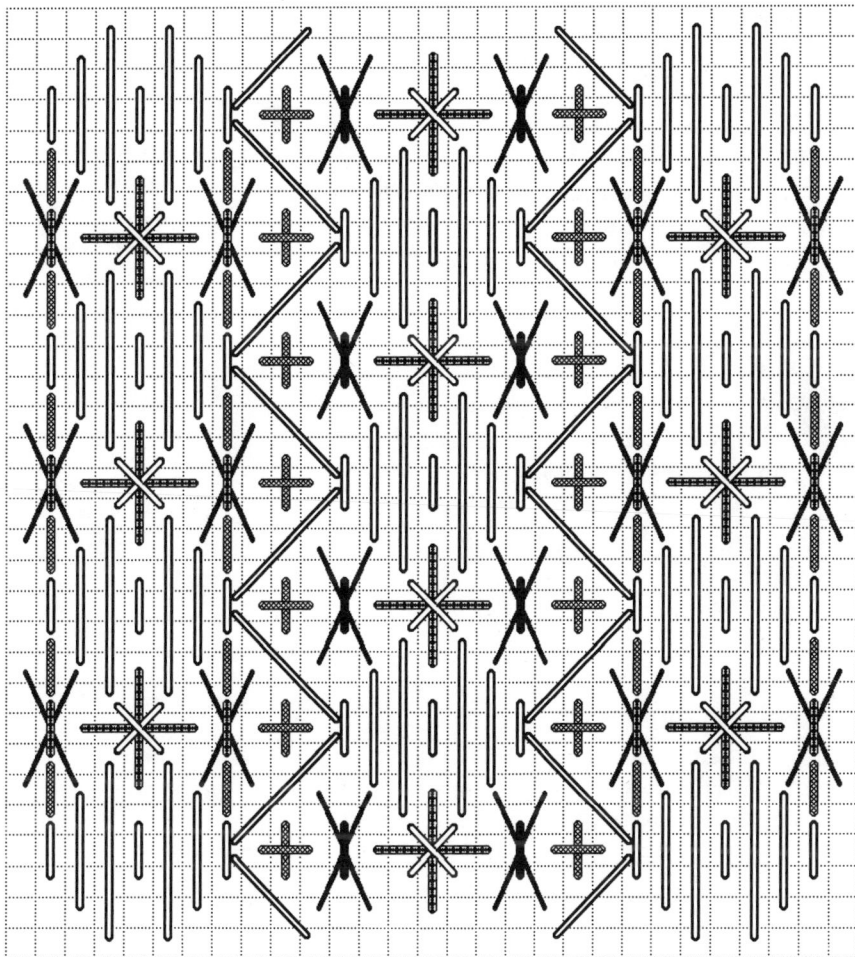

Because of the color distribution as well as the alignment in this arrangement, I recommend that the left and right sides of the fillings be worked in separate vertical paths. Add the two-color Oblong Crosses before the Brick stitches, but all the other paths are independent, so no particular order is needed. These busy color patterns are among my favorites, so I hope you enjoy them as an exciting family of composite treatments. The doodle cloth deliberately shows a wide variety of value ranges in the complementary colors used to interpret these patterns. Contrasts are important to the success of a pattern; as long as different values are used, almost anything goes. Patterns with extreme contrasts or varying intensities sometimes seem to have more than just two colors present, and certainly it is not necessary to limit yourself to two. However, multicolor patterns have greater challenges since there are more variables to manage.

5. Open Network of Flip-flop Double Tent Units Combined with Four-way Brick Stitches. This pattern is quite simple, but its small scale makes it extremely useful in small shapes.

I used this pattern in *Flurry of Butterflies* (Color Plate VII) in the corners of the border as a filling in front of and behind the small butterflies. I used red perle for the diagonal stitches and a gold metallic for the straight stitches, so the patterning is dramatic even though the two areas are small.

Step 1. The Flip-flop Double Tent units are laid first. These stitches can be executed in horizontal paths, but in the narrow tail area I found the diagonal path shown in the sequence chart below more efficient. Either choice will place the traveling path behind the straight stitches eventually.

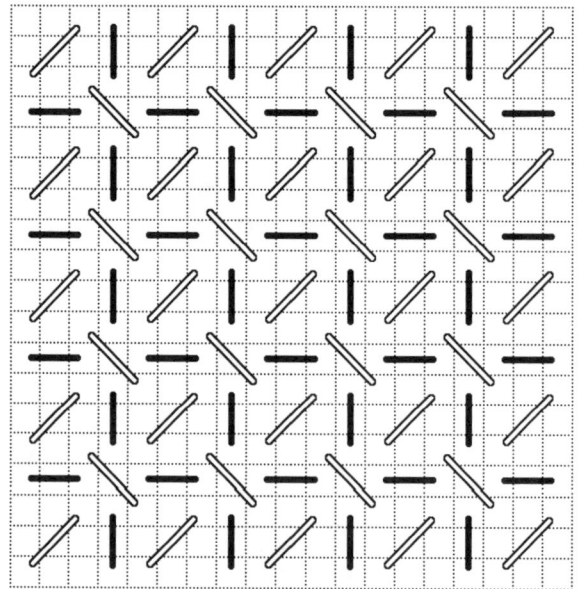

Step 2. The straight stitches can also be added in two different sequences. A running stitch path in both directions will make the stitches look longer since there is no tension on them. If you prefer a snugly wrapped look, work the rows in both directions with a back stitch path. Since I used a metallic, it was more economical to use the running stitch sequence. Having the gold stitches appear longer is also favorable.

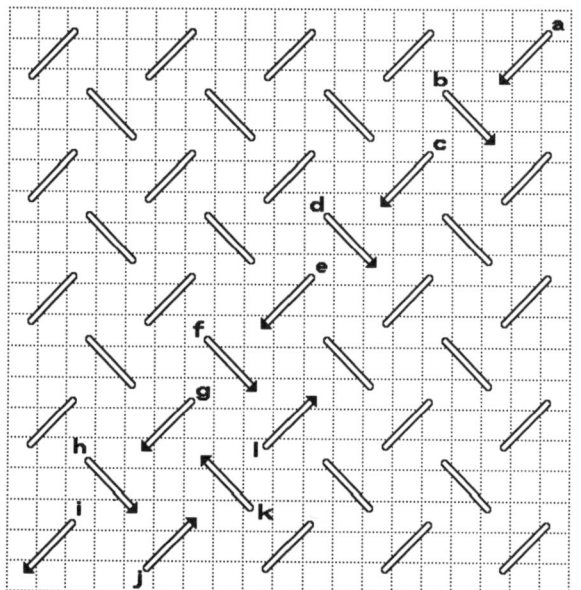

This pattern is a combination of two complete networks, but the diagonal network could be used by itself as a background treatment. It is a small version of Pattern 10 on page 56, and it produces a negative space of smaller diamonds. I have never used the Brick stitch pattern by itself, but if the stitches are laid in zigzag diagonal paths of running stitches, the traveling threads are concealed.

6. Open Network of Alternating Hungarian and Smyrna Cross Units with Accents of Four-way Double Tent Clusters. This combination pattern is a square network. Inside each "window" or square, I added another Smyrna Cross to add density, but these units should be added as a

90

separate step even if the same thread is used. The alternating units of the square "outline" connect nicely in a combination sequence, and a sequence chart is provided below that shows one complete path around a single square.

Step 1. Use the lettered chart below to execute the square lattice of alternating units. Do not work the outlines in small squares. Merely use the "abbreviated" sequence as a guide to change the stitch construction when the row direction changes. You will reach "dead ends," but travel to new starting points by weaving through existing paths. It is also possible to execute the lattice in vertical paths and to add the sideways units of Hungarian that are between these paths as side trips along the way. A Smyrna Cross provides great flexibility in changing directions, and it is possible to pivot in the Hungarian sequence to return to the main path. A similar side trip is discussed in Pattern 2 on page 68 so refer back to this discussion, if needed.

Step 2. Add the inside Smyrna units in diagonal paths. These traveling threads will be concealed by Step 3.

NOTE. If you want to use a different thread weight for the Hungarian and Smyrna units (or different values of the same color), a separate sequence of vertical and horizontal paths must be used for the Hungarian units as Step 1. Then all of the Smyrna Cross units are executed in diagonal rows. If a different color is used for these two elements, the pattern will no longer appear to be an obvious square lattice, but it will have an interesting new dominance.

Step 3. Add the four-way clusters of Double Tent stitches, using horizontal paths of running stitches. If two strands of floss are used for this step, the filling will look like blackwork. The hexagonal shapes formed with the side stitches of the Hungarian units will appear as attractive circles if two values of the same color are used for these elements.

91

CHAPTER 5 – OPEN PATTERNS WITH COUCHING TREATMENTS

The open patterns in this chapter will all have one-way or two-way rows of tramé as the foundation layer of the pattern. A tramé is a long laid thread, not a stitch. Parallel rows are usually laid back and forth as Step 1 of the pattern, and Step 2 is always a stitch overlay that will tie down or secure these long unstable rows. Remaining steps generally embellish the open areas between the laid rows, but some patterns may have more than one tiedown stitch. Patterns with such laidwork or tramé rows are usually called couching patterns, and the tiedown stitches are called couching stitches.

EXAMPLES OF VERTICAL AND HORIZONTAL ARRANGEMENTS

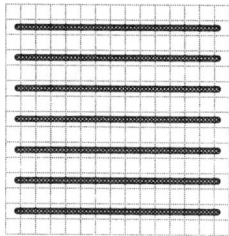

Horizontal One-Way

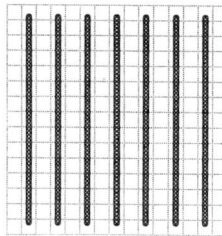

Vertical One-Way

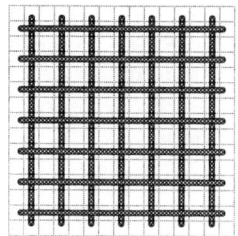

Combined Square Lattice

EXAMPLES OF DIAGONAL ARRANGEMENTS

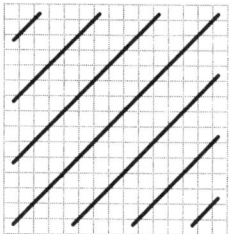

One-Way Tramé - Diagonal Layouts

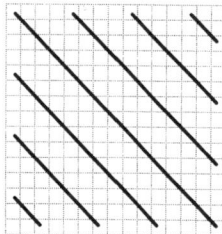

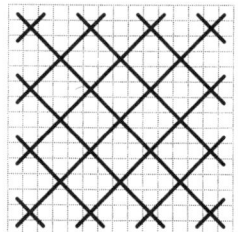

Combined Diamond Lattice

Horizontal and vertical tramé rows are easy to lay. They cover an open channel of the canvas and all of the crossed intersections remain clearly visible. It is easy to read the placement of the stitches that surround or overlap these rows. Diagonal rows, however, can be confusing since the diagonal tramé covers the intersections of that row. In the enlarged diagonal arrangement to the right, notice that there are four exposed threads between the sinking holes of each row in both the horizontal and vertical directions. Diagonally, however, these threads have only two exposed intersections between the <u>holes</u> that are covered by the tramé. The distance between the diagonal rows, as measured between <u>intersections</u>

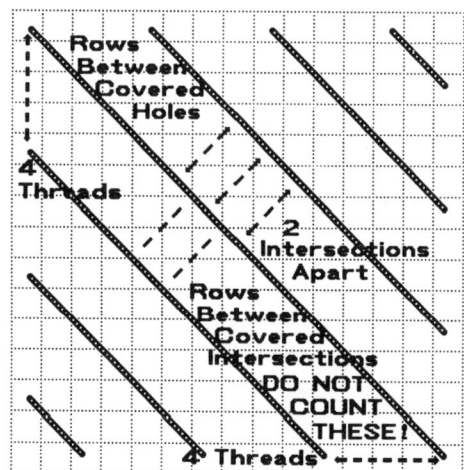

Rows Between Covered Holes

4 Threads

2 Intersections Apart

Rows Between Covered Intersections

DO NOT COUNT THESE!

4 Threads

covered, will always be one less than the number of exposed intersections between the holes that are covered, but I find it better to ignore this relationship and focus on the "hole-to-hole" measurement. This ratio between the hole-to-hole measurement and that of the horizontal and vertical spacing is always consistent **when the thread distance is an even number,** so one can say that arrangements with even spacing will have twice the number of open threads between the sinking holes of parallel rows as there are intersections between the sinking holes of the parallel threads. This ratio does not apply when the spacing is an odd number of threads, however; if one wants only one useful approach, **always count the <u>thread</u> distance between diagonals to assure accuracy every time in transferring stitches from a chart to a canvas or evenly woven fabric.**

When trying to fit a pattern into an irregular shape, it is sometimes necessary to count around the outlines that interrupt the spacing. If the spacing of the tramé rows is four threads apart in an indentation, this distance can also be measured by counting down three threads and over one thread (or down two and over two, or down one and over three) to align the next couching thread. Then move the needle up or down the diagonal to find the correct sinking hole along the edge.

Two-way arrangements (as shown in the "combined" examples on the previous page) are usually tied down at the overlapping intersections since these sections have two layers of thread. These long laid threads tend to make the pattern appear somewhat crooked until the couching stitches are in place. It is also possible to combine a square lattice pattern with a compatible diamond lattice pattern for an "ultra-dimensional" effect. The example on the left below shows the diamond lattice on the previous page superimposed on the square lattice to make a four-way arrangement. This pattern is quite dense and would be difficult to couch, however, so I have provided a second example from my *Heart of Blackwork* book to illustrate a larger scale pattern with double networks of tramé.

EXAMPLES OF FOUR-WAY COUCHING PATTERNS

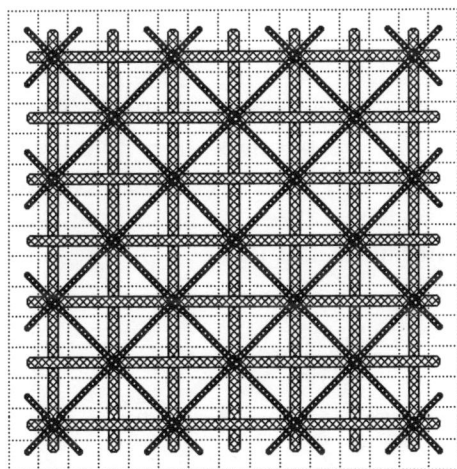

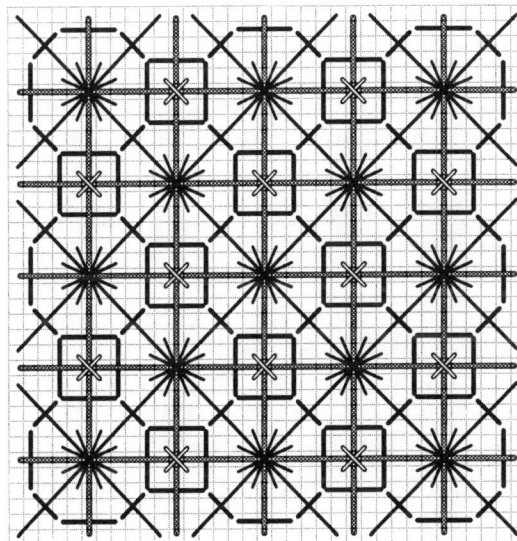

In this case, the blackwork is behind the couching layers, and the dark recessive background makes the raised layers even more prominent. Fine metallic threads are used for the dual layers to both minimize bulk and to not obscure the patterning underneath.

1. Web Variations. The first series of patterns presented are all variations of Web stitch, which is one of the few stitches found in stitch encyclopedias that have a tramé foundation. Three others are Burden stitch, Roumanian Couching and Bokhara Couching. Regular Web stitch has always been a special favorite of mine because it will fit in a tiny area and still create an interesting bumpy texture, especially when done in two colors or contrasting threads. Only Tent and Encroaching Gobelin are small enough to maneuver well in small tapered shapes, but both of these stitches create a relatively smooth flat surface, and they are usually executed in a single color. Therefore Web stitch is the best choice when delicate patterning is desired.

WEB STITCH

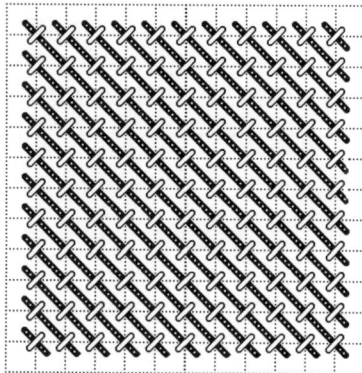

Most couching patterns complete all of the Step 1 tramé rows before adding the Step 2 tiedown stitches. Web stitch is an exception, however, and an alternating sequence must be used instead. Since the tiedown stitches sink behind the tramé rows, it is easier to lay one row of tramé and follow it immediately with a row of couching stitches. The stitches lay smoothly, and once the pattern is completed, it is solid and will appear woven.

WEB ALTERNATING SEQUENCE, USING A SINGLE THREAD

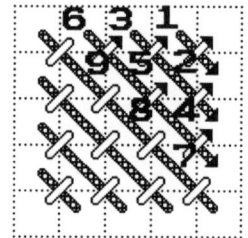

Over the years I have developed a number of Web variations for different uses, and they have become basic staples in my repertory of stitches since they are versatile and adapt well to challenging shapes. Small scale patterns are difficult to develop since the choices of small stitches are limited, but a logical way to vary Web is to spread out the rows of tramé.

The two examples below show Open Web variations with tramé rows that are two threads apart instead of one. A sequence is included in the upper right corner of each chart. Both patterns show separate paths for a two-thread combination, and two needles should be used to execute the alternating steps. The tramé rows are indicated with lettered sequences and the couching rows are indicated with numbered sequences. Keep the idle needle on top of the canvas so that it will not tangle with the working thread as the pattern progresses.

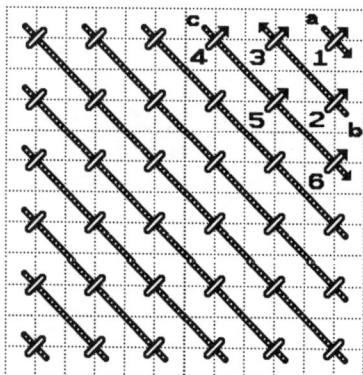

OPEN WEB VARIATIONS

EXAMPLE 1

EXAMPLE 2

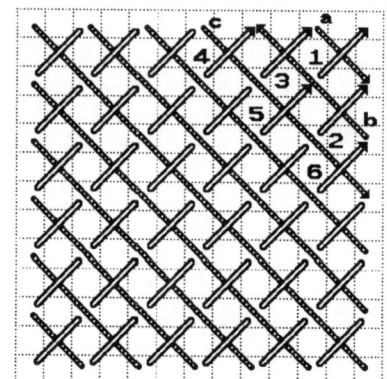

Example 1 uses Tent stitch couching like regular Web, and the placement is staggered or bricked in the same way. The patterning is quite open and delicate. Example 2 uses a longer Double Tent to couch the tramé rows, and its patterning is bold and dense but still slightly open.

Example 1 is used in the *Dresden Heart* design in the narrow right triangles around the diamonds (soft pink area in Color Plate IX). I have also used this pattern in the triangles around the diamonds in the center band of the sampler on the front cover. Contrasts are greater in this example since the couching thread is a darker value, and the canvas behind the pattern is a contrasting green rather than a blending pink.

Example 2 is used in the dark narrow section of the wings of *Oriental Butterfly* (Color Plate X). It is used again in the body of the upper left butterfly in *Flurry of Butterflies* (Color Plate VII). This combination forms a pattern of small diamonds when both layers are done in the same color. The holes of the canvas show between the outlines, but the canvas threads are almost totally covered. This one-color version resembles Alisha Lace, but it is much faster to stitch since all of the diagonal stitches in one direction of each row are accomplished with a single tramé. Each perpendicular couching stitch also covers the same distance as two Tent stitches in Alisha Lace.

ADDITIONAL WEB VARIATIONS

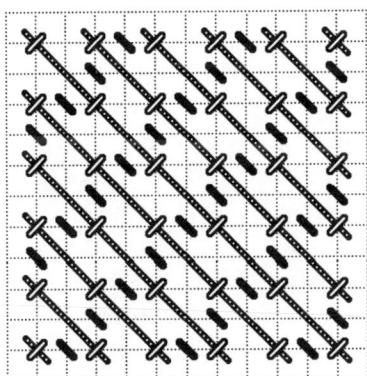
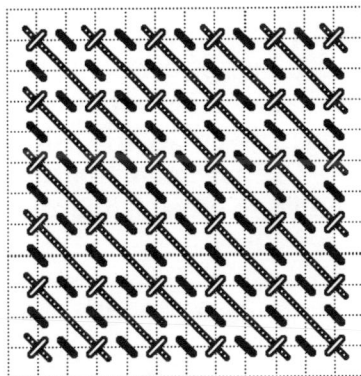
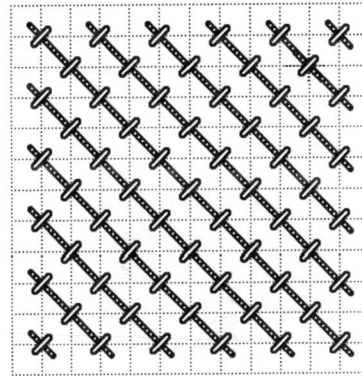

Example 3　　　　　**Example 4**　　　　　**Example 5**

All three of the patterns above have the same spacing for the tramé as Examples 1 and 2 do, and Tent stitches are used to secure the rows. Examples 3 and 4 have bricked rows, but additional Tent stitches are added between the couched rows as Step 3. Example 3 is used in the body of the upper right butterfly in *Flurry of Butterflies (Color Plate VII)*, and the additional Tent stitches between the couched rows form an interesting undulating pattern since they are stitched in the same color as the tiedown stitches. These stitches should be laid in diagonal rows in a lower left to upper right direction. Example 4 is used in the body of the lower butterfly. This pattern is solid and can also be used to copy a biased plaid. I learned it years ago as Alternating Tent, but I do not think it is a "published stitch." I prefer to call it a Web Variation since this describes its structure better. The dark Tent rows between the couched rows are added as Step 3 in diagonal back stitch rows in an upper left to lower right direction.

Example 5 has no added rows of Tent between the tramé, but the spacing of the Tent couching stitches is denser and no longer bricked in alternating rows. This variation is used for the black slippers of the male figure in *Just Plain Folks* (Color Plate IV).

2. Two-way Square Lattice with Cross Stitch Tiedowns. This pattern is so simple, but I am featuring it here because it is one that I have used in different ways to get unique effects.

In *Underwater Ballet* (Color Plate V), it fills the trapezoid area that forms the sides of the border. I used a medium value blue floss for the vertical tramé rows (shown as the numbered sequence in the chart to the right). A slightly lighter value of blue floss is used for the horizontal tramé (shown as a lettered sequence of capital letters). The Cross stitch tiedowns are executed in a fine silver metallic (in the lower case lettered sequence).

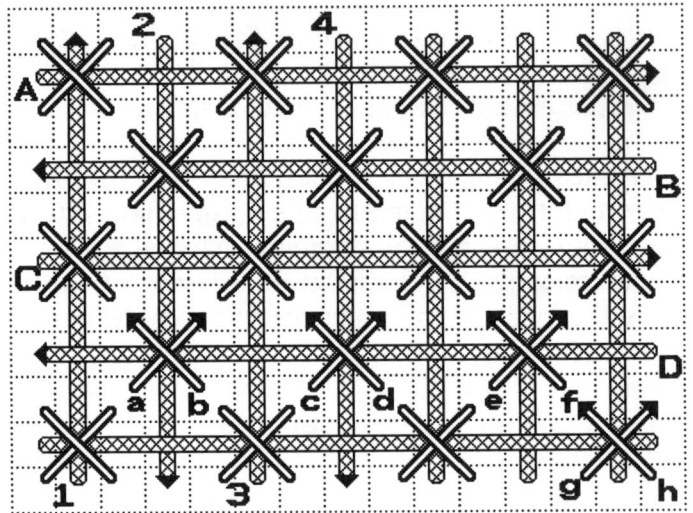

The light reflection from the laid floss and the glistening of the metallic stitches make this pattern a perfect combination to suggest the wet shimmering quality of the water. Since all three threads are similar in value, contrasts are minimal, and the patterning is subtle. It is also dense, but some open perforations are visible where the Cross stitches share holes.

In *Flurry of Butterflies* (Color Plate VII), this pattern is used in the narrow bands that form the circle outline in the border. Two close values of dark blue floss are used for the tramé rows, but the gold crosses form a more obvious diamond network on top of the floss layers since contrasts are greater. The small scale pattern maneuvers well in odd shapes and combines well with the other diamond networks in this piece. In *Hungarian Hootenanny* (Color Plate XII), the pattern is used in the triangles that form the star. Again, the diamond pattern is bold, and it also "punctuates" the triangle shape well.

I have also used this pattern as a shading device, and in spite of its geometric structure, I was able to achieve surprisingly naturalistic effects. In *Strawberry Delight* (Color Plate VIII) the pattern is used to shade the strawberries in three shades of perle cotton. A medium value pink is used for the vertical tramé, and a light pink is used for the horizontal tramé. Then the medium value pink and a dark cranberry shade are used for the crosses in the ripe strawberries (only the light and middle values are used in the less mature berries). At viewing distance, the regular spacing created soft curves even though every cross is a "whole" stitch with no color changes. The indentations in the cross stitch create this illusion, and compensation occurs only along the outside edges.

After succeeding in this treatment, I used the same technique to shade the hibiscus in *Hummer Huddle* (Color Plate VI). Three shades of red perle are combined in the petals, and two shades of red are used for the laidwork throughout the flower. To suggest the deep dark recess of the throat, the top crosses are done in a custom braid that combines red, gold and black metallics. The pattern compensated nicely inside the tight curves of the petals, and the shading is sophisticated even though it is based on a formula. Most shading methods on canvas are somewhat rigid and stylized, and nothing duplicates the lovely soft shading accomplished with long and short technique on fabric. This couching treatment comes close, however, so try it.

In silk and metal embroidery, there is one shading technique called "or nué." Rows of metallic are laid and then couched with different colors and different densities of colored stitches to shade a motif. Uncolored areas are couched in a thread that matches the metallic, and one-way tramé rows are laid one at a time. The effect is beautiful, but the technique is tedious and slow. The four-way technique described above is quick, and one does not have to be an artist with trained skills to get realistic results.

3. Traméd Hungarian Variations. The following series of patterns have a foundation of horizontal tramé couched with Hungarian stitches. By spreading out the placement of the Hungarian units and by adding horizontal rows of tramé behind the units, an attractive layered pattern results. By changing the spacing of the tramé rows, one can get different amounts of exposed canvas; additional accents can be added to these open areas to get beautiful variations.

Example 1. Traméd Hungarian with Accents of Flip-flop Tent. This pattern has tramé rows that are three threads apart. In the remaining open areas, tent stitches are scattered in flip-flop units, and these pairs are mirrored in the alternating rows. This arrangement forms an interesting four-way motif in this pattern, and the other variations that follow will have similar flip-flop treatments.

This pattern can be used to suggest a brocade fabric if the Hungarian units are stitched in floss and the other two steps are executed in the same color or in close shades of the same color. When floss is used for Hungarian units (or any other units that have flat satin stitches of varying lengths), the units will look more uniform if the side stitches are executed before the center stitch.

In a normal horizontal path, stitches are executed in sequential order. Each stitch will lean slightly towards the previous stitch due to the tension on the traveling thread. With some thread weights, there will even be a slight overlap. This tendency should be corrected when floss is used. If the middle stitch is done last, it will spread out evenly over both side stitches and appear uniform and straight. Such a sequence is shown in the chart to the right in lower case letters. If twisted threads like perle cotton are used for the Hungarian units, slight discrepancies will not show so no alterations are needed.

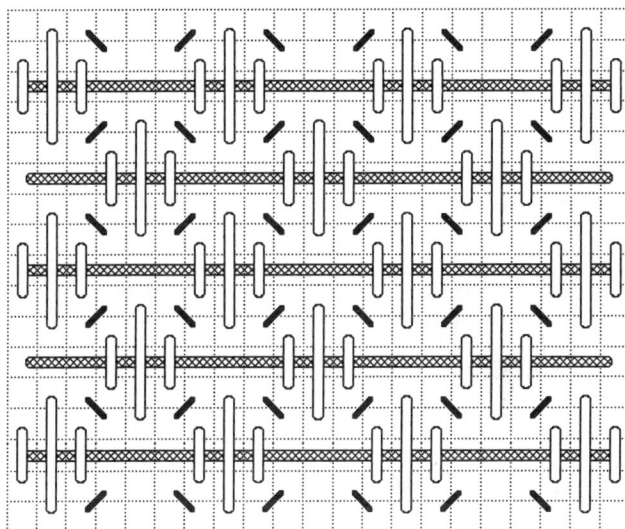

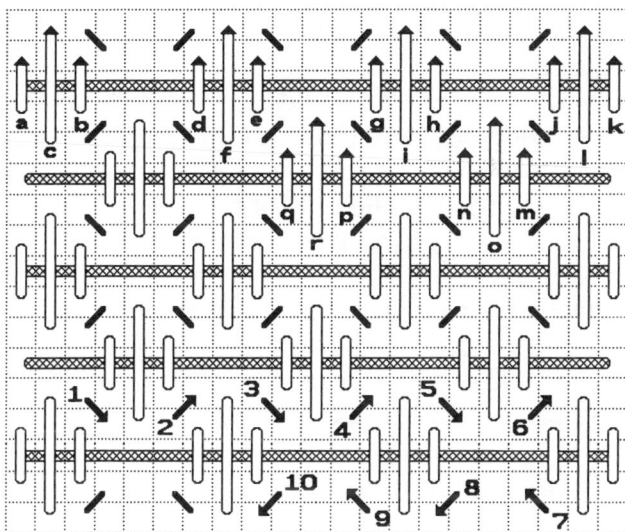

Add the Tent stitches in horizontal paths of running stitches, as shown above in the numbered sequence. The traveling threads will fall behind the middle stitches of the Hungarian units and will be concealed.

NOTE. Stitches 6 and 7 have a back stitch pull on both ends of the stitch. It is convenient to travel this way in this pattern, but be careful not to seat these stitches too firmly or they will look

97

slightly different from the others. Total consistency is the name of the game; any time a rhythm is broken, discrepancies may result that are noticeable. A uniform tension control can offset occasional unavoidable breaks, so evaluate your work and adjust accordingly.

The next two examples use tramé rows that are four threads apart. In Example 2 undulating outlines are added to the open areas, and these outlines mirror in alternating rows. The visual effect created is a wave of soft curves around the couched rows. The coverage is dense but not 100%. A rhythm of alternating running stitches and back stitches is used to outline these waves. A numbered sequence is provided for one direction, and a lettered sequence is provided for the reverse row.

EXAMPLE 2

EXAMPLE 3

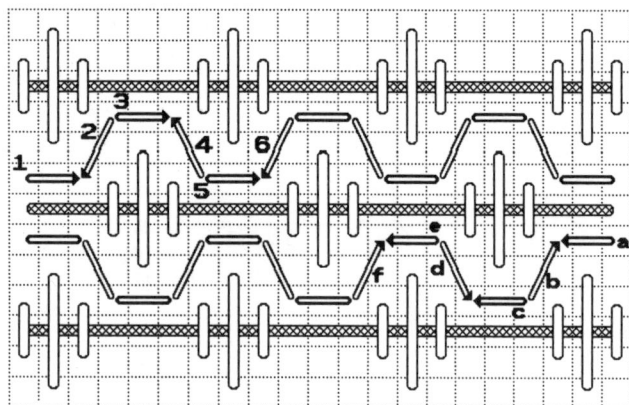

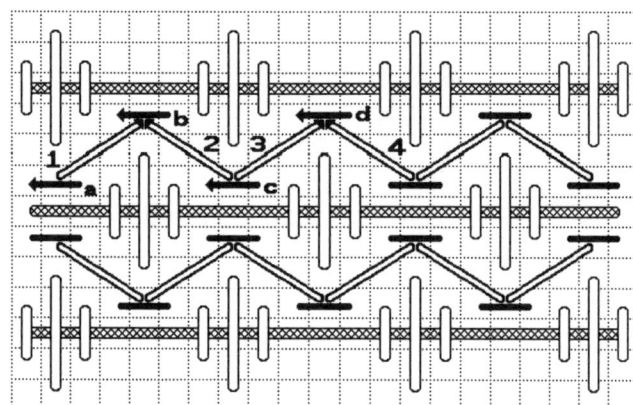

Example 3 has an accent filling of horizontal rows of zigzag slanted stitches. Horizontal Brick stitches cover the ends of these stitches, and the effect resembles smocking when done in two colors, so keep this in mind. A similar alternating sequence of running and back stitches is used to execute the slanted stitches (see the numbered path above). Add the Brick stitches in back stitch paths, as shown in the lettered sequence.

These two patterns do not compensate well as allover fillings in an irregular shape because of the slanted stitches. They can be used in controlled geometric shapes, however, and look at the attractive border stripe to the right that is a combination of the wave rows of Example 2 with a single repeat of Example 3.

Compatible networks can always be combined in an interesting way, and this possibility makes the potential for variations that much greater. Patterns with one-way tramé rows also tend to produce stripe patterns unless the couching treatments interrupt the linear thrust. Conversely, arrangements with two-way tramé networks will usually form allover patterns.

BORDER VARIATION

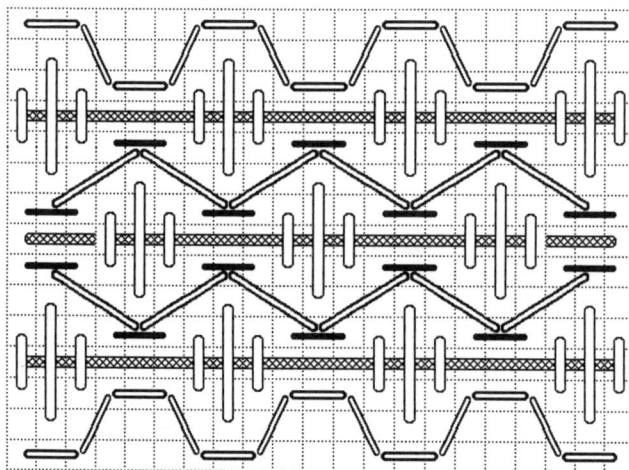

The next pair of variations have tramé rows that are spaced five threads apart. Larger open areas allow bigger stitches to be used in the open areas. Since the arrangement of the Hungarian units is staggered, I again used flip-flop or mirrored placements for the inner fillings. Only one repeat of both examples is featured, but both patterns can be expanded by adding additional repeats to the existing networks.

EXAMPLE 4   **EXAMPLE 5**

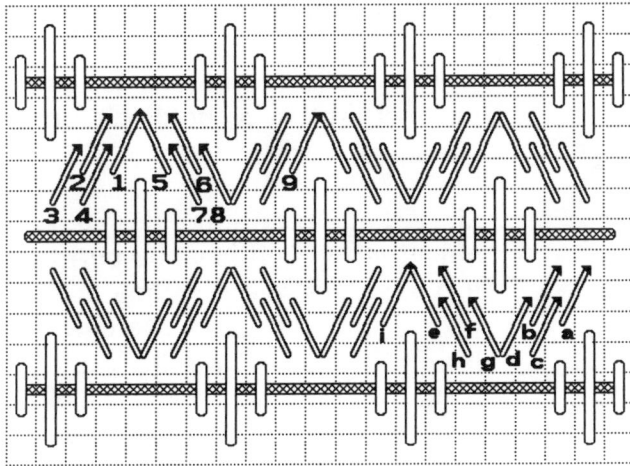 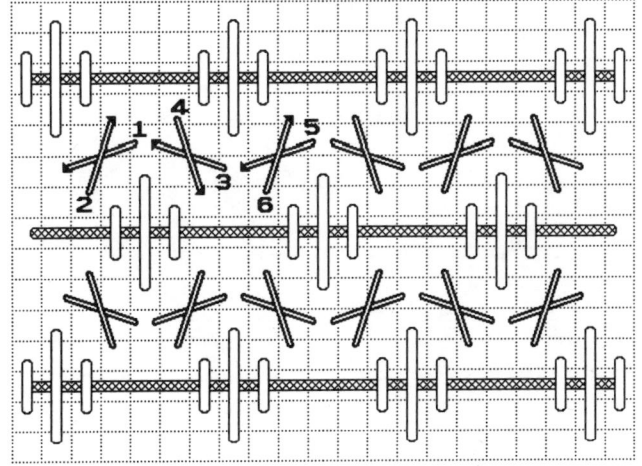

Example 4 has accent clusters of Encroaching Gobelin. Execute the flip-flop groups in horizontal rows with the numbered sequence provided. Keep the pattern upright, and use the lettered sequence for the rows in the opposite direction. This pattern is quite dense and creates the illusion of ovals around the Hungarian units. The "corded" look of the encroaching stitches is also quite unique, especially in contrast to the satiny look of the Hungarian units if they are done in laid floss. Varied textures within a single pattern can further enhance or change its visual impact.

Example 5 has accents of Diagonal Oblong Crosses in the open areas. Again, these are arranged in flip-flop units, and the "more vertical stitch" should be on top in all the units, so proceed cautiously and use the numbered sequence carefully. To execute the rows in the other direction, rotate either the chart or the canvas 180° and use the same sequence.

NOTE. All of the fillings in this pattern form soft curves. Oblique and diagonal stitches are more apt to create the illusion of curves when they are used on a grid, but this tendency is seldom obvious from a printed chart.

To alter the spacing of the tramé is also an excellent way to vary a couching pattern. The basic network still looks the same, but changes in the open areas create new opportunities for different accent fillings.

4. Diamond Lattice with Upright Cross Tiedowns and Four-way Mosaic Units. The next pattern illustrates an alternative way to lay tramé that is ideal for particular situations. This pattern is used in some of the background areas of *Santa Sampler* (Color Plate III). The figures are outlined in red back stitches, and the open red pattern in the center and corner sections are added to mimic the effect in Assisi embroidery, where similar outlines are surrounded by a solid mass of Cross stitches. I designed this pattern to fit the repeats in the border, so the spacing of the Upright Cross tiedowns and the Mosaic units is determined by this count.

99

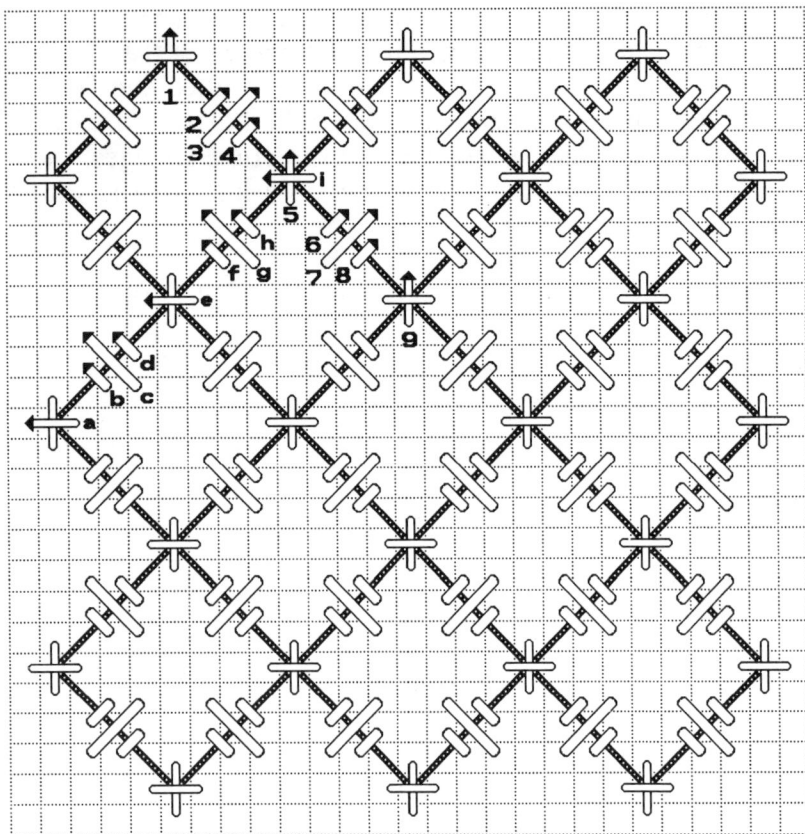

Without the diamond lattice foundation the stitches arranged here would be too far apart to use as an open filling. The laidwork creates the necessary density to connect the units and make the combination work.

NOTE. The negative space in the pattern is a bold Greek cross.

Since the border of the design is open and worked in white perle, it is wise to avoid traveling in it with a red thread. Therefore laying the tramé rows back and forth the usual way is not desirable. The solution chosen was to do what I have since labeled "mock" darning. Partial segments of the tramé are stitched in zigzag paths of alternating running and back stitches, as shown below.

MOCK DARNING SEQUENCE

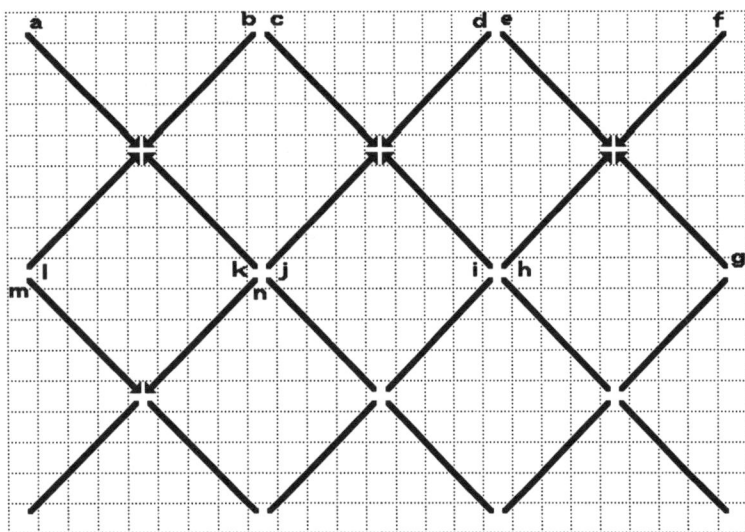

No traveling is needed along the edges since one can change direction at any juncture with this sequence. The likelihood of making errors laying shorter diagonal threads is not only less, but handling compensation around the figure is also easier since side trips can be used.

Another advantage of this method is that any excess bulk from "crossed" tramé threads is eliminated. The Upright Crosses will cover "sinking holes" rather than layers of thread, and the flatter surface is less apt to distort the couching stitches. These stitches also camouflage the method used so "purists" will not realize that the tramé is stitched not laid!

After the mock tramé is completed, the Upright Crosses and Mosaic units can be added in either separate or combined sequences as a one-color pattern. The overall pattern above shows a combined sequence where all the rows from upper left to lower right (the numbered sequence)

100

are executed before the perpendicular rows are added in the lower case lettered sequence. A more random maze path also works well for this step, and I recommend completing the Upright Crosses as you go if this is done because it is easy to omit one and not notice the "sin of omission" until the design is mounted! As long as you remember to keep the horizontal stitches on top and to adjust the direction the stitches are laid when the row direction changes, most lattice patterns can be executed with a less structured sequence. The solid lines of the tramé conceal the paths and give you more freedom to improvise.

5. Diamond Lattice with Upright Cross Tiedowns and Four-way Partial Scotch Units. This pattern is placed here because it is an enlarged version of the previous pattern. The structure is similar, so apply the same sequence instructions. The length of the "mock couching" stitches is now five threads rather than four to allow the larger Partial Scotch units to fit comfortably in the same four-way arrangement as the Mosaic units.

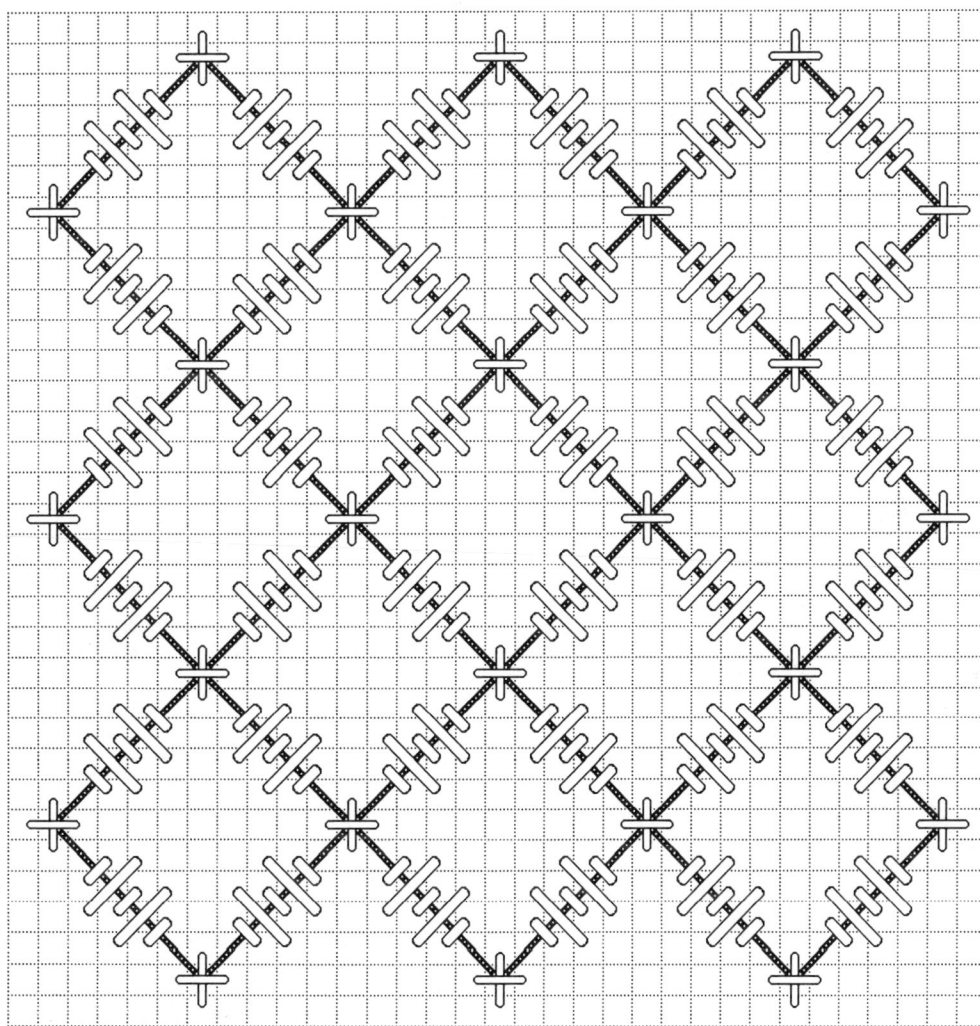

In one color, both patterns make attractive backgrounds, but two-color treatments can be used as interesting fillings. A lighter weight thread can also be attractive in patterns with couched foundations (#8 perle on 18-mesh canvas or #12 perle on 24-mesh). If regular weights are used, it looks nicer to change the Upright Crosses to simple Brick stitches.

6. Caning Pattern. The pattern to the right developed from my attempt to mimic caning on canvas. Vertical rows of tramé are laid first in pairs that are two threads apart. These pairs are arranged four threads apart (see the Step 1 layout below). Then three rows of weaving or darning are added to form a pattern; instead of just passing over and under the tramé threads as in regular caning, these stitches pass through the canvas as well.

The tramé rows are actually secured by the horizontal paths of darning, which are added as Step 2 (see the chart on the next page). The stitches straddle five threads, and notice that the stitch placement shifts in the pairs of horizontal rows. One end of every stitch is also in an open hole whereas the other end is behind a tramé thread.

For this reason, it is important to work the lower row of the darning path from right to left and the top row from left to right. The needle will then come up in an exposed hole and can be slanted to sink comfortably into the covered hole.

Steps 3 and 4 will add the diagonal rows of darning, and these are more attractive on canvas if they are done in a contrasting color or shade. The stitches of these rows both come up and sink behind the horizontal stitches or the tramé, so proceed carefully until you are familiar with the placement.

One helpful clue is that the diagonal rows that lay from lower left to upper right will straddle the vertical pairs of tramé, whereas the diagonal rows that lay in the opposing direction will straddle the pairs of horizontal darning.

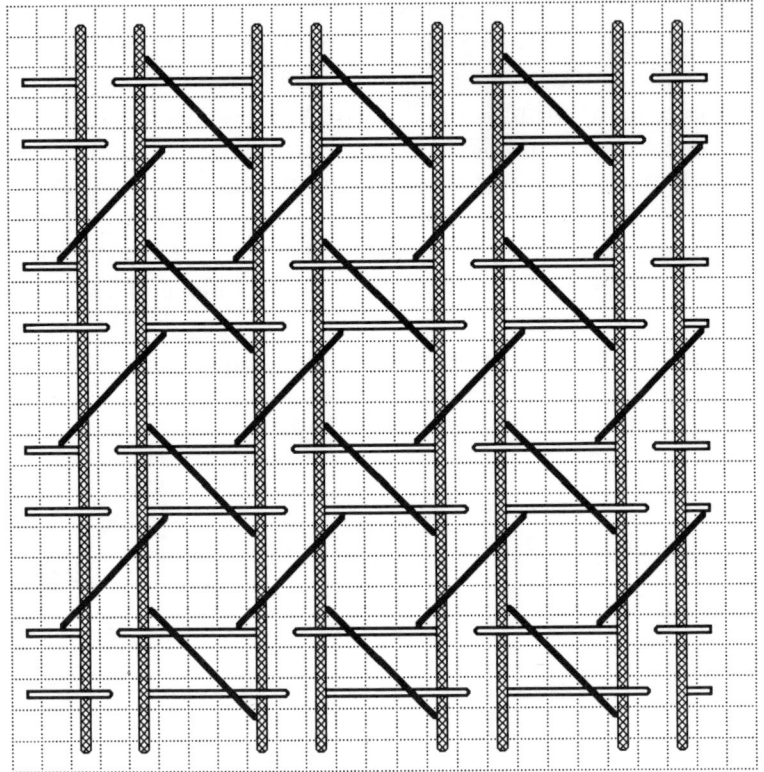

STEP 1 TRAME ROWS

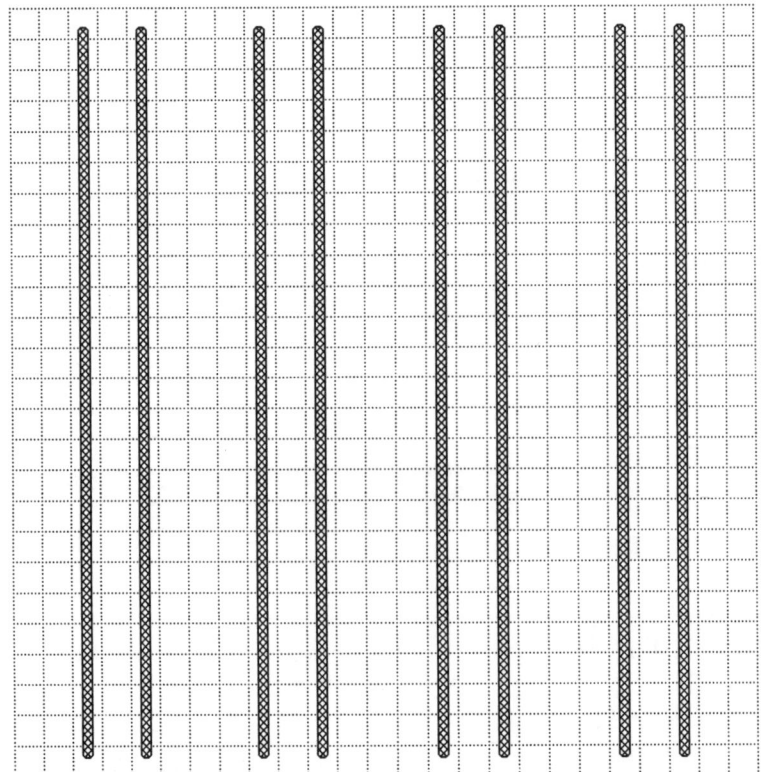

102

Do all of the Step 3 rows of diagonal darning, as shown in the sequence chart below. Then add the Step 4 rows, using the overall chart on the previous page to place these.

This pattern is used in *Hummer Huddle* (Color Plate VI) in the trapezoid shape along the border sides. The first two steps are done in #8 white perle on the ecru ground, and Steps 3-4 are done in a star green Balger metallic. The pastel treatment is effective here, but I have also used the filling in another geometric design combining two values of one color in a high contrast arrangement. A dark shade is used for the top layer, so the "circle" motifs dominate the pattern.

Use the same thread weight for every step to keep the proportions balanced. Since caning is done with a continuous thread, there are no variations or contrasts in the traditional craft. Since the ground is present on fabric or canvas, however, contrasting layers are more attractive whether they are subtle or dramatic.

In *Hummer Huddle* (Color Plate VI), I also needed a background pattern behind the birds. It occurred to me that just the diagonal rows of darning might make an appropriate treatment. My instincts proved right, and this pattern is on page 52 since it uses only diagonal stitches. The point I want to make is that parts of an intricate pattern can be attractive by themselves. Using two or more variations of a pattern in a single design will usually create a nice balance, so I often use related patterns together. The scale and feeling of such patterns will be similar but not identical; therefore this is an effective but subtle way to unify a design.

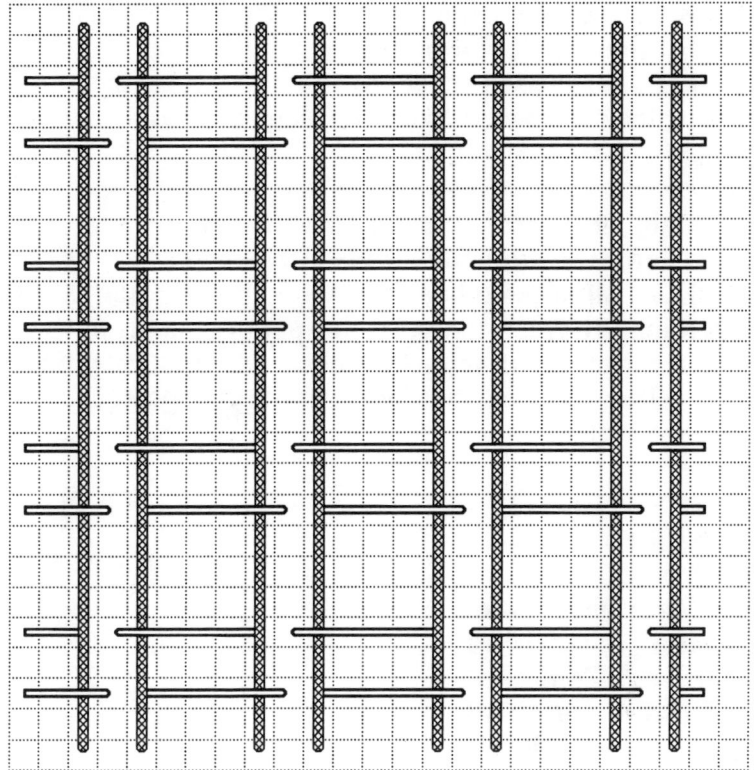

STEP 2 DARNING ROWS - HORIZONTAL

STEP 3 DARNING ROWS - DIAGONAL

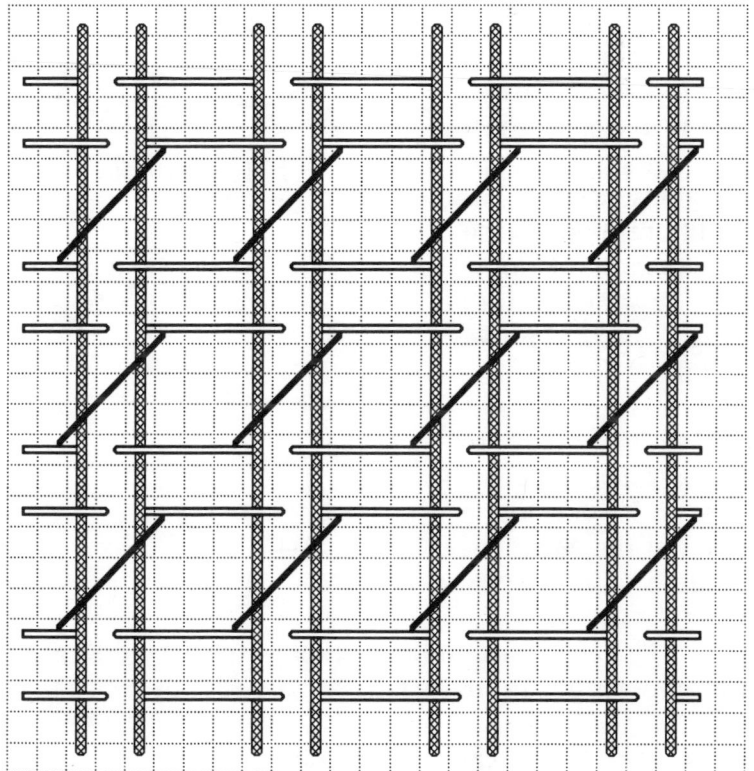

7. Open Network with Tramé Rows Couched with Mirrored Milanese Units. Milanese is one of my favorite stitches to use in composite patterns since its triangular shape is unique. It is a bold stitch, and in the pattern to the right I have used mirrored units to couch the tramé rows, which are spaced four intersections or eight threads apart.

This main network is combined with several additional steps to form a dramatic stripe in *Dresden Heart* (Color Plate IX). All of the other fillings are allover patterns with predominantly green tones, so this pattern stands out with its concentration of intense pinks and its strong linear thrust. The same balance of contrasts is repeated in the border as well.

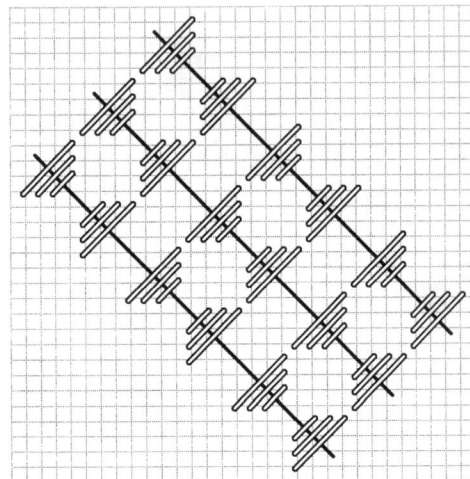

VARIATION 1 - OVERALL PATTERN

Variation 1. Composite Pattern with Main Network of Traméd Mirrored Milanese Combined with Rows of Tied Blackwork and Mosaic Stitches and Perpendicular Rows of Darning. The chart to the right shows the complete overall pattern just described in *Dresden Heart* (Color Plate IX). On the following page, there is a second chart that shows only Steps 1-4. This pattern has six different steps, so the isolation of some of the secondary fillings will prove helpful.

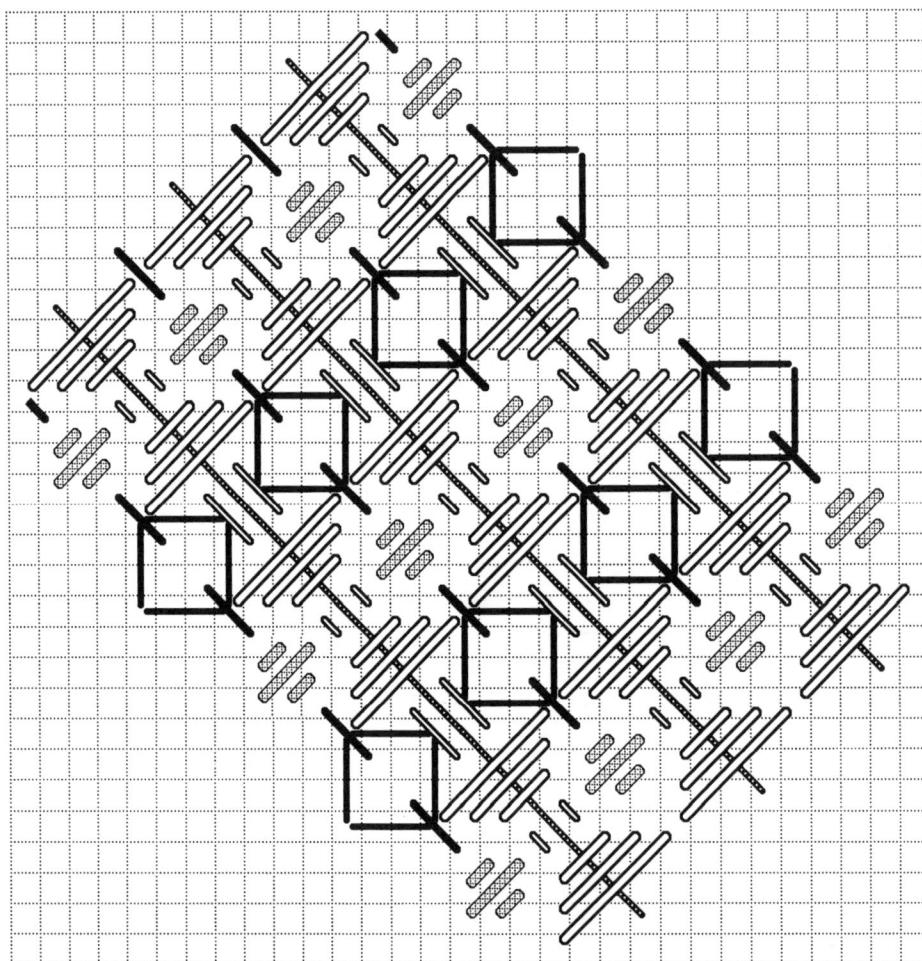

Steps 1-2. Use the Main Network chart above to lay the tramé rows and the Mirrored Milanese units.

Step 3. Use the chart on the next page to add the Mosaic stitches. Work these in diagonal paths from upper right to lower left.

Step 4. Add the blackwork sequence which is also shown isolated in the chart on the next page. A lettered sequence is provided for this step. A combination of alternating running and back stitches is used in the main path (stitches 1-2), but a side trip in a double running path (stitches 3-4) enables the needle to complete the square and to return to the bottom of the shape in order to travel efficiently to the next unit.

Step 5. Add the Double Tent stitches that overlap the upper left and lower right corners of the blackwork squares. Use the matching thread, and work them in diagonal rows of darning stitches.

Step 6. Using a contrasting thread, add the remaining rows of darning that parallel the tramé rows. These include the Double Tent stitches that overlap the other corners of the blackwork and the Tent stitches between the Mirrored Milanese units.

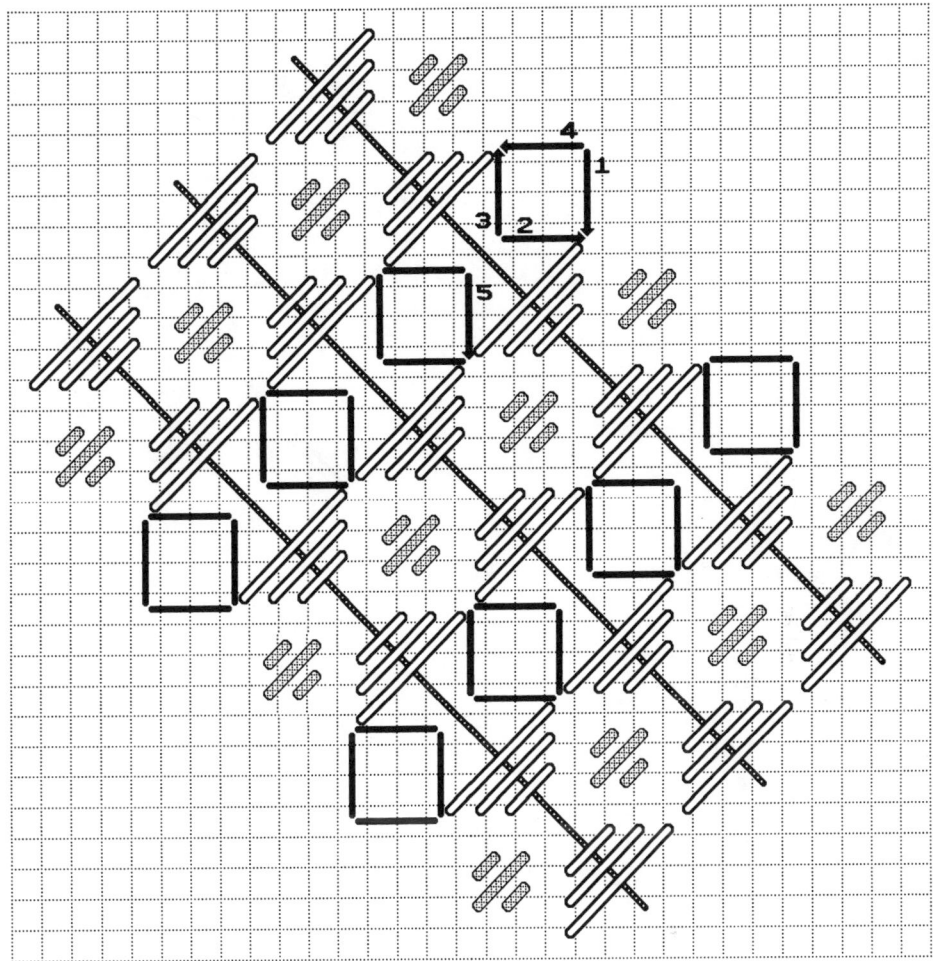

NOTE. The reverse rows of darning actually dilute the diagonal thrust suggested by Steps 3-4. However, the boldness of the Milanese units tend to dominate, so the finished appearance of the pattern suggests a stripe even though the pattern is technically an allover arrangement. The weaker lines of the reverse rows get wiped out by the alignment of the stronger Milanese rows. The blackwork appears to dominate on the black and white chart, but in reality, the Milanese units are denser and overpower the darker lines. This is why patterns have to be stitched to be fully assessed, and I am constantly surprised by what happens with the actual color and thread interpretations.

Variation 2. Main Network of Traméd Mirrored Milanese Units with Accents of Blackwork and Alternating Units of Double Tent and Smyrna Cross. This time I used Watercolours for the Milanese units and a bold metallic ribbon for the tramé so the Milanese stitches no longer dominate as a strong stripe. The added elements are both stripes, however, and their strength becomes the focal point if they are done in a medium or dark value. Steps 1-2 are the same as that of the parent pattern, so only the remaining steps are included in the sequence instructions.

The overall chart for this pattern follows on the next page, and no charts for partial segments are needed.

Step 3. Add the alternating sequence of Double Tent and Smyrna Cross units in diagonal rows, using traditional sequences for these stitches.

Step 4. Add the blackwork rows, as lettered in the chart to the right. Again a combination sequence is used. The main path is executed with alternating running stitches and back stitches, but the side trips (stitches g-i) are added with a double running stitch path. I find this method more efficient for single rows or isolated units of individual blackwork motifs. The double running stitch (reversible method) is superior for only overall patterns.

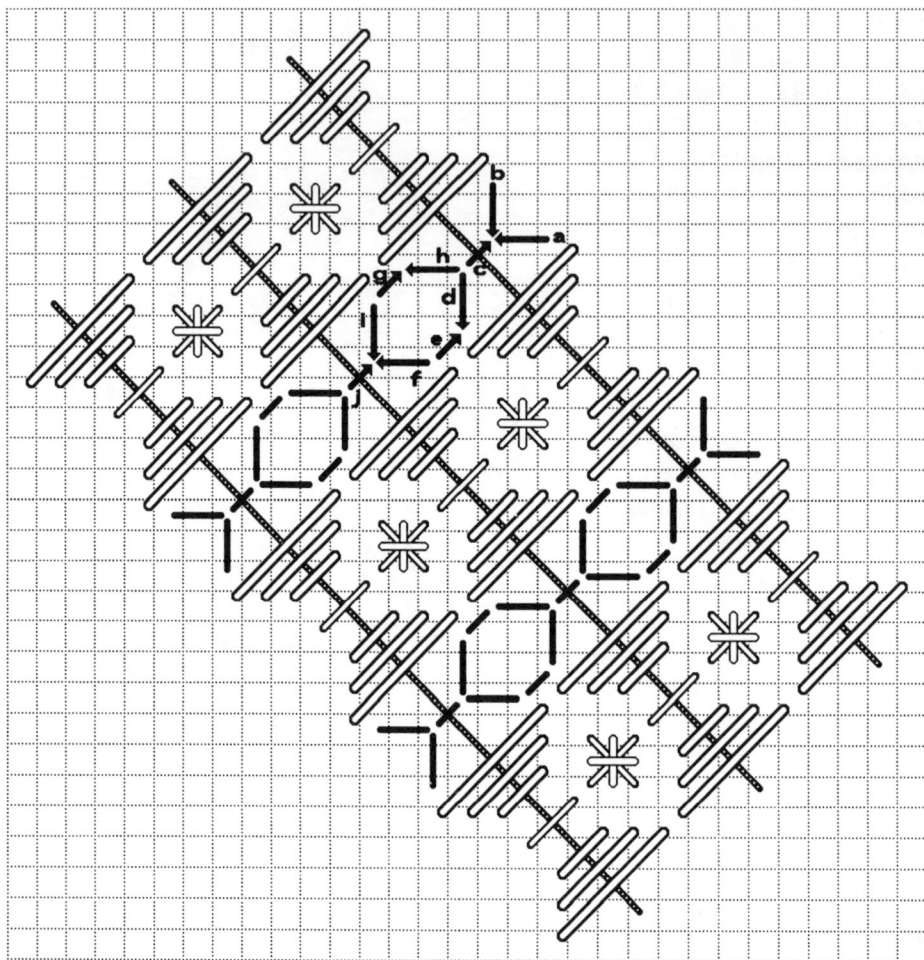

Variation 3. Main Network of Traméd Mirrored Milanese units with an Allover Blackwork Pattern. In this combination (shown on the next page), the blackwork is actually superimposed on top of the Steps 1-2 pattern. Even though the blackwork motifs have separate shapes that align in diagonal paths, they also connect to each other with perpendicular stitches, so the linear thrust is diluted and the pattern becomes an allover repeat.

Step 3. Blackwork Sequence. In spite of what I stated earlier regarding double running stitch being superior for allover patterns, I have presented a combination sequence for this pattern. This is not a book about blackwork, so it is included only as an occasional accent filling. I do not want to add a section on the intricacies of the double running method when this has already been covered in my blackwork book; therefore the sequences provided are merely numbered as single repeats that should be continued until the area is filled. No in-depth knowledge of the technique is needed to add this simple outline. If you are proficient at double running technique, however, please be my guest and use it here.

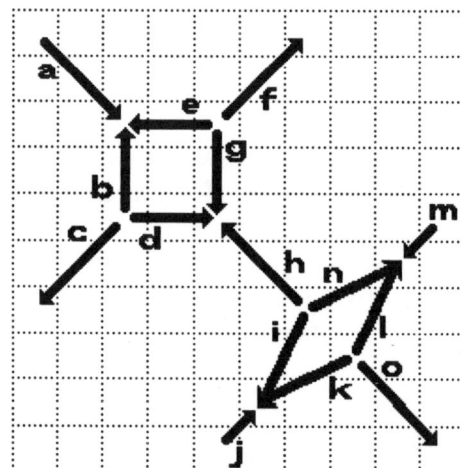

106

NOTE. There are some compensation stitches along both sides of the pattern sample. Add these pairs of partial stitches off of stitches f and m on one side and off of stitches c and j on the opposite edge. The second row of blackwork will only have one set of "couching stitches." Stitches f and m are already done so only stitches c and j must be added.

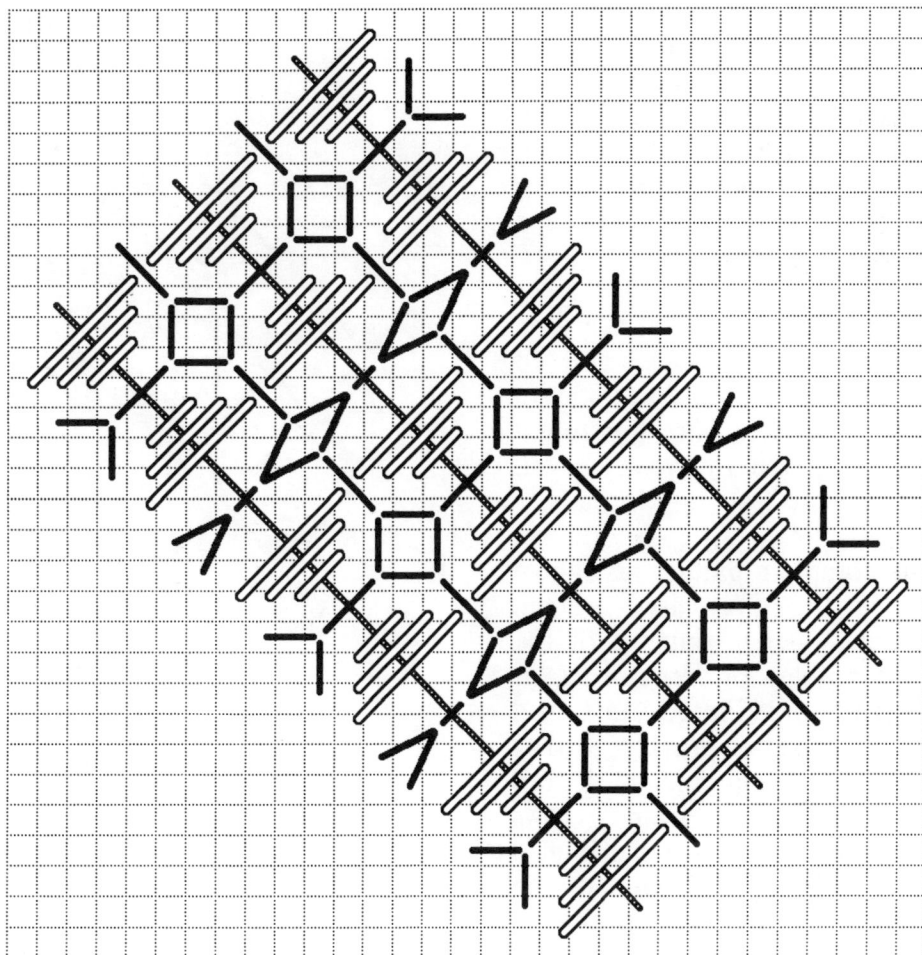

The tramé rows in all of the previous patterns have been secondary accents or foundation layers in the patterning. Therefore I want to include one pattern where the tramé is the major focus.

8. Two-way Couching Pattern with Added Elements of Upright Crosses, Double Straight Crosses, and Flip-flop Tent Units. The pattern to the right is a fancy two-way arrangement of tramé with uneven spacings. Pairs of tramé rows that are four threads apart are arranged in repeats that are six threads apart. When reverse rows of the same spacing are added, a pattern develops that has alternating shapes of large and small diamonds with interesting rectangles that zigzag between these shapes in both directions.

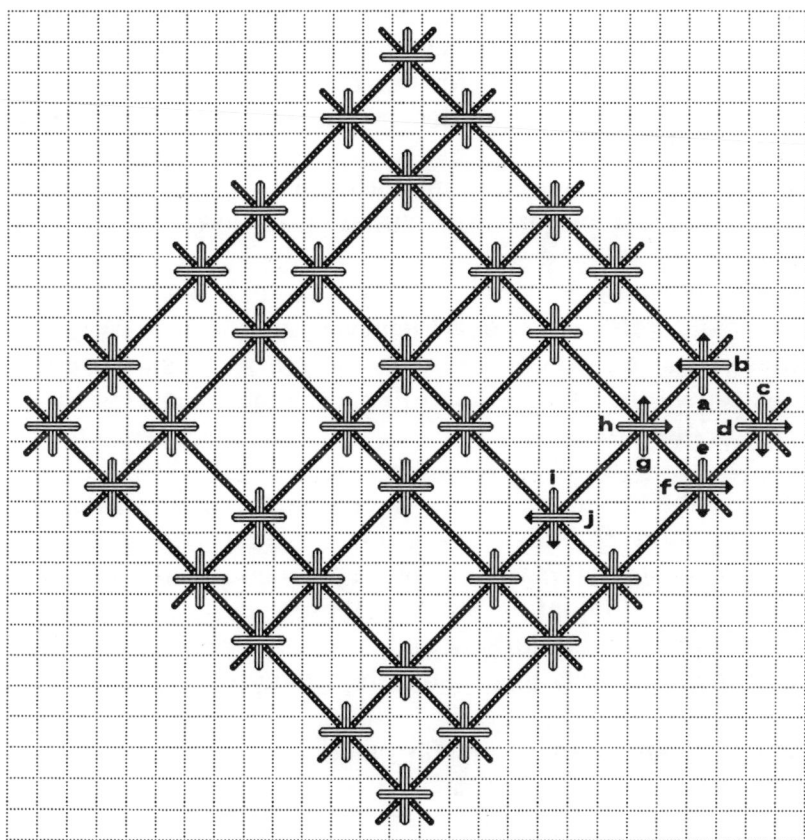

Clusters of Upright Cross units tie down the perpendicular tramé rows at the overlapping intersections. Add these in diagonal paths, using the lettered sequence shown.

Once these two steps are completed, alternating units of Upright Cross and Double Straight Cross are added to the diamond shapes either in vertical or horizontal paths. Use the traditional sequence for these Step 3 additions.

Flip-flop units of Tent are then added to the rectangles as Step 4. These should be done in either vertical or horizontal running stitch rows, which will conceal the traveling threads.

The complete pattern, as shown to the right, is used in the center scalene triangles of the border sides of *Dresden Heart* design (Color Plate IX). I used a monochromatic color treatment, and the dark red lines of the tramé rows dominate. This pattern is also used in the green band of the sampler on the back cover.

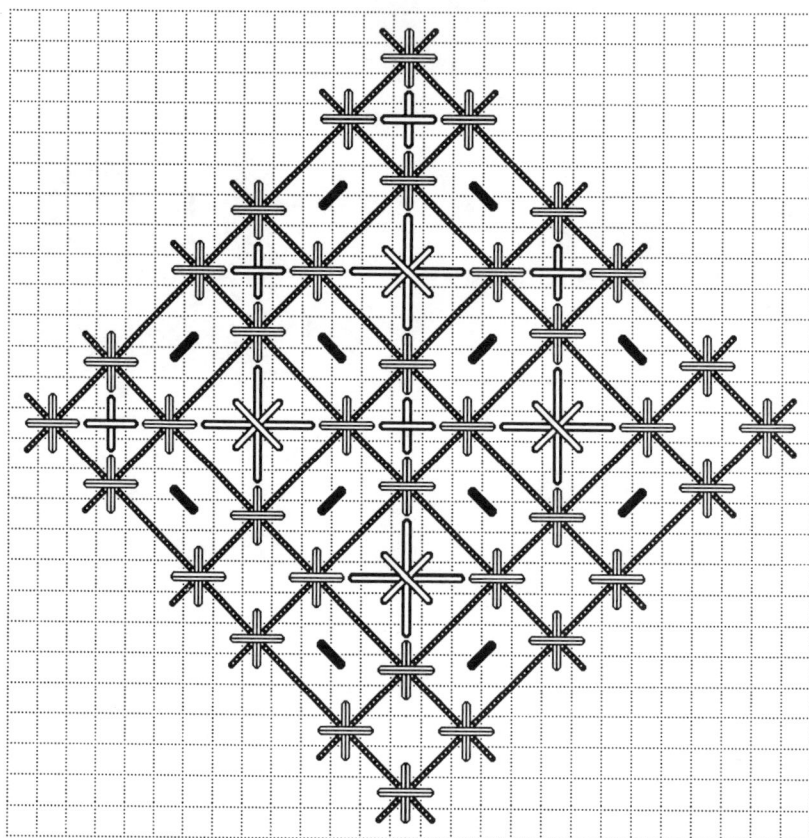

The pattern fits two sides of the irregular triangle comfortably so the uneven compensation on the slanted side is less conspicuous. This trick illustrates one of the basic concepts regarding pattern. **If a pattern is centered strategically or placed so that attention is drawn to the balanced elements, any irregular or compensated edges will recede and be less noticeable. If patterning is not manipulated in this way, it can be a distraction.**

This pattern is also used in monochromatic green shades in the sampler on the back cover. This time the dark Upright Cross clusters used to couch the tramé dominate the pattern.

9. Open Network with Two-way Tramé Rows Couched with Brick Stitches and an Open Composite Pattern. Added Elements Include Four-Way Upright Cross Units and a Blackwork Filler. The overall chart for this pattern follows on the next page. It is a bold pattern with a large repeat that makes it an effective "centerpiece," so I used it in the middle section of *Dresden Heart* (Color Plate IX).

Because the tramé rows are eighteen threads apart, a single Brick stitch is not adequate to couch the long loose threads. Therefore a second "compatible" pattern provides additional couching stitches. This pattern is a modified version of the pattern on page 72. The repeat has been enlarged by eliminating some of the clusters of Four-way Diagonal Hungarian stitches in the parent pattern. Some Smyrna Crosses have also been replaced by Mosaic stitches, which are positioned four-way to straddle the tramé rows.

Step 1. Tramé Rows. A heavy metallic is appropriate for this large scale diamond lattice.

Step 2. Brick Tiedown Stitches. Use another heavy thread to make these stitches prominent. Add them in diagonal paths to force the traveling threads to fall behind the tramé rows.

Step 3. Diamond Lattice. Composite Pattern Using Four-way Diagonal Hungarian Units Around Smyrna Cross Centers and Connecting Units of Four-Way Mosaic Stitches. Add this pattern in diagonal paths, using traditional sequences to construct the stitches. If side trips are preferred, review the sequence of the parent network on page 72.

Step 4. Add the Upright Cross clusters in diagonal rows from upper right to lower left, using a clockwise path. Use a counterclockwise path if rows are worked in the other direction.

Step 5. Add the blackwork hearts, using a double running stitch path from the center of each cluster to form outlines. A chart for one heart outline is shown to the right. Each heart is split into a separate path for each half because this makes a cleaner outline. Both long diagonal stitches at the top will be outside of the traveling path underneath, and this would not automatically happen in a continuous sequence. Work these four-way fillings in diagonal rows, using clockwise or counterclockwise paths. Whip in the backing to hold the traveling thread behind the tramé rows.

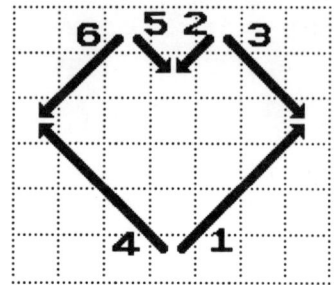

10. One-Way Tramé Rows Couched with Cross Stitches. Additional Accents of Hungarian, Double Straight Cross and Four-way Tent Stitches. The pattern to the right decorates the wing of the lowest butterfly in the center of *Flurry of Butterflies* (Color Plate VII). There are six different stitches in the pattern so it is colorful and intricate in spite of its small scale.

Use the partial overall chart below to execute Steps 1-3. Refer back to the chart to the right to add the remaining steps.

Step 1. Lay the vertical tramé rows six threads apart.

Step 2. Tie down the tramé rows with Cross stitches that are two threads apart. Lay these in vertical paths.

Step 3. Add the alternating units of Hungarian with the foundation crosses of the Double Straight Cross units. Work these in vertical rows.

Step 4. Add the Cross stitches to the Double Straight Cross units in a combined sequence with the Four-way Tent clusters. Use horizontal paths. Execute the crosses the normal way. Then use two separate running stitch paths to add the Flip-flop Tent stitches.

Another color could be used for either of these two accents. I combined them only for the specific pattern cited.

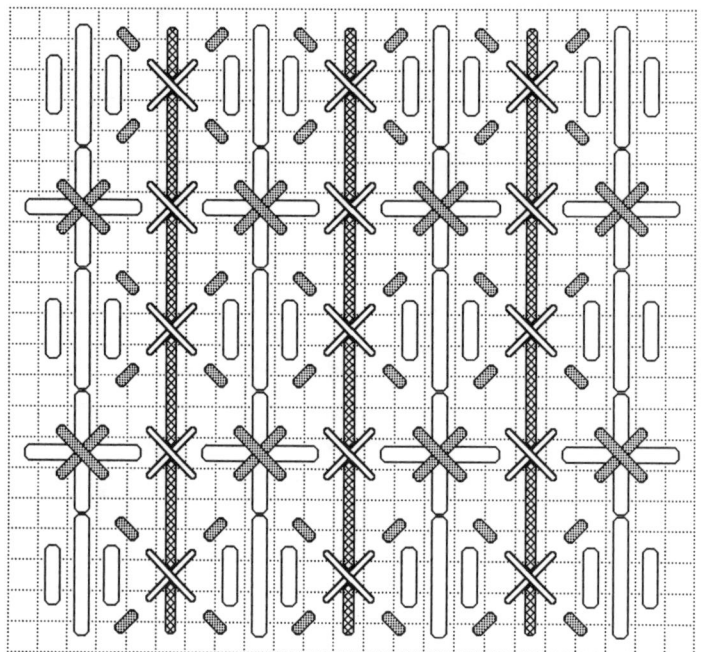

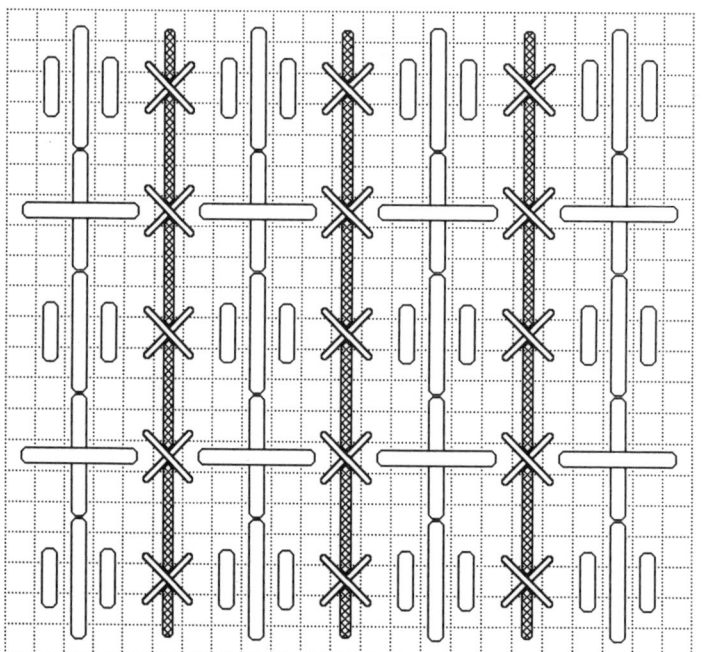

11. Tramé Rows Couched with Oblong Cross Units Combined with Tied Double Cross units and Horizontal Brick Stitches. This pattern is used to embellish the wing of the upper left butterfly in the center of *Flurry of Butterflies* (Color Plate VII). It is possible to manipulate this pattern to form either a stripe or an allover pattern. If the Oblong Crosses and the foundation crosses of the Double Cross units are done in the same color, the pattern will become an allover repeat, but any treatment that separates these two vertical fillings will appear to be a stripe.

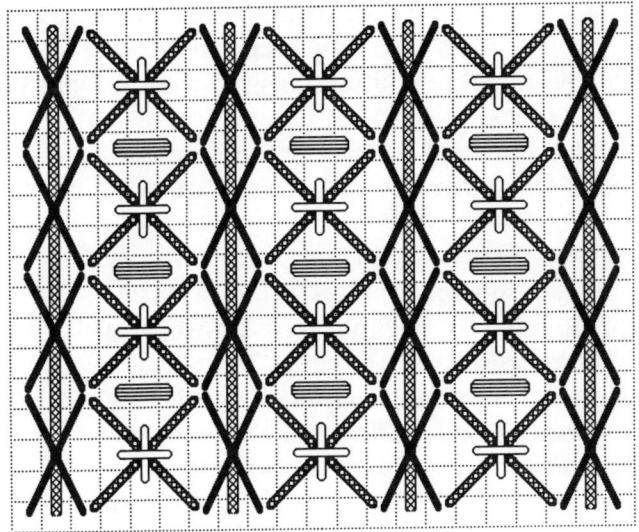

Step 1. Lay the vertical tramé rows six threads apart.

Step 2. Secure the tramé rows with Oblong Cross tiedowns. Lay all of the underneath stitches in one direction first, and then add the top crosses on the return trip. Traveling threads are concealed by the tramé.

Step 3. Add the foundation crosses of the Double Cross units. Use the "eyelet method" to conceal the traveling paths. Split rows of vertical double running paths will also work.

Step 4. Add the Upright Cross stitches in vertical paths.

Step 5. Add the Horizontal Brick stitches in horizontal rows of running stitches.

12. Tramé Rows Couched with Mirrored Milanese Variation. Accents of Tent Clusters. This couching pattern is a simple one that is used in *Tease Time* (Color Plate XI) to embellish the cat in the middle of the bottom row and the cat on the right side of the middle row. All of the patterns used in the cats are bold calico treatments with strong value contrasts and intense colors that show up well on the bright aqua ground.

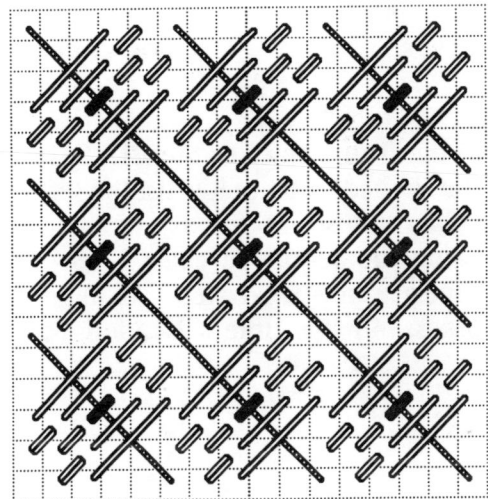

The Mirrored Milanese unit in this pattern is different from that used in the Pattern 7 series. The separate pairs have been "condensed" or merged into one unit with a shared center stitch. The tramé rows are spaced five threads apart in this pattern, and the Mirrored Milanese stitches are staggered in the alternating rows.

The alignment of these units also forms a strong "undulating" diagonal thrust in the pattern from upper right to lower left, and this overshadows the diagonals of the couched rows.

Step 1. Lay the tramé rows.

Step 2. Add the long diagonal stitches of the Mirrored Milanese units. Work these in horizontal rows. Lay the stitches "uphill" on the right-to-left rows and "downhill" on the left-to-right rows.

Step 3. Add the dark center stitches of the Mirrored Milanese units. Work these in vertical rows of back stitches. The bright contrasting color used for the center stitch makes this pattern

111

dramatic. Steps 2-3 both straddle the tramé rows and would normally be stitched in diagonal paths. The straight rows recommended have shorter travel paths, however, so they are more efficient. The use of two different directions for the dual paths also spreads out the traveling threads.

Step 4. Add the Tent clusters in diagonal rows from upper right to lower left, using a basketweave or back stitch rhythm to keep the units snugly wrapped.

13. Open Network of Tent Outline Ovals Separated by Diagonal Rows of Double Tent, Beaded Tent and Cross Stitches. Side Border Rows of Diagonal Tramé with Diagonal Oblong Cross Tiedowns Surrounded by Diagonal Rows of Alternating Units of Double Tent and Cross Stitches. The last couching pattern is used in *Underwater Ballet* (Color Plate V) in the four corner quadrants. The stripe pattern suggests the motion of waves behind the fish and directs the viewer to the mysterious object that the fish are studying.

Space considerations made me abbreviate the pattern here. The pattern in the design has three repeats. Each repeat has three rows of Tent ovals, but I have shown only two. This pattern appears complex, but it builds nicely. Priority must be given to the Oblong Cross size when using it, however, since it does not compensate well.

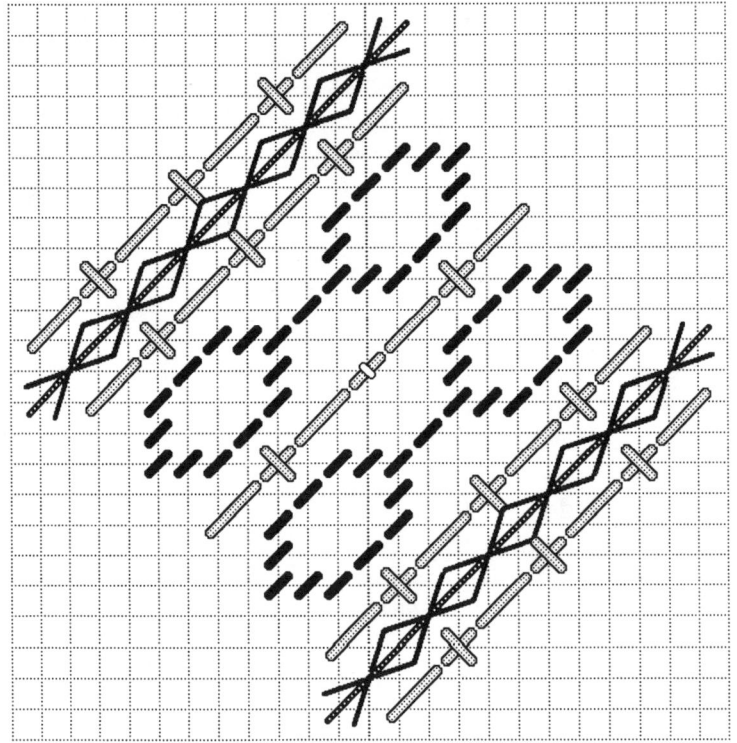

Add the tramé rows as Step 1. Secure these with the Diagonal Oblong Cross rows as Step 2, using the sequence chart below on the left side. Add the surrounding diagonal rows of alternating Double Tent and Cross stitches as Step 3, using a normal sequence. Add the Tent oval outline next as Step 4, using the sequence chart below on the right side. Add the stripe row between the Tent oval outlines as the final step. It aligns with the border rows around the Traméd Diagonal Oblong Crosses, but this time a Beaded Tent stitch is substituted for every other Cross stitch.

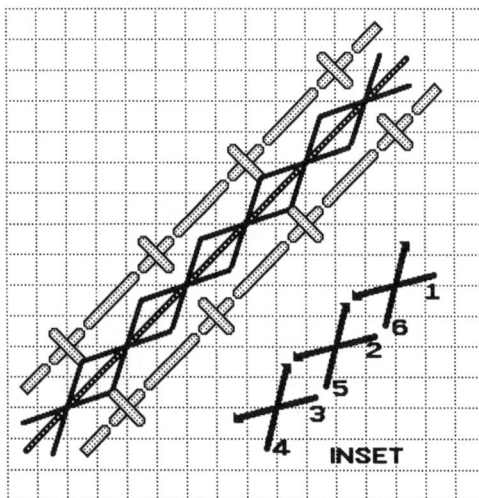

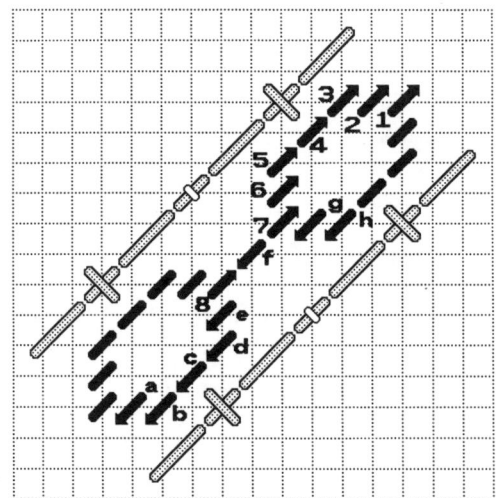

This chapter features open patterns that are formed with different Cross stitches. I often use Cross stitches as one of the units of an alternating sequence or as accent fillings in multinetwork patterns. It is also possible to create open patterning with just Cross stitches. Because crosses have indentations, they do not form smooth geometric shapes, but the jagged quality of the edges is especially attractive in patterns with clusters of crosses.

1. Open Networks of Tied Oblong Crosses with a Half-Drop Placement of the Alternating Rows and Color Variations to Define Shapes. This pattern has a wonderful texture since the half-drop placement creates pairs of slanting stitches throughout the pattern. The arrangement to the right is a stripe with a wide center band surrounded by dark narrow bands on both sides. By varying the color treatments of the crosses, interesting shapes can be defined. I usually use the same color for all of the tiedown stitches, but this is not a rigid rule.

Work the crosses in diagonal paths as Step 1, starting in the upper left corner. Complete all of the foundation crosses before adding the Brick stitch tiedowns in a contrasting thread as Step 2. No alterations are needed except along the side edges where threads will show, so use the "eyelet method" to eliminate clutter there.

NOTE. It may be helpful to use Hi-Liter pens to mark the color distinctions of the next few patterns before you start stitching.

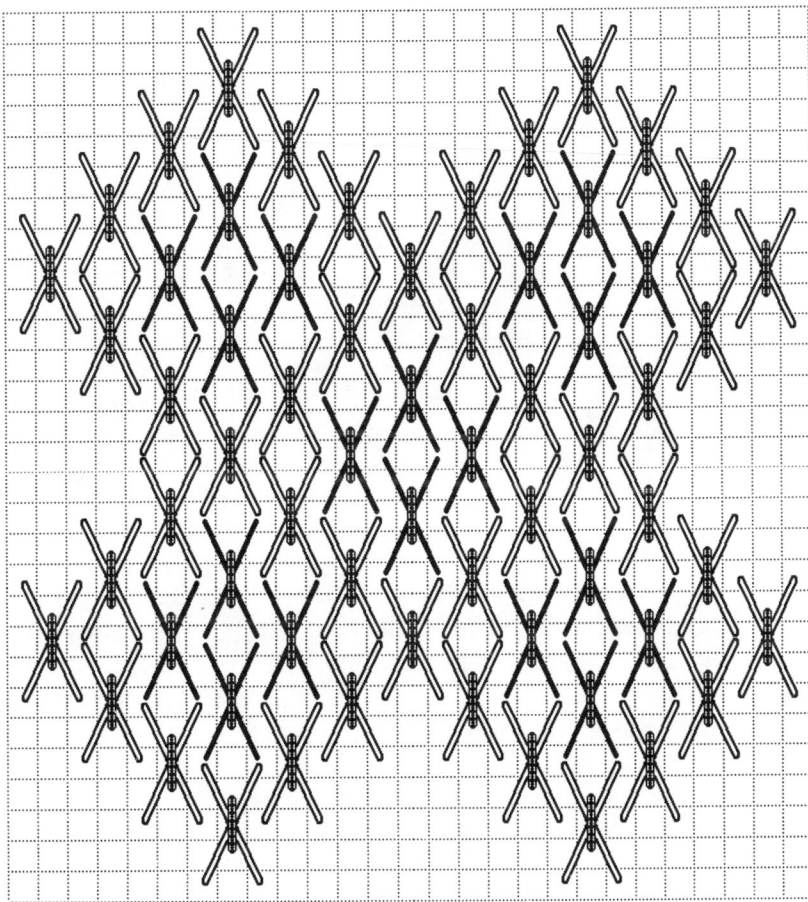

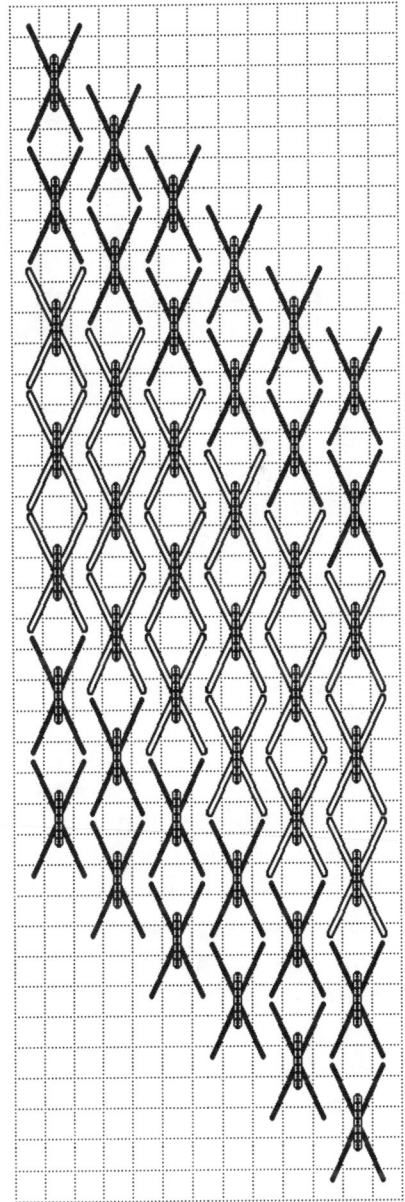

Variation 1. The arrangement to the left is identical to the previous one, but changes in the color placement and in the overall shape have created a network of framed diamonds. Execute the outlines of the light stitches first, and then add

the contrasting units to the open diamond spaces. Add the tiedown stitches in a different thread after all the crosses are completed.

The next series of patterns includes stripes or borders created with Tied Oblong Crosses. The patterns are simple open networks with arrangements of different sizes of the units. Other texture stitches are added to the negative spaces as accent treatments. I used only #8 perle on 18-mesh canvas for these doodles. This sampling illustrates the versatility of this remarkable stitch. Mere changes in the scale of the stitch and the simple layering of one Oblong Cross on top of another can produce unique effects.

Variation 2. Tied Oblong Cross Border. Open Diamond Areas Embellished with Crossed Long Upright Stitches. This pattern creates a strong stripe or border. Solid horizontal rows of Tied Oblong Cross surround an open row in the middle. Add the scattered units in the middle row as side trips off of the solid rows (when convenient) to keep the open areas uncluttered.

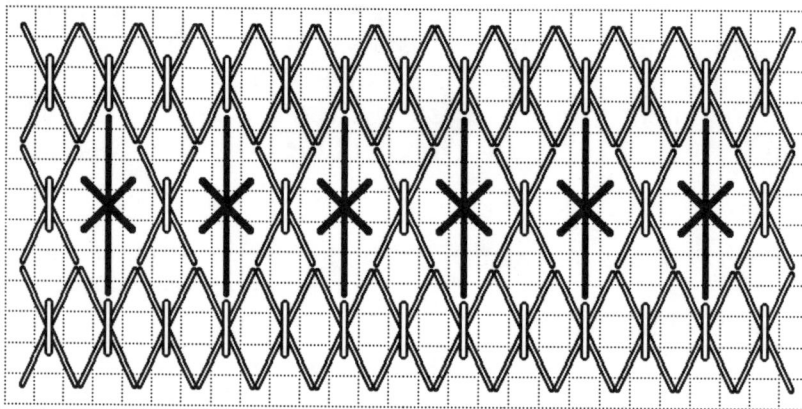

Add the Crossed Long Upright stitches to the negative spaces of the middle row after the Tied Oblong Cross rows are established. Use horizontal paths to execute both sequences. If additional colored accents are desired, add Brick stitches between the Oblong Crosses of the edge rows. These will also conceal the traveling threads from earlier sequences.

Variation 3. Tied Oblong Cross Border. Open Center Row with Accents of Partial Pavillion. This pattern is similar to the previous one. This time the middle row has crosses that are two units apart rather than one so the space remaining is larger. Add the simple satin stitch units of Partial Pavillion in horizontal rows after the Tied Oblong Cross network is completed.

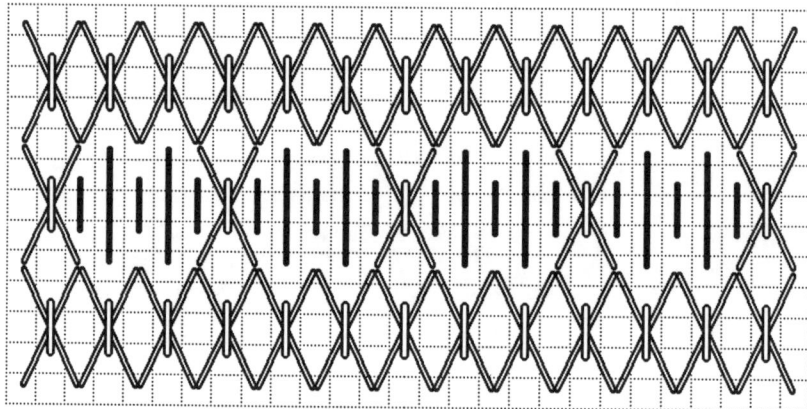

The next two variations will have superimposed layers of one Tied Oblong Cross on top of another. Larger units must be used to make this patterning effective; therefore the first pattern has units that are six threads high and four threads wide. The second pattern has units that are 8 threads tall and four threads wide. Both patterns leave open areas of diamond shapes between the outlines of the units. It is logical to use a dark value thread for the bottom layer to give the pattern more dimension, but either two colors or two values of the same color may be used.

The two patterns presented are both allover arrangements rather than stripes. The elongated diamonds are especially attractive if light weight threads are used for both layers.

114

Variation 4. Open Pattern of Superimposed Tied Oblong Cross Networks. This pattern has two rows of Enlarged Oblong Cross units. The underneath row (shown in dark stitches) is tied down with Brick stitches, which should be done in the same color. Add the second layer of light stitches after the foundation layer is completed. These stitches are tied down with Upright Cross units.

Use the second overall pattern chart shown to the right to lay out the rows of Oblong Cross. The additional tiedown stitches that I added between the rows have been removed so that the sinking holes of the Oblong Cross units can be seen. Instead of doing the Oblong Cross units the traditional way, try doing the top and bottom halves of the units as two separate double running paths (thus splitting the stitches in the middle hole like the "eyelet method" would). With this method, it is possible to connect the entire "maze" without a thread showing in an open area, but you must use some creative pivots and/or side trips to start each new row (a fun puzzle for advanced students!).

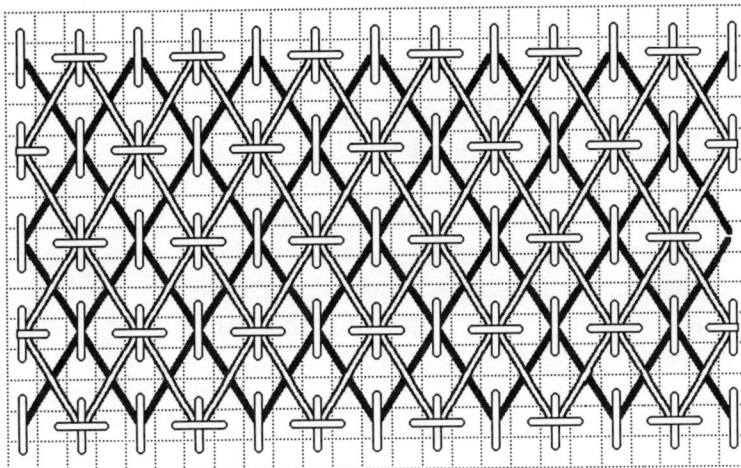

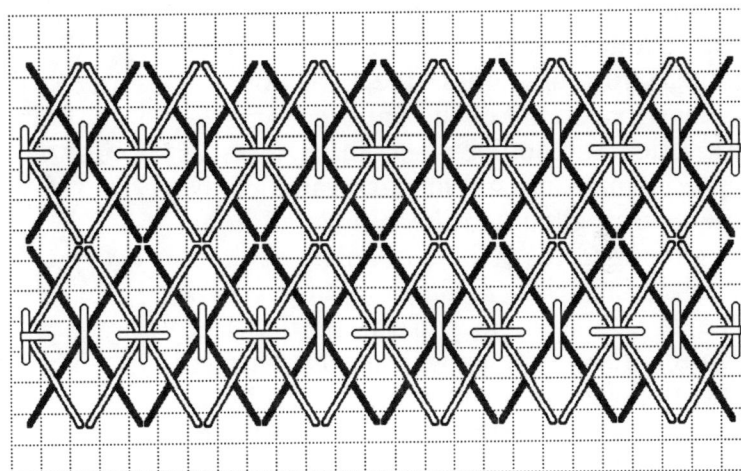

After both layers are completed, use the same thread to add the tiedown stitches and the "extra" stitches to each layer in horizontal paths. The "extra" top stitches cover the sinking holes of all of the crosses and disguise the fact that the pattern is really two separate couching patterns!

Variation 5. Open Network of Superimposed Tied Oblong Cross Networks. The units of Oblong Cross in this pattern are the same width as the previous one, but the stitches are longer and the diamond shapes formed are more elongated. The previous pattern also had no open holes, but this pattern has both open holes and open threads in the exposed areas. For this reason definitely use the split double running sequence recommended in the previous pattern for both layers of crosses.

Again do the tiedowns and extra stitches as a separate Step 2 sequence of horizontal rows after the cross

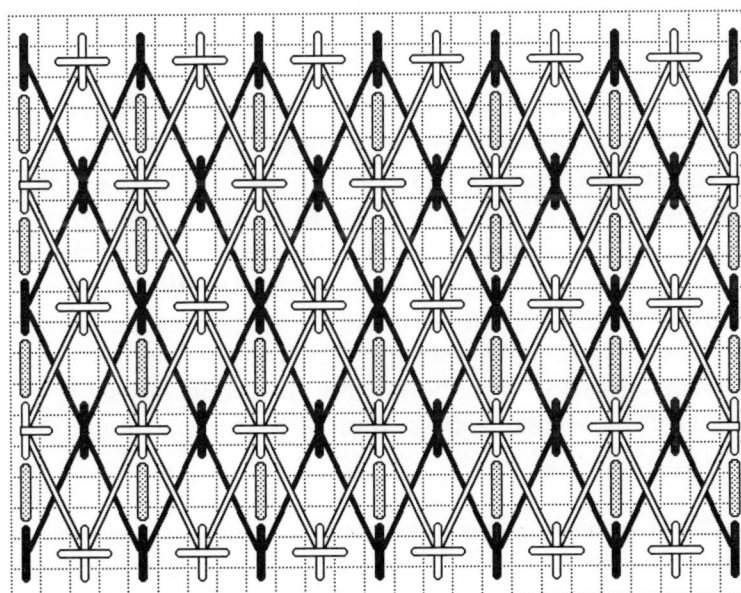

115

sequences are completed. No traveling threads will show since the Brick stitches and the Upright Crosses of the different layers still line up in the same horizontal rows.

Step 3. Add the bold Brick stitches between the tiedown stitches of alternating rows. Use a contrasting color for these stitches, and add them in vertical paths of back stitches.

Variation 6. Border of Tied Oblong Cross Units Shaded to Form Elongated Diamond Repeats. Inner Fillings of Four-way Oblong Cross Units. The last pattern in this series is another border pattern that uses color contrasts to set up the interesting zigzag lines that form the diamond outlines. In addition, the pattern uses Tied Oblong Crosses that encroach or overlap each other to create the sharp diamond points and steep slanted lines. Execute the Tied Oblong Cross diamonds (the light units on the chart) as Step 1 of the pattern. Add the dark Brick stitches between these units as Step 2, using a middle or dark value of the same color. Then add the Elongated Four-way Oblong Cross centers in a light value of a contrasting color as Step 3. Use a dark value of this color to add the border Tied Oblong Cross units as well as the Upright Cross tiedowns and radiating Brick stitches around the Elongated Four-way Oblong Cross centers (Step 4).

This pattern has open holes as well as open threads in the exposed areas whereas the previous pattern only had exposed threads. Therefore any casual traveling is dangerous. The "eyelet method" can be used for the Oblong Crosses to keep the areas around them clean, or the split sequence discussed on pages 52-53 may also be used. The split double running paths will not work since the rows are interrupted by color changes. A more random combination of sequences will work best, so use logical solutions for each situation. Definitely use the "eyelet method" for the radiating stitches in the center filling.

Variation 7. Four-Way Arrangement of Tied Oblong Cross Clusters combined with Brick Stitches, Double Straight Cross Units, and Four-Way Oblong Cross Units Tied With an Upright Cross with Radiating Brick Clusters. This pattern sounds intricate, but it builds nicely in sequential order. One color is used for several different stitches so only four sequences are needed. The main network of this pattern forms a square network. The chart to the right shows only the Main Network of Tied Oblong Cross. The complete pattern is shown on the next page.

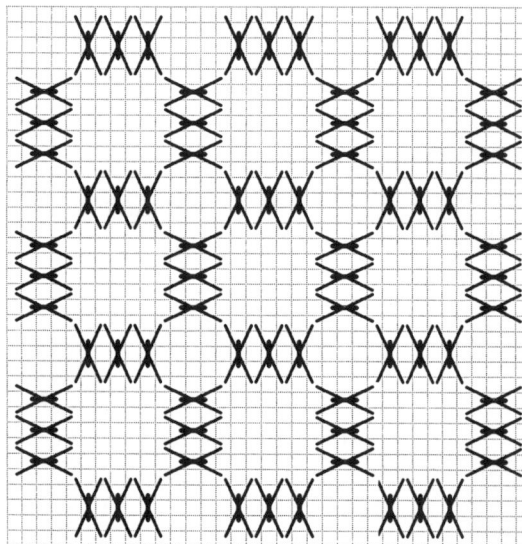

Execute these units in zigzag paths of flip-flop clusters as Step 1. Use one color for both the crosses and the tiedowns of the units. Execute these units the normal way but adjust the direction of the tiedown stitch in anticipation of the direction of the next cluster on the third unit of each cluster. Work the remaining steps, using the chart below.

VARIATION 7 - SQUARE NETWORK OF TIED OBLONG CROSS CLUSTERS

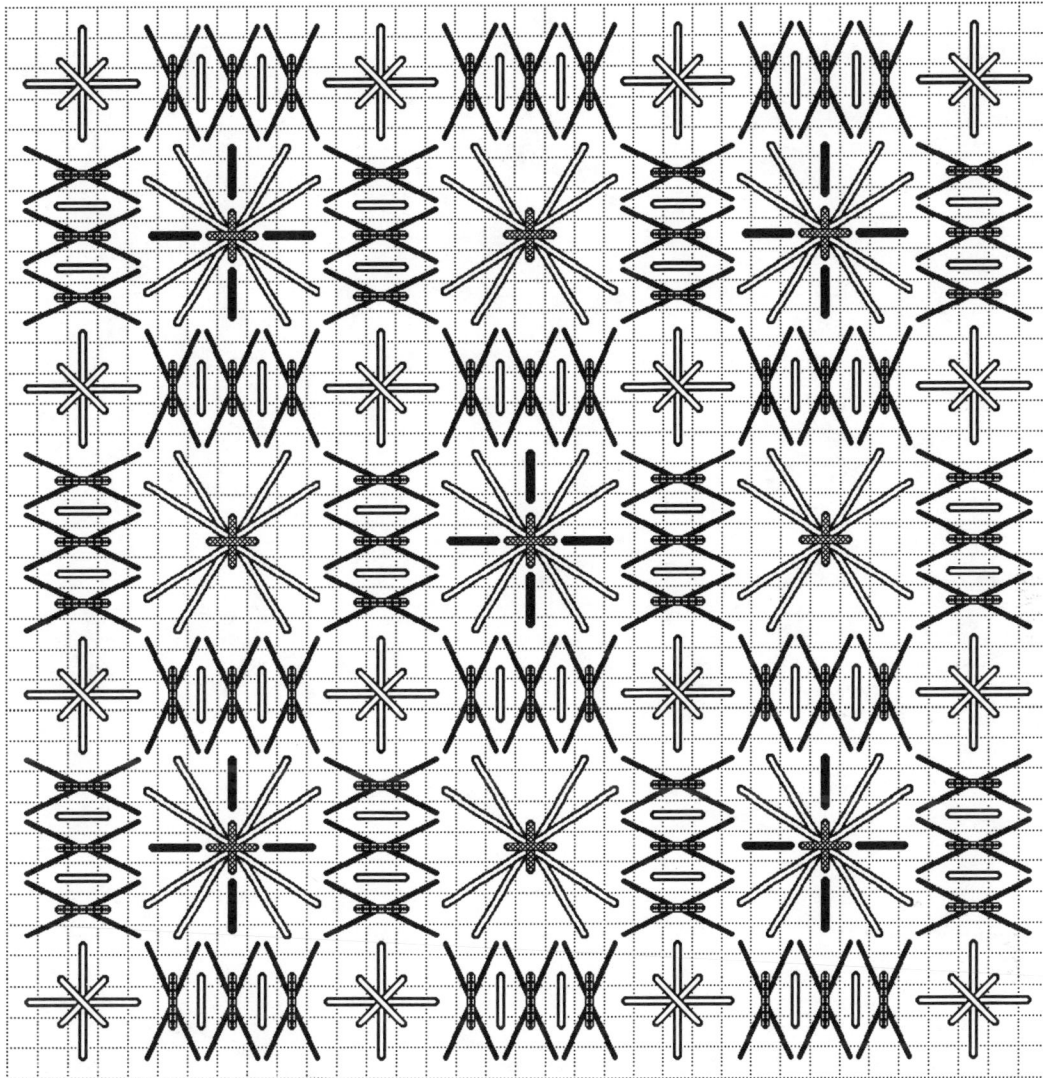

Step 2. Add the Four-way Oblong Cross units in the center of the open "squares." Use the "eyelet method" and add them as radiating "split" stitches. Use a light value of a second color for these accents.

Step 3. Add the radiating Brick stitches around the Four-way Tied Oblong Cross units. Work these from the outside in clockwise or counterclockwise paths. These are added only to alternating squares in the chart but can be used in every square, if preferred. Use a dark value of the same color used in Step 1.

NOTE. These stitches will also serve to conceal some of the traveling paths of Step 4, so there is an advantage to having them surround every Four-way Oblong Cross unit.

Step 4. I used a combined sequence to add the final accents, and these are done in a dark value of the same color used for Step 2. Add the Double Straight Cross units inside the octagonal shapes along with the Brick stitches inside the clusters of three Oblong Cross units. Also include the Upright Cross tiedowns on top of the Four-way Oblong Cross units. A number of strategies can be used to add these combined elements. I would suggest doing one complete path around the

117

outside border of the square. Then add the inside units in vertical rows. One row will add the Upright Cross Tiedowns with the Upright Brick stitches. The alternating row will add the sideways Brick stitches with the Double Straight Cross units.

2. Open Pattern of Four-way Diagonal Oblong Crosses. This pattern forms a striking one of alternating shapes. On the chart the octagons appear to be angular, but once stitched these lines soften to form curves or circles.

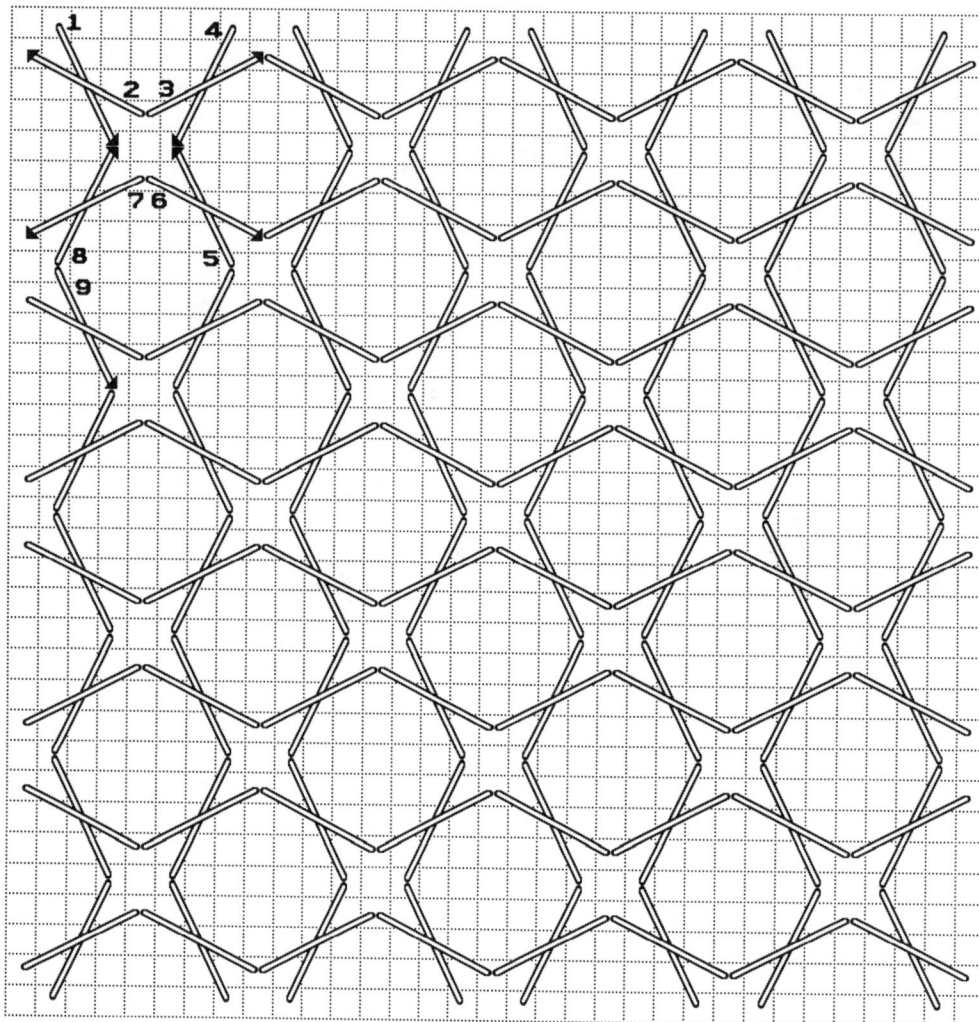

This pattern is particularly stunning on a dark canvas. Its interesting "outlines" make it appear to be blackwork at first glance, but it is much faster to execute the shapes with the crosses shown.

**VARIATION 1
SINGLE REPEAT**

Sequence. The large overall chart above shows a numbered sequence that executes the four-way clusters in a vertical row, using a clockwise path. These Oblong Crosses are not tied, and the more horizontal stitch of each unit must be on top. There is no sequence that can meet this criteria and still conceal all of the traveling threads. By weaving stitches 4 and 8 under the previously laid stitch, however, the pattern will look totally consistent, and the traveling threads will not show. I try to avoid this tedious extra step as a routine measure, but in this pattern, it is the only way to attain a consistent appearance.

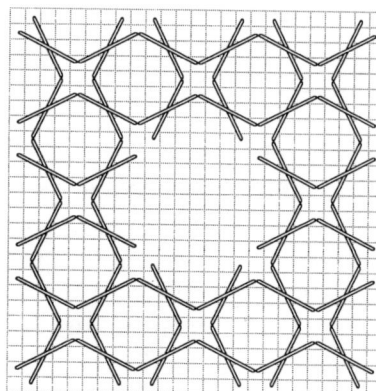

Variation 1. The small chart on the previous page shows a second example using the same Four-way Diagonal Oblong Crosses. This time the center cluster of the nine-repeat arrangement has been eliminated, and a beautiful quatrefoil outline results. As a single repeat, this pattern could be enlarged to an attractive overall pattern. One could further embellish the octagons and the stars to create a circular edging, but I would not embellish the curved centers since they are stunning by themselves.

3. Open Network of Large Tied Oblong Crosses with Inside Fillings of Brick Stitches and Tied Long Upright Stitches. This pattern is an allover arrangement of Enlarged Oblong Cross units. However, a different tiedown stitch is used in every other vertical row, so a stripe is produced. A simple Upright Cross is used in one row, but five parallel Brick stitches are used in the alternate rows, so the pattern is dense. The outside stitches actually wrap or squeeze the cross units together.

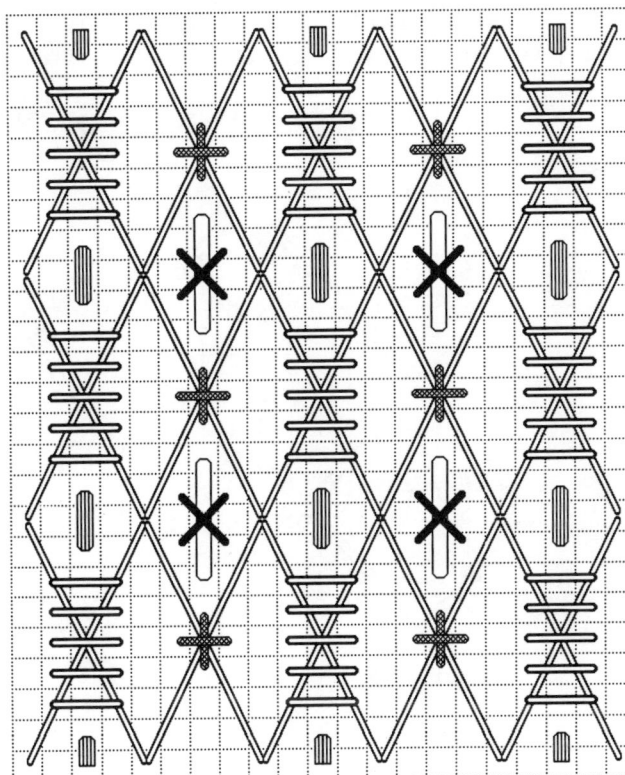

Step 1. Oblong Cross Rows with Upright Cross Tiedowns. Since there are accent stitches between these units, use the running stitch method to lay the crosses. Lay all of the underneath stitches in one direction first. Then add the top crosses on the return trip.

Step 2. Oblong Cross Rows with Brick Cluster Tiedowns. Add these stitches in vertical rows, using the same thread used for Step 1. A numbered chart is provided below of this combined sequence.

NOTE. The canvas can be rotated 90° to stitch these clusters more comfortably in the normal position, using horizontal paths.

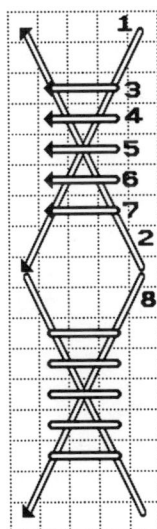

Step 3. Add the Upright Cross stitches to tie down the Oblong Crosses of the Step 1 rows.

Step 4. Add the Tied Long Upright stitches in vertical rows, using either one sequence for solid units or two sequences for a two-color treatment.

Step 5. Add the Brick stitches in vertical rows.

I used this pattern as an attractive border in a small geometric design. Since the top edge is twenty threads wide it is easy to plan a corner motif for the border. Any checkerboard combination of alternating box units is appropriate, so try your hand at several possibilities. I used a fancy multicolor arrangement of Dotted Scotch units (see page 26) as a solid rather than an open pattern, and I repeated the colors and/or values used in the border bands in the corner motif.

Oblong Crosses can be used both as upright units and as diagonal units. They can be resized to suit any scale or need as well. I have provided several different

119

examples of their use in open patterning to exhibit their enormous potential not just as fillers but as complete networks by themselves.

4. Open Network of Herringbone with Accents of Upright Cross, Double Straight Cross and Blackwork. This pattern is unusual in that Herringbone is normally considered a line or outline stitch. In *Tease Time* (Color Plate XI) I used this stitch in multicolor layers to create the border. The main network shown below uses mirrored rows of Herringbone to create a beautiful open network that forms interesting staggered rows of "bow tie" shapes. The pattern is large scale, so only two repeats are included in the overall charts below and on the next page.

STEP 1 SEQUENCE - OPEN HERRINGBONE NETWORK

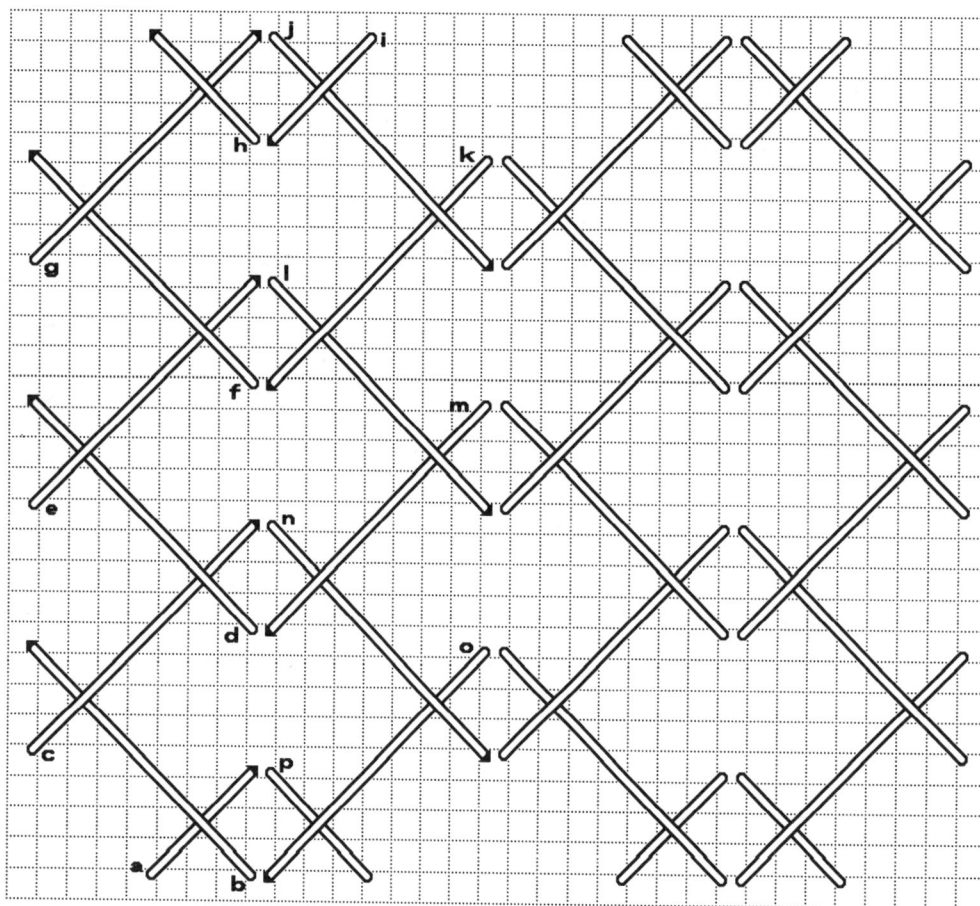

Step 1. Add the criss-cross rows, using the lettered sequence shown on the left side above. You will notice one inconsistency in that stitches j-p are shown underneath rather than on top of the stitches they follow. This would be the correct position for the normal rhythm, but if the pattern is used with exposed crosses, these stitches must be woven under the previously laid ones to make them mirror the adjacent crosses consistently, as shown.

In the composite pattern on the next page, I have camouflaged these "incorrect" crosses by covering them with Upright Cross stitches as one of the additional accents. If this is planned, ignore the weaving and merely stitch the sequence without this tedious step. As mentioned several times earlier, many of my additional embellishments are not just ornamental. They are often devices that conceal inconsistencies and allow me to take liberties with the sequences that will accomplish other priorities. In my opinion, the ultimate goal is to achieve the best final presentation to an embroidery, and any measures taken to achieve a sophisticated look is justifiable as long as any shortcuts or unorthodox measures taken are not obvious. I like to think of these concepts and problem solving devices as stitch refinements, and "the end justifies the means" when such liberties are taken with traditional approaches.

OVERALL PATTERN - OPEN HERRINGBONE COMPOSITE PATTERN

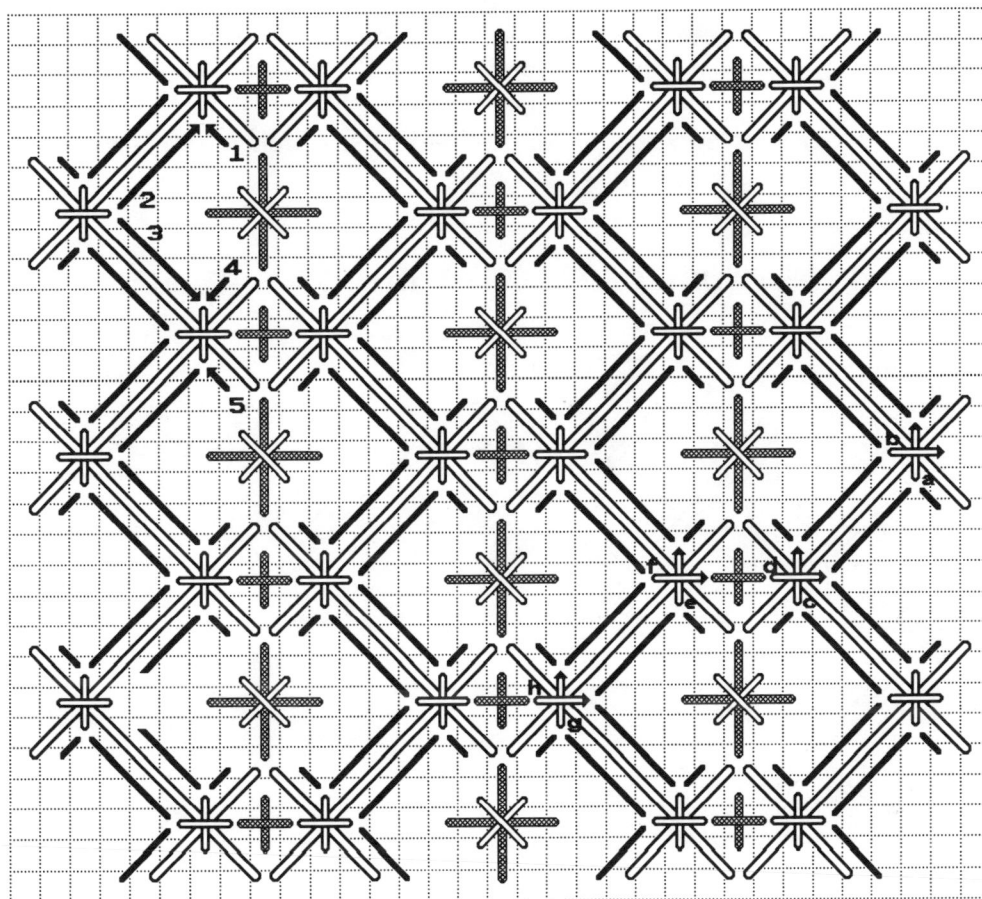

This pattern is used in the sampler on the back cover in the top and bottom bands, so you can see how bold and striking it is.

Step 2. Add the Upright Crosses inside the small diamonds in a combination sequence with the foundation crosses of the Double Straight Crosses. Work these in vertical rows.

Step 3. Add the top crosses of the Double Straight Cross units in the same thread as the blackwork or in a contrasting thread. Work these in vertical paths as well.

Step 4. Add the blackwork, using the numbered sequence shown in the upper left corner of the chart above. I added the left side fillings in one vertical path and the right side fillings as a second path, using the same sequence.

Step 5. Add the Upright Cross "tiedowns" on top of the Herringbone crosses, using the lettered sequence shown on the right side above. These rows are done in what I call a "step diagonal" path. I used a matching metallic in a finer weight for this step in the pattern on the sampler, but a matching perle in a lighter weight is also suitable. I have worked this part of the pattern in a slightly contrasting value in another sample. Instead of using Upright Crosses inside the small diamonds, I added beaded Brick stitches as part of the Step 5 sequence.

Someday I hope to write a book just about borders because borders are a wonderful way to use original patterning. Some patterns miter nicely without the need for a corner motif. Other patterns can be used in combination with an interesting corner motif, and it is fun to design a compatible arrangement. Many of the designs featured in the color plates have borders. Several borders are also included in the samplers on the inside covers and in the band samplers on the front and back covers. This chapter will include a few of these treatments just to whet your appetite for more. Most use stitches that have already been explored, but some of the accent fillings are new.

BORDER 1 - MAIN NETWORK OF FLIP-FLOP DIAGONAL HUNGARIAN - STEP 1

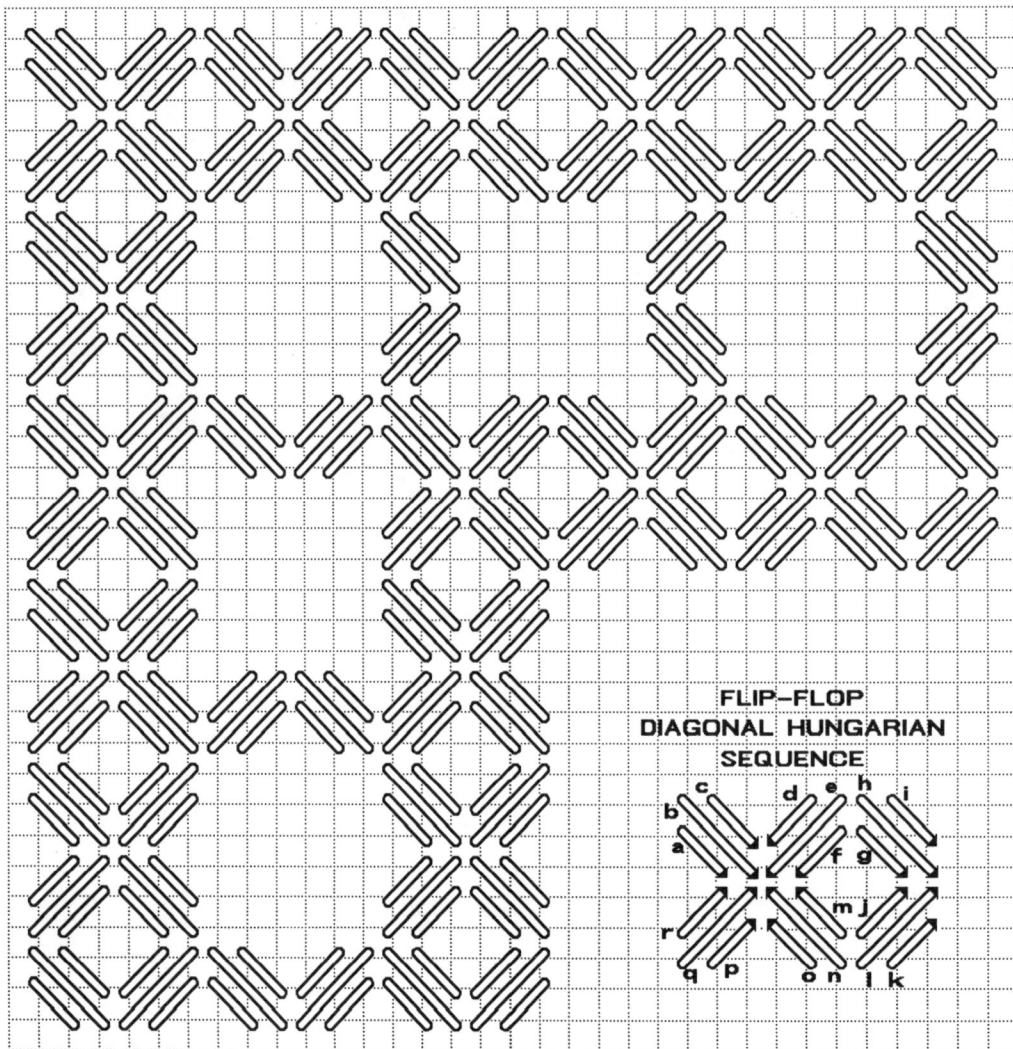

FLIP-FLOP
DIAGONAL HUNGARIAN
SEQUENCE

The edges of this border have continuous repeats of four-way clusters of Diagonal Hungarian. In the center area, some units are omitted, so two unusual shapes alternate to form an interesting border. Inside the overall chart, there is a sequence chart for executing the outlines as Step 1. In the allover patterns discussed earlier on pages 45-47 each cluster is done as a total entity, but in this border, it is better to use what I call a flip-flop sequence to do each zigzag row separately. Usually the stitches in each unit are stitched in sequential order; however, when traveling to a new row, do what is necessary to make a graceful transition.

Along the edge, the units have open areas that are shaped like diamonds. I added two-color units of Double Straight Cross here. The same thread that is used for the top cross is also used to add Upright Crosses to the center "seams" of the four-way clusters between the diamonds. The chart below shows the placement of these embellishments. Since the area around these units is dense, they can be added in horizontal and vertical paths with no adjustments. Lay the foundation crosses of the Double Straight Cross units first as Step 2. Then add the combined sequence of Regular and Upright Crosses as Step 3.

BORDER 1 - OVERALL PATTERN OF STEPS 2-3

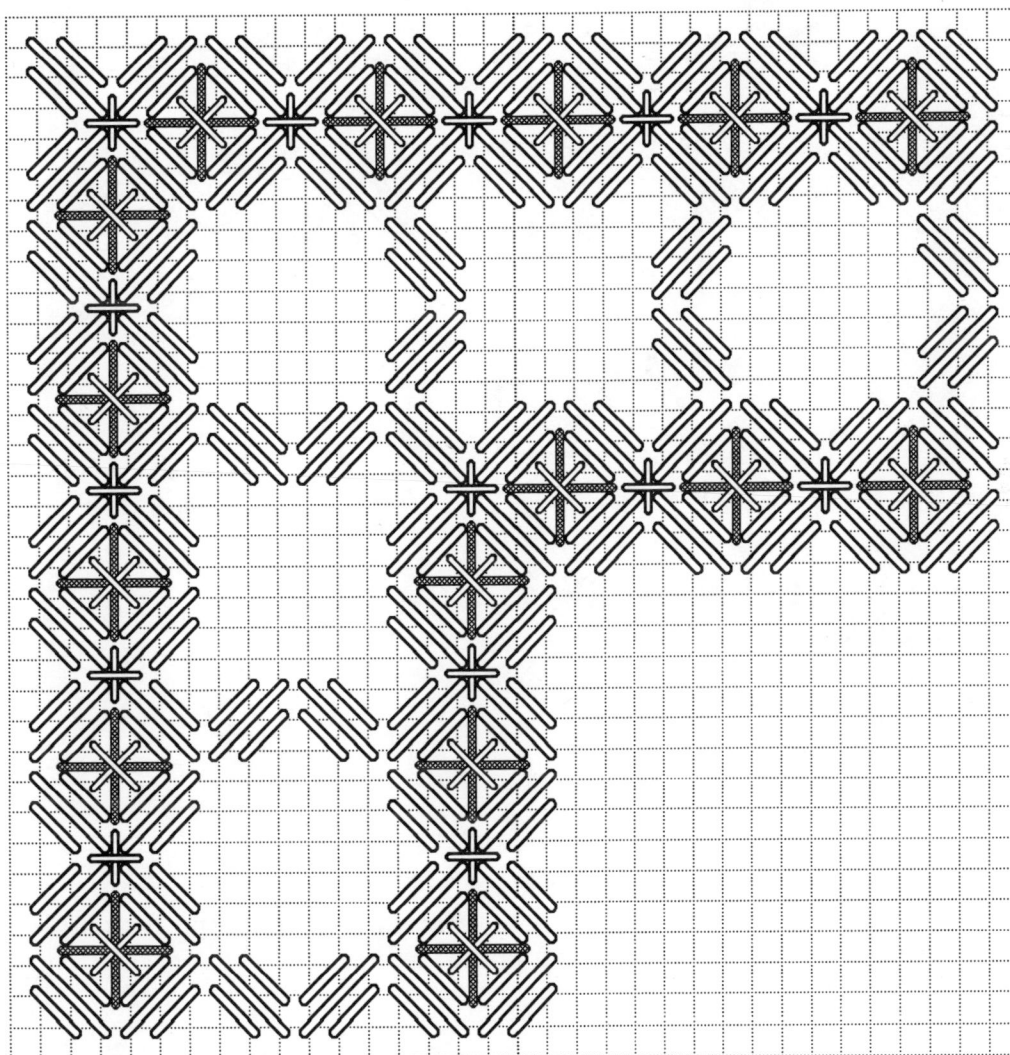

The final addition to this border includes two fillings that embellish the open areas in the middle of the band. The same thread is used for both stitch treatments, and my example is shown in the sampler on the inside of the front cover. The filling that forms a star in the center looks like blackwork at a first glance, but it is actually a four-way arrangement of Diagonal Oblong Cross units. The other filling is a four-way arrangement of Ray Variations.

BORDER 1 - OVERALL PATTERN - MAIN NETWORK OF FLIP-FLOP DIAGONAL HUNGARIAN WITH UPRIGHT CROSSES AND DOUBLE STRAIGHT CROSS UNITS ACCENTS OF FOUR-WAY RAY VARIATIONS AND DIAGONAL OBLONG CROSSES STEP 4 SEQUENCE INCLUDED FOR THE OBLONG CROSS CLUSTER

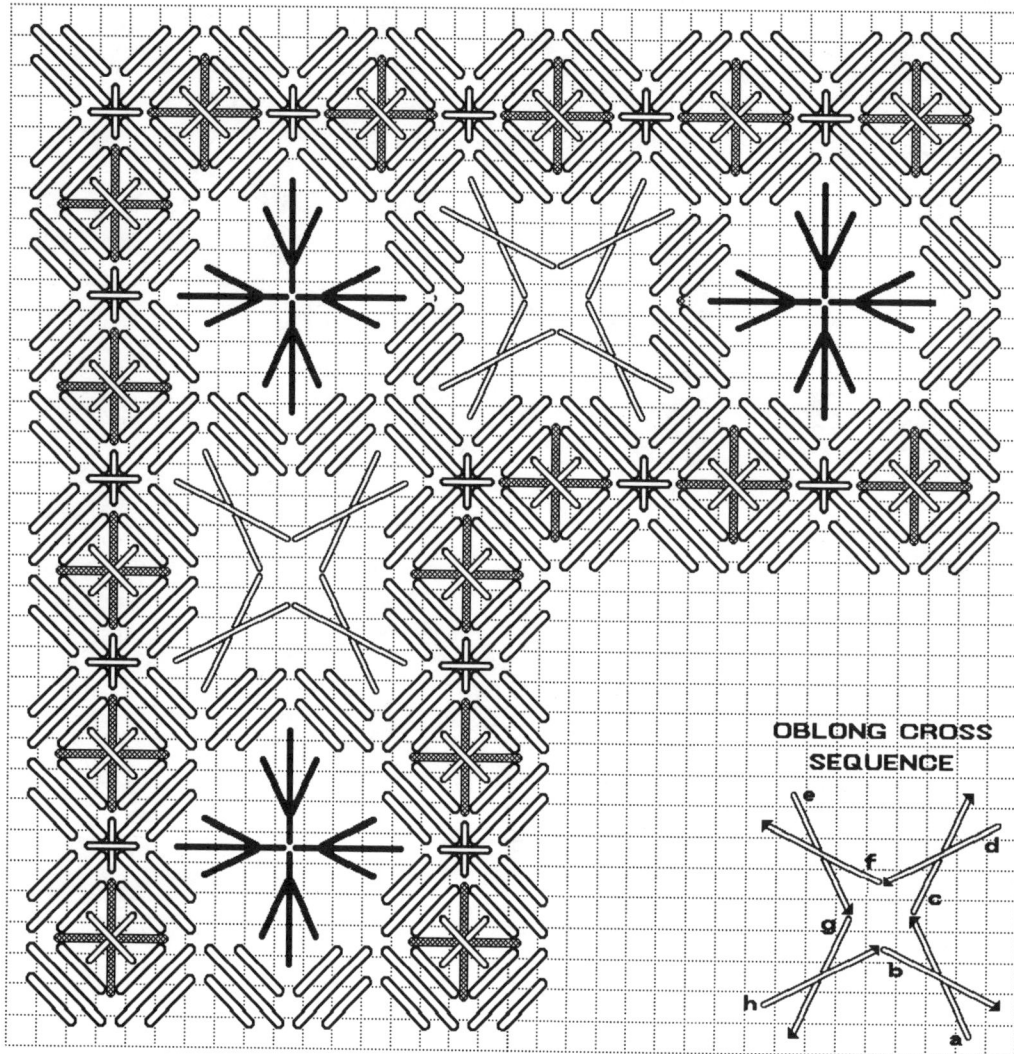

OBLONG CROSS
SEQUENCE

Add these clusters together if the same thread is used. The Ray Variation unit should be executed in radiating paths. Lay the side stitches first in each unit, and then add the long center stitch. Adjust the starting and ending points, as needed, to travel efficiently in the pattern.

The Oblong Cross units must all have the more horizontal stitch placed on top for a consistent and attractive look. Therefore use the prescribed lettered sequence to add these clusters. The sequence shown is ideal for the upper section when rows are stitched from right to left. Rotate the chart 180°, as needed, to add additional repeats; however, if the chart is rotated 90°, the wrong crosses will be on top – so beware!

124

BORDER 2 - OVERALL PATTERN - OPEN PATTERN COMBINING EXTENDED DIAGONAL HUNGARIAN WITH DIAGONAL HUNGARIAN VARIATION

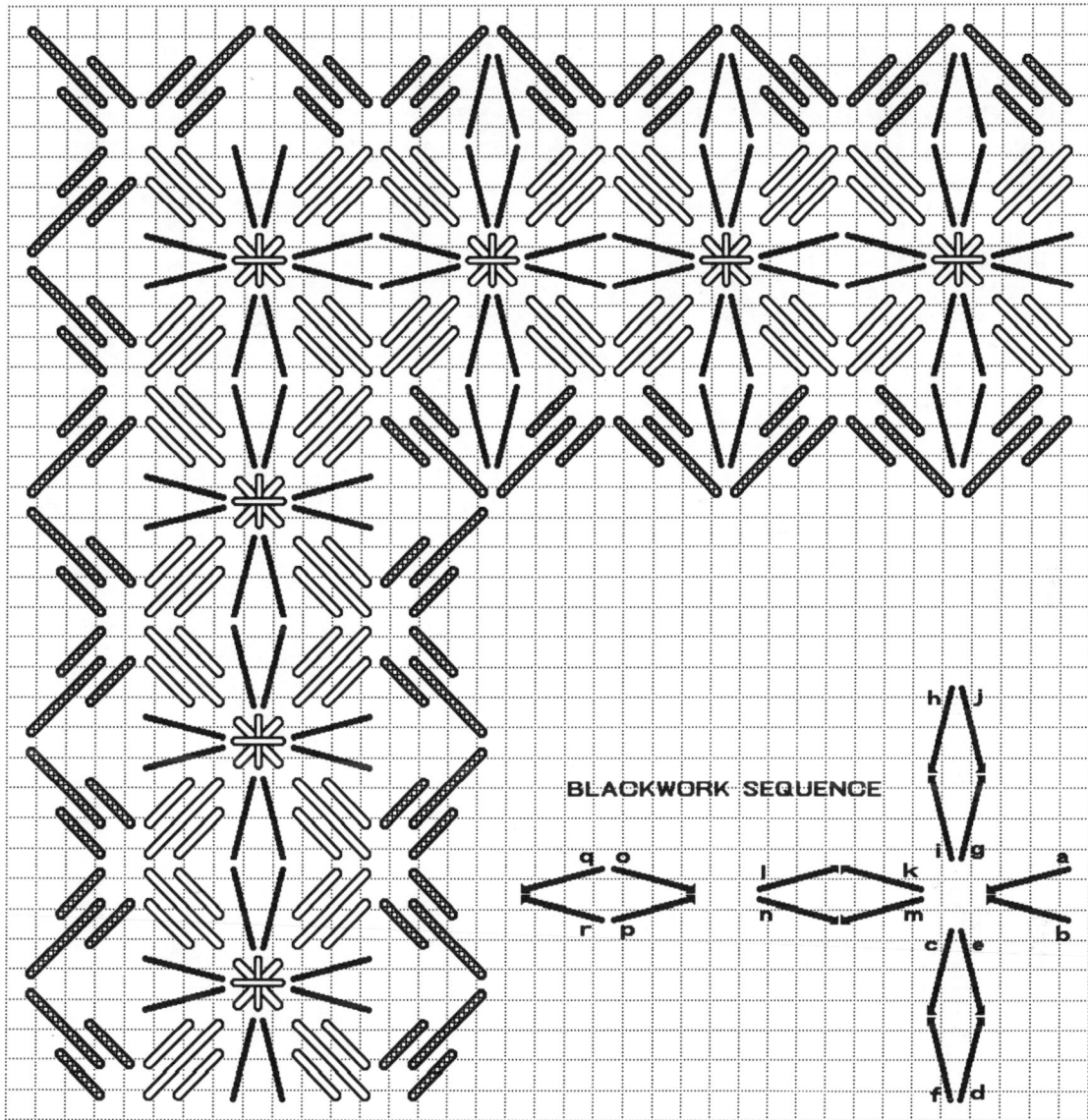

This border combines two compatible networks. The outside edge of the border has flip-flop units of Extended Diagonal Hungarian (Step 1). The interior pattern is a combination of Four-way Diagonal Hungarian units with Smyrna Cross centers (Step 2) and a star blackwork pattern (Step 3). No instructions are needed for the first two steps since they were discussed earlier on pages 61 and 72.

A sequence is provided for the blackwork outline, however, in the lower right hand corner of the chart. The sequence is a combination of running stitch and back stitch paths to connect the four-way stars. The main path is the center row, and the side "points" are added as side trips off of the main path. The left side of the border shows a four-way partial star arrangement, and this is the version of the border that appears in the sampler on the inside back cover. Either option is nice; just skip the extra stitches in the sequence to use the partial pattern.

125

Variation 1. An abbreviated version of this border is also featured in the sampler on the inside back cover. Only the outside band of the Extended Diagonal Hungarian is used. The inner outline is a zigzag path of only half of the Diagonal Hungarian with the Smyrna Cross centers. This is a simple but elegant border, and the inside pattern produces an unusual wave that is similar to that produced in some bargello patterns.

This border was discovered while the first version was "in progress." I liked what emerged as I was interpreting my doodle graph, and I decided the partial pattern was notable by itself. It is shown to the right.

The next border was actually planned for the pattern that it is shown with (which is discussed on pages 75-76). It is featured between the two previous borders in the sampler on the inside back cover. The color balance between the two compatible elements is obvious, and this is essential to a border's success.

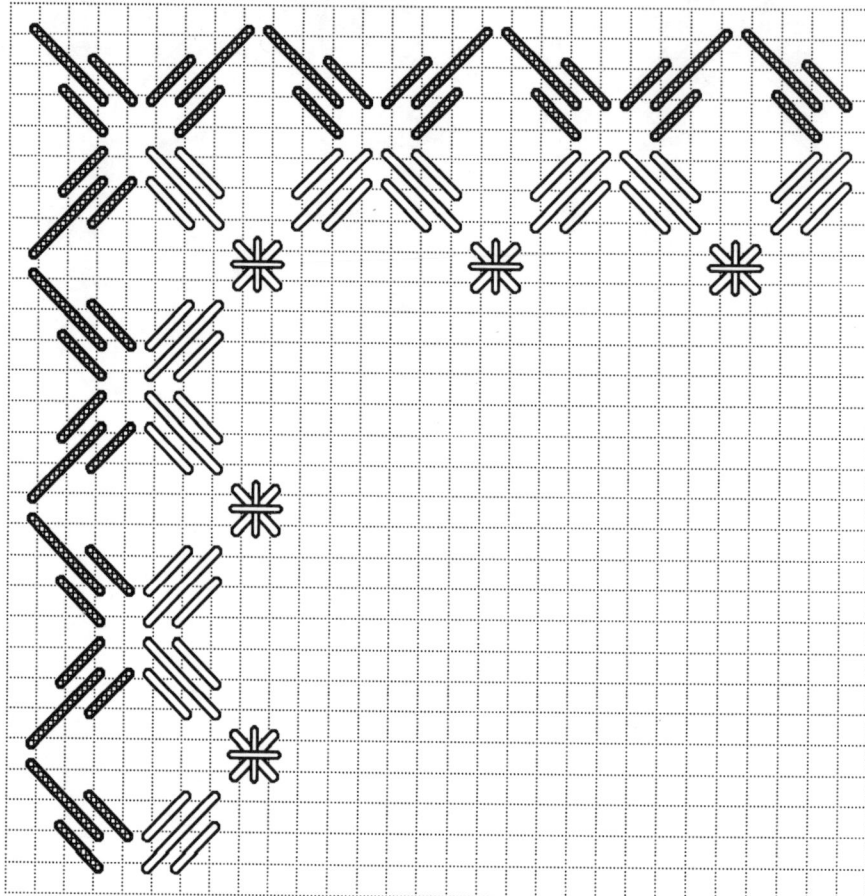

Border 3. Edging of Alternating Units of Flip-flop Diagonal Hungarian and Upright Crosses in a Zigzag Path with Blackwork Accents. The chart for this border is shown on the next page. The band echoes the main structure of the interior pattern with its use of a flip-flop row of Diagonal Hungarian units along the inside edge. The additional embellishments are blackwork outlines that include a flower that alternates with a star motif. This border also tends to "undulate" like the variation shown above.

Step 1. Execute the zigzag paths of Diagonal Hungarian along the inner edge of the border first. Add the units of Upright Cross between these units along the way. These stitches were substituted for the Smyrna Crosses of the original pattern. No sequence chart should be needed for this simple outline row.

Step 2. Add the blackwork elements after the canvas stitches are completed. A sequence chart is shown on the next page. It shows a lettered sequence of one complete repeat. The sequence is a combination of alternating back stitches and running stitches with double running paths.

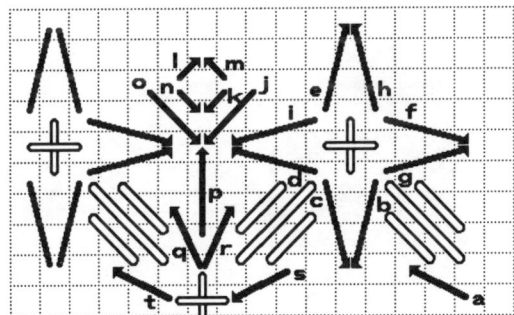

Blackwork Sequence. This pattern is continuous, and stitch t is the repeat point of the sequence. The small stem flower in this border adds a touch of realism to an otherwise geometric pattern. I thought the inner pattern suggested a trellis of small flowers in spite of its formal arrangement, so this association was suggested by the original pattern.

In the example on the sampler, I used a two-color treatment for the blackwork, so the flowers were done separately in pink perle. To do this, just skip stitches j-o in the main outline and proceed from i to p in each repeat. Add the flowers in a separate sequence, using the j-o sequence for these. The sequence is equally efficient for either option, and all thread tails should be ended in the denser canvas stitches.

Border 4. Flip-flop Extended Diagonal Hungarian Outline with Accents of Double Straight Cross Units and Beaded Brick Stitches. Corner Motif of Blackwork and Beaded Brick Stitches. This border is used in *Santa Sampler* (Color Plate III). A wreath shape developed when I added extra rows of the Extended Diagonal Hungarian to the corners. By using a dense blackwork pattern to suggest the foliage, and by adding red bead clusters, I was able to make the wreaths look realistic. The side bands are decorated with additional elements to complete the elegant border.

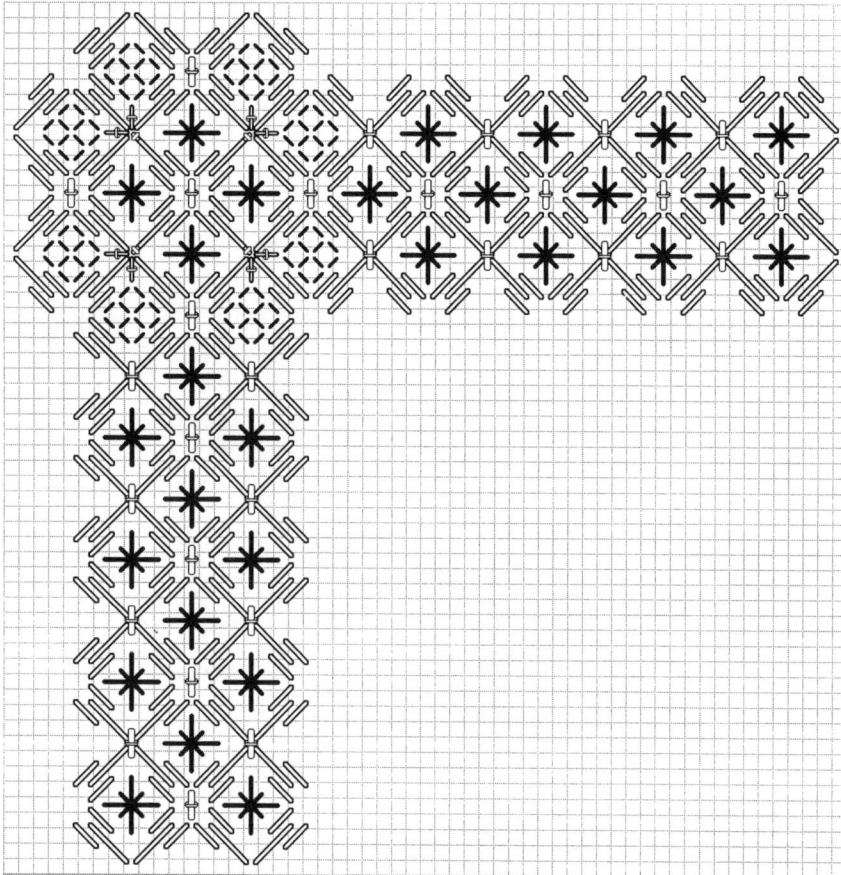

**SEQUENCE OF STEPS 2-3
HORIZONTAL BAND OF BORDER 4**

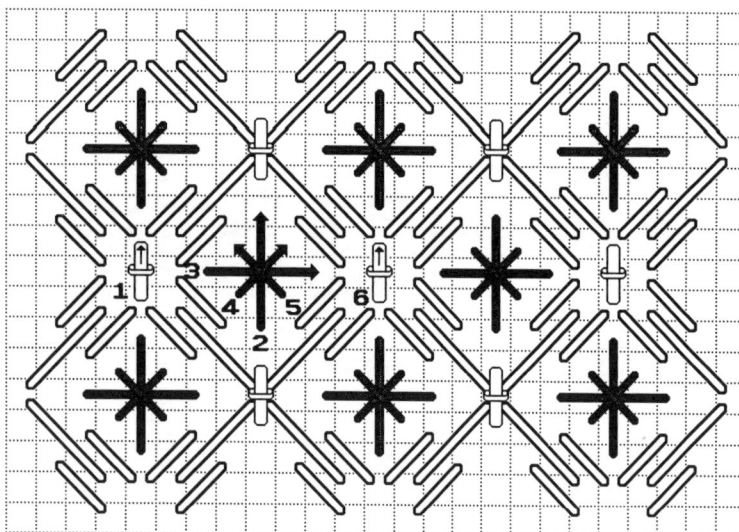

Step 1. Use the sequence chart on page 61 to lay the main network of the border as shown to the left.

Steps 2-3. Use a combined sequence to add the Double Straight Cross units and the Beaded Brick stitches to the border bands. There are three separate rows of these fillings in each band, and the arrangement is staggered in the alternating rows.

Keep the top crosses of the Double Straight Cross units and the Beaded Brick stitches upright throughout the pattern. Use the enlarged sequence chart below and the one on the next page to add these fillings.

NOTE. This filling is also used in the center diamond of each corner motif.

In *Santa Sampler,* a #8 white perle is used for the border outline on a 24-mesh Congress canvas. These side fillings are executed in #8 light gray perle, and the beads added are silver.

The blackwork filling in the corner motif is done with a #12 kelly green perle, and a #12 red perle is used to attach the red beads.

This concept of a large corner motif is also used in *Tease Time* (Color Plate XI), which is another nine-patch design. Notice how the corner motif is not a square but a flower

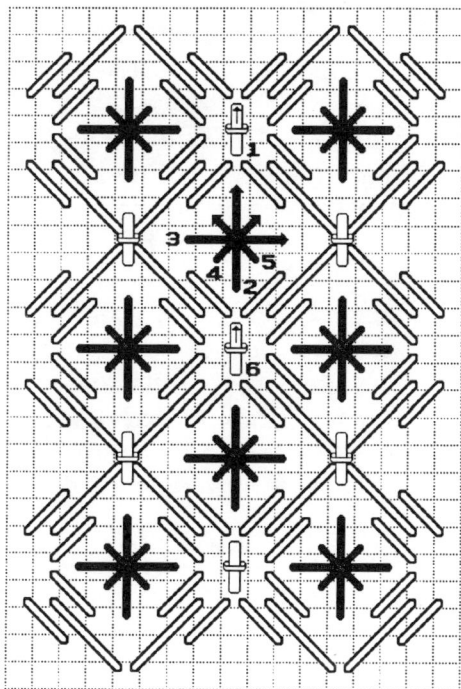

The charts on the next page are large, so discussion of the Variation 1 border will continue here. Execute Steps 1-5, as outlined in the parent pattern, but omit the side rows of Steps 4-5.

Because an overdye is used for the outline of this border, more definition of the negative space is needed to reinforce the shapes. Therefore a Tied Oblong Cross is used in the side rows with "long" open areas (the middle row has "wide" shapes). Add these units to both rows with the Beaded Brick stitches as Step 6.

Then a dark blackwork outline is added that defines the shape further. The dark value of this thread creates dimension as well and recedes nicely inside the heavier "embossed stitches" of the border outline. Add the Step 7 rows, using the charts on the next page.

shape, which I formed by taking advantage of the existing color arrangements in the converging side bands. These are repeated along the outer border.

Step 4. Add the blackwork filling, as shown in the enlarged charts of the corner motif below. There is a sequence chart in lower case letters on the next page for both this step and Step 5.

Step 5. Add the Beaded Brick stitch clusters, using the sequence shown in capital letters on the next page.

Variation 1. Border of Flip-flop Extended Diagonal Hungarian Units with Different Fillings in the Side Bands. This border variation is used in the sampler on the back cover. The same corner motif is used, but this time it resembles a large flower rather than a Christmas wreath. Watercolours is used for the Step 1 outline. This time the Double Straight Cross filling is used in just the middle row of each band. A different filling is used in the side rows.

DETAIL VIEW OF THE CORNER MOTIF

BORDER 4
CORNER MOTIF SEQUENCES

BLACKWORK SEQUENCE
VARIATION 1 BORDER

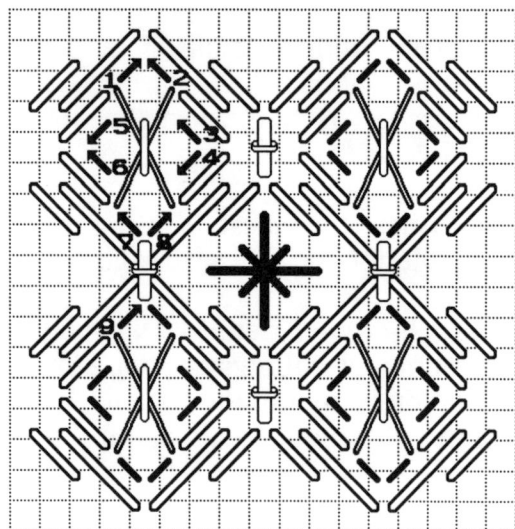

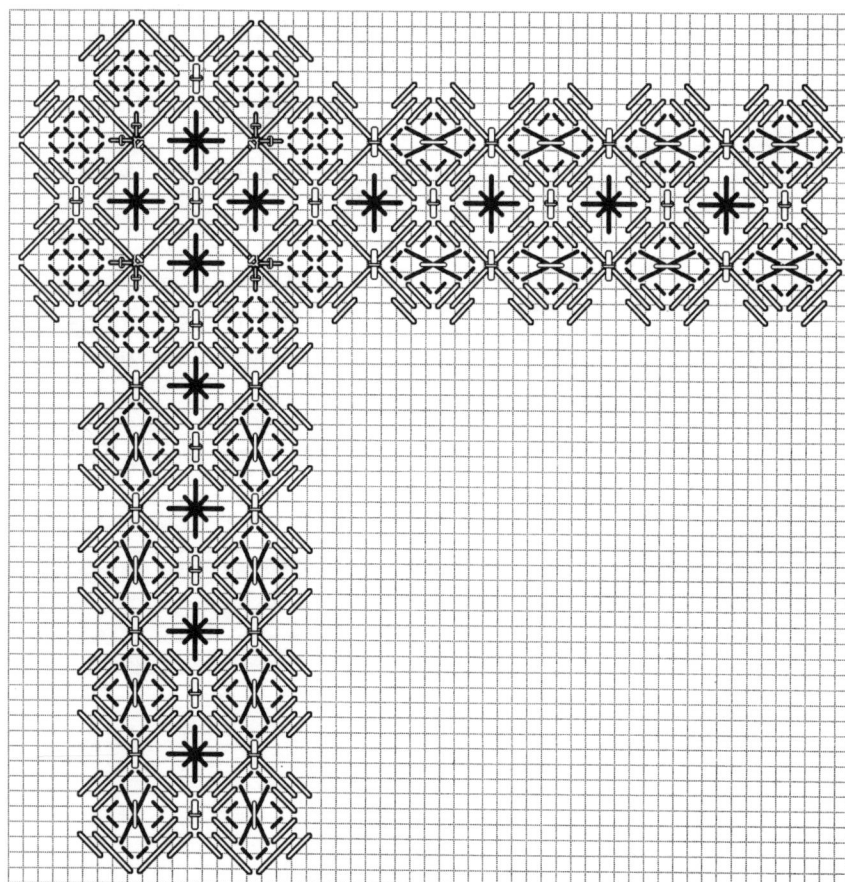

VARIATION 1 BORDER

NOTE. In the blackwork outlines of the chart above, I have provided complete paths for the first two diamonds. Thereafter, I have indicated the starting stitch of each new diamond with an a. The logical ending stitch is indicated with a z. Other paths are possible, but use these as a guideline.

This is the last pattern in the book. I hope I have given you more than just some unusual open patterns to use in your future projects. I hope the ideas shared will inspire you to experiment on your own.

This "potpourri" is just a beginning. Please use my concepts as a springboard to add new dimensions to your personal work and to gain fresh insights into the versatility of pattern. You will develop a deeper understanding of the issues raised in the text and greater satisfaction from using stitches in a new and original way. The pleasure of pattern is endless - enjoy!

PATTERN

Selected Bibliography

Christie, Archibald H. *Pattern Design.* New York: Dover Publications, 1969.

Day, Lewis F. *Pattern Design.* New York: Taplinger, 1979.

Edwards, Edward B. *Pattern and Design with Dynamic Symmetry.* New York: Dover Publications, 1967.

Justema, William. *The Pleasures of Pattern.* New York: Reinhold Book Corporation, 1968.

McDowell, Ruth B. *Symmetry - A Design System for Quilters.* Lafayette, California: C & T Publishing, 1994.

Messent, Jan. *Design Sources for Pattern.* Morecambe LA4 5PZ: Crochet Designs, 1992.

Phillips, Peter and Gillian Bunce. *Repeat Patterns.* New York: Thames and Hudson, Inc., 1993.

Proctor, Richard M. *The Principles of Pattern.* New York: Van Nostrand Reinhold, 1969.

Robinson, Jackie. *Tessellations.* Durango, Colorado: Animas Quilts Publishing, 1992.

Schoenfeld, Susan. *Pattern Design for Needlepoint and Patchwork.* New York: Van Nostrand Reinhold, 1972.

Stevens, Peter S. *Handbook of Regular Patterns.* Cambridge: MIT Press, 1981.

Wade, David. *Geometric Patterns and Borders.* New York: Van Nostrand Reinhold Publishing, 1982.

Ware, Dora and Maureen Stafford. *An Illustrated Dictionary of Ornament.* New York: St. Martin's Press, 1974.

Waterman, V. Ann. *Design Your Own Repeat Patterns.* New York: Dover Publications, 1986.

Waterman, V. Ann. *Surface Pattern Design.* New York: Hastings House Publishers, 1984.

CANVAS EMBROIDERY

Selected Bibliography

Ambuter, Carolyn. *Carolyn Ambuter's Complete Book of Needlepoint.* New York: Thomas Y. Crowell Co., 1972.

Ambuter, Carolyn. *The Open Canvas.* New York: Workman Publishing, 1982.

Bucher, Jo. *Complete Guide to Creative Needlepoint.* Des Moines: Meredith Corp., 1979.

Christensen, Jo Ippolito. *The Needlepoint Book.* Englewood Cliffs, NJ: Prentice-Hall, Inc., 1976.

English, Mindy. *The Canvas Embroidery Notebook (Backgrounds).* Self-published, 1994.

English, Mindy. *The Canvas Embroidery Notebook (Stitches).* Self-published, 1988.

Fischer, Pauline and Anabel Lasker. *Bargello Magic.* New York: Holt, Rinehart and Winston, 1972.

Hilton, Jean. *Borderlines.* Self-published, 1994.

Hilton, Jean. *Needlepoint Stitches.* Self-published, 1988.

Ireys, Katherine. *The Encyclopedia of Canvas Embroidery Stitch Patterns.* New York: Thomas Y. Crowell Co., 1977.

Lantz, Sherlee and Maggie Lane. *Pageant of Pattern for Needlepoint Canvas.* New York: Atheneum, 1973.

Lantz, Sherlee. *Trianglepoint.* New York: The Viking Press, 1976.

Pendray, Shay. *Stitching Toward Perfection.* Self-published, 1989.

Ritter, Marnie. *Canvas Patterns.* Self-published, 1992.

Strite-Kurz, Ann. *The Heart of Blackwork.* Self-published, 1992.

Strite-Kurz, Ann. *The Science of Canvas Embroidery.* Self-published, 1994.

Taggart, Jean. *Laid Fillings for Evenweave Fabrics.* Self-published, 1995.

Zimmerman, Jane D. *The Canvas Work Encyclopedia.* Self-published, 1989.

Open Network of Extended Diagonal Hungarian with Four-way Diagonal Hungarian with Smyrna Cross Centers - Border 2 - Page 125

Open Network of Four-way Diagonal Hungarian with Smyrna Cross Page 72

Open Network of Double Cross and Tied Diagonal Oblong Cross Variation 3 Page 79

Open Network of Double Cross and Tied Diagonal Oblong Cross Variation 2 Page 78

Open Network of Four-way Diagonal Hungarian and Smyrna Cross (Variation 5) Combined with Border 3 Page 127

Border 2 - Variation 1 - Page 126

Open Network of Double Cross and Untied Diagonal Oblong Cross Variation 1 Page 77

Open Network of Double Cross and Tied Diagonal Oblong Cross Variation 4 Page 80

Open Network of Extended Diagonal Hungarian with Four-way Diagonal Hungarian and Smyrna Cross

Open Network of Reverse Mosaic (Four-way) Variation Page 45

Open Network of Reverse Mosaic Page 44

Open Network of Reverse Mosaic (Four-way) Variation 1 Page 44

Tied Oblong Cross Stripe Page 113

Open Network of Partial Pavillion Variation Page 37

Open Network of Four-way Reverse Mosaic with Double Straight Cross Variation 3 Page 50

Open Network of Four-way Reverse Mosaic with Upright Cross Clusters and Single Units Variation 2 Page 49

Open Network of Four-way Reverse Mosaic with Tied Oblong Cross and Upright Cross Variation 1 (Stripe) Page 49

Partial Pavillion Stripe Page 38

Tied Oblong Cross

Variation 1 Page 113

Open Variation of Partial Pavillion with Tied Oblong Cross and Brick Stitches Page 38

Open Network of Four-way Chain Link Page 51

Open Network of Four-way Chain Link with Large Oblong Cross Filling (Tied with Upright Cross Clusters) Variation 1 Page 52

Open Network of Four-way Chain Link with Oblong Cross Variation 2 (Stripe) Page 52